NATIONAL GEOGRAPHIC
KiDS

ALMANAC
2020

A red panda eats bamboo in Wolong National Nature Reserve in Sichuan Province, China.

# NATIONAL GEOGRAPHIC KiDS

# ALMANAC
# 2020

NATIONAL GEOGRAPHIC
WASHINGTON, D.C.

National Geographic Kids Books
gratefully acknowledges the following people for their help with the
*National Geographic Kids Almanac.*

Jennifer Leff of the National Geographic Explorer Programs

## Amazing Animals

Suzanne Braden, Director, Pandas International

Dr. Rodolfo Coria, Paleontologist, Plaza Huincul, Argentina

Dr. Sylvia Earle, National Geographic Explorer-in-Residence

Dr. Thomas R. Holtz, Jr., Senior Lecturer, Vertebrate Paleontology, Department of Geology, University of Maryland

Dr. Luke Hunter, Executive Director, Panthera

Dereck and Beverly Joubert, National Geographic Explorers-in-Residence

Nizar Ibrahim, National Geographic Explorer

"Dino" Don Lessem, President, Exhibits Rex

Kathy B. Maher, Research Editor (former), *National Geographic* magazine

Kathleen Martin, Canadian Sea Turtle Network

Barbara Nielsen, Polar Bears International

Andy Prince, Austin Zoo

Julia Thorson, translator, Zurich, Switzerland

Dennis vanEngelsdorp, Senior Extension Associate, Pennsylvania Department of Agriculture

## Science and Technology
## Space and Earth

Tim Appenzeller, Chief Magazine Editor, *Nature*

Dr. Rick Fienberg, American Astronomical Society, Press Officer and Director of Communications

Dr. José de Ondarza, Associate Professor, Department of Biological Sciences, State University of New York, College at Plattsburgh

Lesley B. Rogers, Managing Editor (former), *National Geographic* magazine

Dr. Enric Sala, National Geographic Explorer-in-Residence

Abigail A. Tipton, Director of Research (former), *National Geographic* magazine

Erin Vintinner, Biodiversity Specialist, Center for Biodiversity and Conservation at the American Museum of Natural History

Barbara L. Wyckoff, Research Editor (former), *National Geographic* magazine

## Going Green

Eric J. Bohn, Math Teacher, Santa Rosa High School

Stephen David Harris, Professional Engineer, Industry Consulting

Catherine C. Milbourn, Senior Press Officer, EPA

Brad Scriber, Senior Researcher, *National Geographic* magazine

Paola Segura and Cid Simões, National Geographic Emerging Explorers

Dr. Wes Tunnell, Harte Research Institute for Gulf of Mexico Studies, Texas A&M University–Corpus Christi

Natasha Vizcarra, Science Writer and Media Liaison, National Snow and Ice Data Center

## Culture Connection

Dr. Wade Davis, National Geographic Explorer-in-Residence

Deirdre Mullervy, Managing Editor, Gallaudet University Press

## Wonders of Nature

Anatta, NOAA Public Affairs Officer

Dr. Robert Ballard, National Geographic Explorer-in-Residence

Douglas H. Chadwick, wildlife biologist and contributor to *National Geographic* magazine

Susan K. Pell, Ph.D., Science and Public Programs Manager, United States Botanic Garden

## History Happens

Dr. Sylvie Beaudreau, Associate Professor, Department of History, State University of New York

Elspeth Deir, Assistant Professor, Faculty of Education, Queens University, Kingston, Ontario, Canada

Dr. Gregory Geddes, Professor, Global Studies, State University of New York–Orange, Middletown-Newburgh, New York

Dr. Fredrik Hiebert, National Geographic Visiting Fellow

Micheline Joanisse, Media Relations Officer, Natural Resources Canada

Dr. Robert D. Johnston, Associate Professor and Director of the Teaching of History Program, University of Illinois at Chicago

Dickson Mansfield, Geography Instructor (retired), Faculty of Education, Queens University, Kingston, Ontario, Canada

Tina Norris, U.S. Census Bureau

Parliamentary Information and Research Service, Library of Parliament, Ottawa, Canada

Karyn Pugliese, Acting Director, Communications, Assembly of First Nations

## Geography Rocks

Carl Haub, Senior Demographer, Conrad Taeuber Chair of Public Information, Population Reference Bureau

Dr. Toshiko Kaneda, Senior Research Associate, Population Reference Bureau

Dr. Kristin Bietsch, Research Associate, Population Reference Bureau

Dr. Walt Meier, National Snow and Ice Data Center

Dr. Richard W. Reynolds, NOAA's National Climatic Data Center

United States Census Bureau, Public Help Desk

# Contents

# CULTURE CONNECTION 116

# SPACE AND EARTH 140

# FUN AND GAMES 162

# AWESOME EXPLORATION 182

**NATIONAL GEOGRAPHIC KIDS**

**ALMANAC CHALLENGE 2020**

### THE RESULTS ARE IN!

Which lion poster was the favorite in our 2019 online pole? *See page 191.*

**Want to become part of the 2020 Almanac Challenge?** Go to page 190 to find out more.

# YOUR WORLD 2020

A surfer rides a wave in Fiji. Surfing will make its debut at the 2020 Olympic Games in Tokyo, Japan.

# 10 WAYS THE WORLD HAS CHANGED SINCE THE 2010 ALMANAC

## PANDA BOOM

In 2010, China's Wolong National Nature Reserve was just beginning to rebuild after a devastating earthquake in 2008 that left dozens of pandas homeless. Today, Wolong— home to 10 percent of all living pandas in the world—has been rebuilt, and its breeding program recently welcomed 42 cubs. This panda boom means the beloved animals are now off the endangered list—hopefully for good.

## FINAL FLIGHT

In 2010, NASA announced that its 30-year space shuttle program would fly its final mission in 2011. Now, NASA's focus is on exploring Mars, and scientists are using the Mars rovers to search for signs of life—and to determine if humans could one day live on the red planet.

## OCEAN AID

Since 2010, large areas of the South Atlantic and South Pacific Oceans have been designated as Marine Protected Areas (MPAs). While only some 4 percent of the world's oceans are now protected from human activities like overfishing, it's a positive step toward saving our seas.

## A BIG WORLD

The planet's population is growing— by the billions! It now stands at some 7.6 billion people, nearly a billion more than the population in 2010. And there's no sign of a slowdown: Experts estimate the number to hit 8 billion by 2023.

## POWER UP

There were fewer than 17,000 electric cars on the roads around the world in 2010. Today, there are more than 3 million. While this may not mean the end of gas-powered vehicles for good, the electric car count is estimated to hit 125 million by 2030.

## TABLET TAKEOVER

Back in 2010 when Apple first introduced the iPad, just about 5 percent of U.S. households owned a tablet. Now? More than half of the nation is tuned into such devices. Worldwide, some 20 percent of the population is on team tablet. But far more—66 percent—stick to smartphones.

## POTTER MANIA

Millions of Muggles across the globe flocked to movie theaters in 2010 and 2011 to see *Harry Potter and the Deathly Hallows Part 1* and *Part 2*, the final films in the über-popular series. Today, Harry is as beloved as ever, with the hit play *Harry Potter and the Cursed Child* and several theme parks featuring all things Potter.

## LOST AND FOUND

In 2018, the last remaining male northern white rhino passed away, marking a sad blow to this rare subspecies. While some animals' numbers are dwindling, others are just being discovered: Since 2010, scientists have found a walking catfish, a two-legged lizard, and the adorable olinguito (above), a small mammal native to South America.

## SEEING THE FUTURE

In 2010, virtual reality prototypes were being developed but the tech was not widely available. A decade later, VR is used daily in places like hospitals, classrooms, museums, and in people's homes worldwide.

## VIDEO VIEWS

In the past 10 years, YouTube's popularity has exploded. In 2010, some two billion videos were viewed a day. Today? That number exceeds five billion. One of 2010's most popular clips—a man emotionally showing off a double rainbow in his front yard—has been viewed nearly 50 million times since it was originally posted.

# GOLDEN GATHERING

## BOW, WOW: THIS CELEBRATION HAS GONE TO THE DOGS!

In 2018, the Golden Retriever Club of Scotland welcomed 361 golden retrievers from around the world to an estate in the Scottish Highlands. The occasion? The 150th birthday of the very first litter of golden retrievers, born in July 1868. Golden retrievers were originally bred by a Scottish politician and businessman known as Lord Tweedmouth to be hunting companions that could also swim far distances. Today, golden retrievers rank among the world's most popular and beloved dog breeds, paws down.

# ICY MAZE

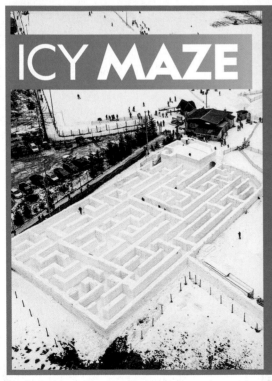

## THIS LABYRINTH IN POLAND

is nothing short of a-*maze*-ing! Constructed out of some 60,000 individual blocks of ice and snow, the maze at Snowlandia Zakopane Park covers an area that's about the size of five basketball courts. Each winter, it takes some 50 workers about one month to build the maze, which features narrow passages with walls taller than most adults. And if you find your way out with time to spare, Snowlandia also offers its visitors a chance to explore a five-story snow castle, complete with an icy throne. Talk about some *royal* fun!

# Olympic Fever

## IN THE SUMMER OF 2020,

Tokyo will become the first Asian city to become a repeat host of the Summer Olympics, having welcomed the games to the Japanese capital in 1964. When the 32nd Olympic Games kick off on July 24, 2020, millions of ticket holders will watch athletes from around the world compete in 33 different sports. Which events are new this year? Women's softball and men's baseball are back on the program after being removed in 2008, and karate, sport climbing, surfing, and skateboarding will be competed on the Olympic stage for the first time ever. So even more athletes will have a chance to go for the gold.

Meet Miraitowa and Someity, the official mascots of the 2020 Olympics and Paralympic Games! Selected by elementary school children throughout Japan, the cheerful mascots are named for the Japanese words for future and eternity (Miraitowa) and mighty (Someity). Together, the mascots are meant to represent both tradition and innovation.

## SPORTS FUNNIES

### OLYMPIC EDITION

Team Canada competes in Team Synchronized Swimming at the London 2012 Olympic Games.

Hey, would you mind scratching my back while we're up here?

Team USA basketball players Kevin Durant and DeAndre Jordan joke on the podium after receiving gold medals at the Rio 2016 Olympic Games.

I can't believe I forgot to wish my mom a happy birthday ...

# Real-Life TRANSFORMERS

## When it comes to some robots, there's more than meets the eye!

Modeled after the popular Transformers toys, the J-deite RIDE robot is programmed to shift into a car and back to a bot again. The robot, which was designed by a team of Japanese engineers, is taller than an elephant and weighs about the same as a rhino. In about one minute, it can switch from a robot to a drivable car that seats two. As for its top speed on the roads? The J-deite RIDE top speeds of 37 miles an hour (60 km/h).

Hit a switch on a remote control and the J-deite RIDE returns to its robot form. While upright, it can walk about 328 feet (100 m) an hour. That pace is not nearly as speedy as the fictional Transformers, but it's not too bad for a real-life robot!

# HOT MOVIES in 2020*

- Trolls World Tour
- Barbie
- Peter Rabbit 2
- Minions 2
- The Croods 2
- Sing 2
- The SpongeBob Movie: It's a Wonderful Sponge

*Release dates and titles are subject to change.

# Walking Gorilla

**WHEN LOUIS THE GORILLA** wants to get around his habitat at the Philadelphia Zoo, he doesn't always move about on all fours like most apes. Instead, he walks on his own two feet, completely upright!

The strange sight is super uncommon for gorillas, who typically walk on two legs once in a while, and just for a few seconds. But six-foot (1.8-m)-tall Louis is seen standing quite often, taking quick strides across the yards, just like a human.

So why does Louis love to walk? Researchers who work with him at the Philadelphia Zoo say it has to do with his preference for keeping his hands clean. He walks when he's gathering food like tomatoes, leading experts to think that he doesn't want to crush the juicy snacks by walking on his hands. Louis also stands up and walks when his yard is muddy, and he has been seen using leaves to wipe dirt off his hands and feet. Sounds like Louis is one particular primate!

## THERE ARE TORNADOES ... AND THEN THERE ARE *LAVANADOES.*

# KILAUEA'S STRANGE PHENOMENON

A lavanado happens when a funnel forms over an active volcano, forming a twister of fire, smoke, ash, and, yes, even lava if it can stay suspended in the air. Recently, a lavanado was spotted over Kilauea on Hawaii's Big Island, the result of intense heat and high winds rising rapidly from the raging volcano. This terrifying twister, measuring some 200 feet (61 m) long, could be spotted whirling over the island from half a mile (800 m) away. Similar columns have been seen over large wildfires, also forming from a combination of high heat and wind.

While lavanadoes are rare, they are fascinating examples of the extreme weather produced around active volcanoes—and proof of just how powerful these forces of nature truly are.

# Cool Events 2020

## GILROY GARLIC FESTIVAL

Garlic ice cream? Why not! That's just one of the fun foods found at this festival showcasing the smelly veggie in northern California, U.S.A.

**July 24–July 26**

## POLAR BEAR SWIM

100 years have passed since the first people plunged into the icy waters near Vancouver, Canada. Today, thousands of brave swimmers jump right into this New Year tradition.

**January 1**

## SUMMER PARALYMPIC GAMES

**LET THE GAMES BEGIN!**
Thousands of athletes with various disabilities head to Tokyo.

**August 25– September 6**

## WORLD FROG DAY

*Ribbit, ribbit!* Show your love for these hopping amphibians today.

**March 20**

## WORLD SMILE DAY

**SAY CHEESE!**
Today, you've got plenty to grin about!

**October 2**

## EARTH DAY

The **50TH ANNIVERSARY OF THIS EVENT** reminds us to protect the planet today—and every day.

**April 22**

## MAYFLOWER VOYAGE

**400TH ANNIVERSARY**
It has been four centuries since the *Mayflower* brought the Pilgrims from England to America.

**November**

## WORLD OCEAN DAY

Celebrate the seas and all of the living things that call our oceans home.

**June 8**

## ROLL ON

As part of a Christmas Eve custom, the locals of Caracas, Venezuela, lace up their roller skates and glide to church.

**December 24**

# ESCAPE ROOM

The lights turn off, and there you are: In a dark, windowless room, with your friends and family ... and no way out. Sound like the start of a scary movie? Not quite. You are in an escape room—and it's all for fun!

Escape rooms, which first started in Tokyo in 2007, have been popping up all around the world as a family-friendly activity. The concept is simple: Your group is locked in a room and is given about an hour to search for clues and solve puzzles to figure out how to exit. Cracking the code is all about teamwork and plenty of problem-solving. Escape rooms have become so popular that there is even an adventure park in Budapest, Hungary, where you can spend an entire day attempting to get out by conquering a series of physical and mental obstacles.

And if you don't crack the code in an escape room? It's okay! You still get to leave the room—and you're always welcome to come back for escape room redemption.

## A Not-So-Great Escape!

While most people try to break out of an escape room, one harebrained burglar in Vancouver, Washington, U.S.A., went the opposite route. After breaking into an escape room (where he allegedly ate a burrito he brought with him and pocketed a remote control and a cell phone), the bad guy began to worry he couldn't actually, uh, escape. Scared, he called 911. And even though he eventually found an exit, the cops still busted him for burglary.

# HIGH-TECH TEACHER

## ROBOTS CAN DO JUST ABOUT ANYTHING THESE DAYS.

Including teach a class full of kids! At least that's what Elias the robot is doing in Finland. As part of a test program, Elias and three other humanoid robots are

programmed to work with students to teach subjects like math and language. He can speak 23 languages, ask questions, and even give feedback on the kids to human teachers. But Elias isn't just about reading and writing. He can break out some serious dance moves! Sounds like one rockin' robot.

A panther chameleon flashes
a threat display in Masoala
National Park, Madagascar.

# AMAZING ANIMALS

# EARTH EXPLORER
## Meet **Krithi Karanth!**

**This conservation biologist and National Geographic explorer is hoping to solve conflict between wildlife and humans in her home country, India.**

From the time she was a kid, Krithi Karanth has been concerned about the need to protect wildlife. In fact, as the daughter of a conservationist, Krithi spotted her first tiger and leopard in the wild when she was just two years old. Today, as a conservation scientist, Krithi is focused on keeping the wildlife in her native India around for future generations.

One way she's doing just that? By trying to limit the conflict between farmers throughout the many villages in India and the wildlife that often wind up on their land. These animals—including feral pigs, tigers, leopards, and elephants—crush crops, mangle fences, and even harm farm animals.

"Spaces for wildlife are shrinking, and people are in closer contact with wildlife," explains Krithi. "As a result, the frustrated and sometimes furious farmers chase or harm animals."

Krithi is working to build tolerance by helping people report and get paid by the government for damage caused by wild animals. She created Wild Seve, a phone reporting system through which people in the field file reports of damage for farmers. Once a report is filed, the farmer receives payment for their losses from the Indian government.

"If farmers are covered for their loss, they will be less likely to retaliate," explains Krithi. She hopes this simple system will be a way to keep humans happy—and animals alive.

Krithi is also intent on raising awareness of India's unique wildlife to the rest of the world. She has even written her own children's book called *Will You Play With Me?* to introduce kids to animals found only in India—like the lion-tailed macaque and the wild dog—and to get kids excited about and to value the animals found in their own countries.

"It's easy to think that all of the discoveries have been done and the species have all been found, but that's not true," says Karanth. "There is still a lot of exploration left to do."

**Female Asian elephants don't have tusks.**

ASIAN ELEPHANTS

> "The big question we have to ask in India is, 'Is there room for wildlife?' And the answer has to be yes.

BENGAL TIGER

**No two tigers have the same pattern of stripes.**

## CALL TO ACTION!

Pick a cause—whether it's saving big cats or boosting the bee population—and look into the ways you can support it. "You don't have to sit back and say 'I can't do anything,'" says Krithi. "Go out and learn everything you can about wildlife. Take pictures of animals and write about them." Who knows, maybe one day you'll play a major role in saving a species.

# Extraordinary ANIMALS

## KITTEN on WHEELS

I rock ... and roll.

**Fort Langley, Canada**
When the TinyKittens Society found a starving kitten suffering from a terrible injury to his back legs, they were shocked he was still alive. But his rescuers refused to give up on him. After amputating part of the cat's back legs, his medical team constructed slings, splints, and eventually a set of mini wheels to give his back end a lift and keep him mobile.

Throughout the process, the team documented the cat's progress on social media. He had tons of fans! Nobody would have guessed that after seven months of intensive physical therapy, the miracle cat— now called Cassidy—would be able to get around without the help of his wheels. These days he scoots around on his two front paws. Except when he's tired, of course—then he hitches a ride on his new family's robotic vacuum cleaner.

CASSIDY NO LONGER NEEDS WHEELS TO GET AROUND.

"Hoppy" to see me?

## TOADZILLA!

**Darwin, Australia**
In the dark of night, a group of citizens set out to hunt down one of Australia's most menacing predators. Their prey? A giant toad nicknamed Toadzilla.

Looking like a cantaloupe with legs, Toadzilla is the largest cane toad on record in Australia, at about eight inches (20.3 cm) long and almost two pounds (0.9 kg). Why the toad hunt? Cane toads were brought to Australia all the way from Hawaii to eat crop-destroying beetles, but instead they gobble down just about anything they can get their mouths around. "Cane toads take away food from other predators and are killing many other native animals," says Graeme Sawyer of FrogWatch, which leads expeditions such as the one that netted Toadzilla.

Luckily cane toads are slow and easy to catch. Once Sawyer's team heard Toadzilla's distinctive mating call—"like a dial tone on a telephone," he says—a tracker grabbed the creature by hand.

Now instead of being a predator, Toadzilla is a teacher, visiting schools to educate kids about invasive species like the cane toad. Better listen to *this* teacher!

TOADZILLA, A GIANT CANE TOAD, IS HANDLED BY THE TRACKER WHO LOCATED THE CREATURE.

The birds ALL call me for fashion tips.

## PARROT wears SWEATERS

**Lecompton, Kansas**

Chilly temperatures never get Javi the bird down. That's because the lesser sulphur-crested cockatoo (a type of parrot) owns plenty of sweaters to keep herself warm!

Normally birds rely on their feathers to stay toasty. But Javi—who was likely raised in harsh conditions before moving to the Tallgrass Parrot Sanctuary—probably plucked out most of her feathers because of stress. Care-takers weren't sure if her belly and chest feathers would grow back, but they knew Javi would be more comfortable with another layer covering her delicate skin. So they fitted her with a sweater.

Today the cockatoo owns more than 20 sweaters. They're made from colorful socks that Tallgrass co-owner Kail Marie makes herself. The fashions have caught the eye of Javi's bird friends, Sassy and Poppy. "Javi's the leader," Marie says. "They'll follow her anywhere." Looks like Javi got more than a new wardrobe—she got new friends as well.

Here we come to save the day!

## PUPPIES save LOST BOY

**Virgilina, Virginia**

Jaylynn Thorpe's family was terrified when the three-year-old wandered off into the woods on a frigid 17°F (-8.3°C) night. Thankfully, Bootsy and Dipstick the puppies wandered off with him—and probably saved his life.

While rescue workers searched for Jaylynn with scent-sniffing dogs and a heat-seeking helicopter, the puppies nestled around the shivering boy. They pressed against him all night and kept him warm—and alive. "They treated him like another puppy in their litter," veterinarian Emily Kinnaird says. "They snuggled to keep warm."

Twenty hours later, rescuers were nearby. But a scared Jaylynn hid beneath a pile of leaves. Once again, the puppies played the heroes, barking to alert the rescue team. Jaylynn was reunited with his family, cold and hungry but unhurt. "The puppies were very important to his survival," fire chief Chad Loftis says.

BOOTSY (LEFT) AND DIPSTICK

RADIO FLYER

# INCREDIBLE ANIMAL FRIENDS

I love ya, but I think your coat needs washing.

## DOMESTIC GOOSE

**ORIGIN** Europe and Asia

**WEIGHT** 5 to 10 pounds (2.3 to 4.5 kg)

**CLAIM TO FAME** The goose is thought to be one of the first animals to be domesticated, probably in Egypt about 3,000 years ago.

**FUN TO KNOW** The wing-span of a domestic goose can be six feet (1.8 m) wide.

Step away from the bull!

## HIGHLAND BULL

**ORIGIN** Scotland; these bulls were brought to Australia (near New Zealand) by Scottish immigrants

**WEIGHT** 1,500 to 1,800 pounds (680.4 to 816.5 kg)

**CLAIM TO FAME** Highland cattle grow two coats of hair. The coarse outer layer protects the animals from wind and rain, and the soft bottom layer keeps them warm.

**FUN TO KNOW** Experts think Highland cattle have been around since the sixth century.

# GOOSE GUARDS BULL

**GISBORNE, NEW ZEALAND**

A big Highland bull like Hamish probably doesn't need a bodyguard, but this goose disagrees. Whenever the bull is grazing in the pasture, the goose watches for cattle that—in the bird's opinion—get way too close. "Then the goose will stretch out his neck, shriek, and chase the other cows and bulls away," says Kees Weytsmans, owner of the Knapdale Eco Lodge where the two live.

Hamish and the goose have been inseparable for 10 years—ever since the bird was found resting on Hamish's leg a week after the bull was born. Since then, the goose has rarely left Hamish's side. Weytsmans once moved Hamish to another rancher's pasture for a few nights. But one evening apart was all the goose could stand. "The next afternoon the goose traveled all by himself to the other pasture to find Hamish," he says. And though Hamish doesn't seem as eager for friendship as the goose, the bull doesn't mind his bodyguard. Otherwise, this bull would ruffle some feathers!

# MONKEY DOTES ON IGUANA

**KREFELD, GERMANY**
This white-faced saki rarely scaled back her affection for her green iguana bestie. The saki, a type of monkey, loved petting and snuggling her reptile pal as they lounged together on tree branches at the Krefeld Zoo.

The saki and iguana met after they were placed in the zoo's Rain Forest House, a tree-filled enclosure that's home to 40 different types of animals from tropical areas. "Both green iguanas and white-faced sakis spend most of their time in treetops," zoo spokesperson Petra Schwinn says. "One day these two crossed paths." The curious saki examined the reptile, patting its skin with her long fingers.

THE FEMALE SAKI PETS HER IGUANA PAL.

The pals continued to have hangout sessions, eating together at the enclosure's feeding station. But most of their "playdates" were in the trees and involved the saki petting the iguana and tickling his chin. The reptile, meanwhile, seemed to soak up the attention.

Recently the animals moved to separate zoos. But keepers and visitors haven't forgotten about their friendship. "They made a good team," Schwinn says.

## GREEN IGUANA

**RANGE**
Central and South America

**WEIGHT**
11 pounds (5 kg)

**TALL TAIL**
If it's caught by a predator, the green iguana can detach its tail and grow another.

**FUNNY NAME**
These animals are sometimes referred to as "bamboo chickens."

> Hey, your beard feels a bit sharp. How about a shave?

## WHITE-FACED SAKI

**RANGE**
South America

**WEIGHT**
around 4 pounds (1.8 kg)

**FACE OFF**
Only male white-faced sakis have white fur covering their faces. The fur on a female's face is mostly brown.

**SWEET TREATS**
Sakis eat fruit, honey, leaves, and flowers.

# WHAT IS Taxonomy?

Since there are billions and billions of living things, called organisms, on the planet, people need a way of classifying them. Scientists created a system called **taxonomy,** which helps to classify all living things into ordered groups. By putting organisms into categories, we are better able to understand how they are the same and how they are different. There are eight levels of taxonomic classification, beginning with the broadest group, called a domain, followed by kingdom, down to the most specific group, called a species.

Biologists divide life based on evolutionary history, and they place organisms into three domains depending on their genetic structure: Archaea, Bacteria, and Eukarya. (See p. 85 for "The Three Domains of Life.")

## Where do animals come in?

Animals are a part of the Eukarya domain, which means they are organisms made of cells with nuclei. More than one million species of animals have been named, including humans. Like all living things, animals can be divided into smaller groups, called phyla. Most scientists believe there are more than 30 phyla into which animals can be grouped based on certain scientific criteria, such as body type or whether or not the animal has a backbone. It can be pretty complicated, so there is another, less complicated system that groups animals into two categories: vertebrates and invertebrates.

HEDGEHOG

### SAMPLE CLASSIFICATION
### KEEL-BILLED TOUCAN

| | |
|---|---|
| Domain: | Eukarya |
| Kingdom: | Animalia |
| Phylum: | Chordata |
| Class: | Aves |
| Order: | Piciformes |
| Family: | Ramphastidae |
| Genus: | *Ramphastos* |
| Species: | *sulfuratus* |

TIP: Here's a sentence to help you remember the classification order: Did King Phillip Come Over For Good Soup?

## BY THE NUMBERS

There are 13,267 vulnerable or endangered animal species in the world. The list includes:

- 1,204 mammals, such as the snow leopard, the polar bear, and the fishing cat.

- 1,469 birds, including the Steller's sea eagle and the black-banded plover.

- 2,386 fish, such as the Mekong giant catfish.

- 1,215 reptiles, including the American crocodile.

- 1,414 insects, including the Macedonian grayling.

- 2,100 amphibians, such as the Round Island day gecko.

- And more, including 170 arachnids, 732 crustaceans, 239 sea anemones and corals, 190 bivalves, and 1,992 snails and slugs.

ROUND ISLAND DAY GECKO

# Vertebrates
## Animals WITH Backbones

**Fish** are cold-blooded and live in water. They breathe with gills, lay eggs, and usually have scales.

**Amphibians** are cold-blooded. Their young live in water and breathe with gills. Adults live on land and breathe with lungs.

**Reptiles** are cold-blooded and breathe with lungs. They live both on land and in water.

**Birds** are warm-blooded and have feathers and wings. They lay eggs, breathe with lungs, and usually are able to fly. Some birds live on land, some in water, and some on both.

**Mammals** are warm-blooded and feed on their mothers' milk. They also have skin that is usually covered with hair. Mammals live both on land and in water.

BIRD: MANDARIN DUCK

AMPHIBIAN: POISON DART FROG

# Invertebrates
## Animals WITHOUT Backbones

**Sponges** are a very basic form of animal life. They live in water and do not move on their own.

**Echinoderms** have external skeletons and live in seawater.

**Mollusks** have soft bodies and can live either in or out of shells, on land or in water.

**Arthropods** are the largest group of animals. They have external skeletons, called exoskeletons, and segmented bodies with appendages. Arthropods live in water and on land.

**Worms** are soft-bodied animals with no true legs. Worms live in soil.

**Cnidaria** live in water and have mouths surrounded by tentacles.

MOLLUSK: MAGNIFICENT CHROMODORID NUDIBRANCH

SPONGE: SEA SPONGE

GARDEN SNAIL

## Cold-blooded
### versus
## Warm-blooded

**Cold-blooded** animals, also called ectotherms, get their heat from outside their bodies.

**Warm-blooded** animals, also called endotherms, keep their body temperature level regardless of the temperature of their environment.

27

# RISE OF THE TIGER

An adult male tiger can weigh the same as eight 10-year-old kids.

Tigers live in both cold and hot climates.

## Scientists find good news with the help of secret snaps.

Recently, scientists have worked to get a current global estimate of how many wild tigers exist. As part of the effort, experts in countries throughout the tiger's range, including Russia, Bangladesh, Bhutan, India, and Nepal, trekked to forests and grasslands where the cats live to set up camera traps—motion-sensing or remote-controlled cameras that snap wildlife pics. They hoped the photos would give clues about the number of tigers in each nation.

### Cats on Camera

To track down tigers, researchers focused on water holes and areas with boar and other tiger prey. There, they fixed multiple camera traps to trees to catch the cats from different angles. The camera's treelike disguise made them less likely to be destroyed by curious animals. After setting up the traps, the researchers journeyed home.

### Take a Number

The cameras snapped pictures of any animal that walked in front of them, using night vision to get good photos in the dark, when tigers are most active. The researchers returned to collect the devices a few months later and uploaded their pictures to computers, which analyzed each tiger's coat pattern and recognized when a certain tiger appeared more than once. The computers then counted how many individuals appeared overall in the photos.

Using this data and other information, teams were able to estimate how many tigers lived in the countries studied. The final tally surprised them all.

### Tiger Time

Researchers estimated that about 3,890 wild tigers exist on the planet. That's up from as few as 3,200, the estimated population in 2010. Experts say this bump may be partly due to conservation efforts made by several of the countries where tigers live, such as laws to protect the cats' habitats.

Still, experts emphasize that the rise in numbers doesn't mean that tigers are out of danger. In fact it's possible that better technology may have allowed researchers to photograph more tigers than before, making it seem as if the population is increasing. Still, analyzing these "selfies" is certainly a step in the right direction for the future of wild tigers.

A TIGER CUB INVESTIGATES A CAMERA THAT'S MOUNTED ON WHEELS AND CONTROLLED REMOTELY BY A RESEARCHER.

# MARGAYS: OUT ON A LIMB

**M**eet the margays! These small wild cats, about the size of a house cat, are native to rain forests of Central and South America. Because of their secretive lifestyle—they spend a lot of their lives in trees, even hunting among the branches—catching a glimpse of these acrobatic cats in their natural habitat is no easy task.

## BUILT TO CLIMB

With a body uniquely adapted to life in the treetops, a margay moves through the canopy like a feline gymnast. Unlike most wild cats, they can go down a tree headfirst. The margay's ankles can rotate all the way around to face backward, which allows the cat to quickly change direction while climbing.

A margay's feet are wide and soft, with flexible toes that allow it to grab branches. Its 17-inch (43-cm)-long tail provides balance as it moves around in the treetops.

## TRACKING MARGAYS

Because they can stay hidden in the trees, experts use radio collars to track these cats and shed some light on their daily activities. As a result, the margay's characteristics and habits aren't a complete secret. Experts have observed that these solitary animals are active mostly at night (their huge eyes help them see in the dark), hunting for birds, snakes, rodents, and even small monkeys. It takes skillful climbing to accomplish that hunting feat.

## SAVING MARGAY HABITAT

Though the overall margay population isn't in immediate danger, the cats are vulnerable. Margays need tropical forests to survive. Habitat destruction, especially clearing forests for farms and ranches, is their biggest threat. Today, scientists are working hard to save the habitat of these acrobats of the rain forest.

**Climbing skills make margays the acrobats of the rain forest.**

CLIMBING HEADFIRST DOWN A TREE IS A RARE ABILITY MARGAYS HAVE MASTERED.

# TURBO-CHEETAH

A cheetah can cover 26 feet (8 m) in one stride.

## SCIENTISTS USE CUTTING-EDGE TECHNOLOGY TO UNCOVER THE CHEETAH'S BIG SECRET.

The fastest land animal, cheetahs have been clocked going over 60 miles an hour (97 km/h). Naturally, scientists have attributed the cheetah's hunting success to its speediness—until recently. Using top-notch technology to research the feline's movements and hunting techniques, scientists found surprising answers to the question of what makes the cheetah a first-rate predator.

## CUTTING-EDGE COLLARS

Until recently, people assumed that the animal's swiftness was what allowed it to snag prey so effectively in the wild. But some experts weren't so sure. So one team, led by Alan Wilson, trekked to Botswana, a country in Africa with one of the world's largest cheetah populations, where they encountered several of the cats on grassy terrain. After zapping them with tranquilizer darts, the scientists fitted them each with a special fashion accessory: a tricked-out radio collar to monitor their movements.

Over the next 18 months, the gadgets sensed when each cheetah was running (which meant that it was hunting), then recorded the cat's location and speed. After 367 runs, the scientists began analyzing the data they'd collected. They knew that the cheetahs were chasing prey. If a cat's run ended with quick, jerky movements and then mostly stillness, they could tell that it had wrestled with and taken down its target.

## SMOOTH MOVES

Looking at the cats' speed and the paths in which they ran, the scientists realized that it's not just speed that makes the cheetah a talented hunter—it's the animal's ability to slow down quickly and make sharp turns. Take the antelope, which runs in a zigzag in an attempt to lose its pursuer. The study showed that, like the antelope, the cheetah slows down, makes a tight turn, and speeds off in the same direction—all within seconds. This is a skill cheetahs start to develop as cubs, and with claws that act like running cleats and a long tail to keep them balanced, a cheetah's body is built for making difficult hairpin turns.

All of this makes the cheetah a champion predator. And now that researchers are more aware of this feline's hunting habits, the data may help conservationists create nature reserves where cheetahs can thrive.

A cheetah can take four strides in one second.

## Collar Connection

The high-tech collars used by Alan Wilson's team had accelerometers to measure increases and decreases in the feline's speed. They also included gyroscopes that could sense when a cheetah twisted or turned to change direction, and GPS to allow the scientists to pinpoint the felines' exact locations on the savanna.

# LIONS OF THE KALAHARI DESERT

**ROARRR!**
On a still night, the sound of lions roaring can carry for five miles (8 km). Roaring often is used to tell other lions, "This is my piece of land."

E yes half-closed against the wind-blasted sand, a sleek, black-and-gold-maned lion (above) strides along a dry riverbed in the Kalahari Desert. He is one of the lions that roam the desolate sand dunes of southern Africa's Kalahari and Namib Deserts. These lions thrive in an intensely hot landscape. They have learned how to go without water for weeks.

Life for a desert lion is very different from life for a lion in the grassy plains of Africa, such as in the Serengeti of Kenya and Tanzania. There, large prides of up to 20 lions spend most of their time together. A pride is very much like a human family.

Fritz Eloff, a scientist who spent 40 years studying the desert lions of the Kalahari, found that desert lions live, on average, in small groups of fewer than six. Family ties are just as strong, but relationships are long-distance. Desert lions often break up into even smaller groups.

## BUSY NIGHTS

Life for Kalahari lions is a constant battle against thirst and high temperatures. In summer during the day, the surface temperature of the sand can be 150°F (66°C). That's hot enough to cook an egg.

Not surprisingly, Kalahari lions hunt mostly after the sun has gone down. The big cats usually rest until the middle of the night, waiting for a cool desert wind. Then they spend the rest of the night walking—looking for food.

In the Serengeti, food is very plentiful. Lions rarely have to walk more than a couple of miles before they find a meal. But life in the desert is not so easy. With only a few scattered animals such as porcupines and gemsboks—horse-size antelopes—for prey, desert lions have to walk farther and work harder to catch dinner.

## DANGEROUS DINNER

When Kalahari lions do find something to eat, it is usually spiky or dangerous. One out of every three animals they catch is a porcupine. The desert lion's main prey is the gemsbok, which can provide 10 times as much meat as a porcupine. But gemsboks are difficult to bring down; they've been known to kill lions by skewering them on their three-foot (0.9-m)-long, saberlike horns.

Water is scarce in the Kalahari, so the desert lions have to be as resourceful at finding a drink as they are at finding a meal. One hot day, just as a light rain began to fall, Eloff watched two lionesses. Side by side, they licked the raindrops off each other.

These lean, strong lions have amazingly learned to survive, and by cooperating, they manage to thrive in an inhospitable, almost waterless world.

31

# Surprise Party!

## Red-eyed tree frogs astonish others with their weird behavior.

Looking for a snack, a 30-inch (76-cm)-long viper slithers down a tree in a steamy rain forest in Central America. Suddenly it sees a tasty-looking, three-inch (7.6-cm)-long red-eyed tree frog resting on a nearby leaf. The reptile lunges forward and snatches up the tiny croaker in its fanged mouth. But the snake's in for a not-so-pleasant surprise—the frog tastes terrible! The snake immediately spits out the amphibian. Landing unharmed on the forest floor, the frog blinks its big red eyes, then hops off to safety.

Red-eyed tree frogs have some features and behaviors that surprise other animals in their rain forest home, as well as the experts who study them. Discover how these jaw-dropping jumpers turn their habitat into one big surprise party.

The red-eyed tree frog oozes stinky, slightly toxic slime through its skin when a predator is near. It also doesn't taste very good!

A FROG LEAPS TO CAPTURE A TASTY CRICKET.

LUNCH

CAUGHT IT!

Males may wrestle over territory or mates.

## Ambush and Eat

A red-eyed tree frog might jump through the air to get closer to an insect it wants to eat. This animal also uses the element of surprise. Known as an ambush predator, the amphibian sometimes hides among the leaves in its rain forest home. The frog waits patiently until a tasty-looking moth or cricket comes within striking distance. Then it fires out its long, sticky tongue to capture the insect and pull the meal into its mouth. Now *that's* some fast food.

## Eye Spy

These nocturnal animals may spend the day lazing on plants, but they can still spy on their habitat. Thanks to a see-through third eyelid

that closes over their eyeballs when resting, the amphibian can stay on the lookout for trouble while it reenergizes. If a hunter does approach, the frog can leap away, startling its pursuer. The eyelid's stripes also may help hide the frog's bright red eyes from would-be predators.

## Stick to It

Slick surfaces aren't a problem for this frog. It can easily clamber across wet leaves. Instead of hopping, the animal takes careful steps like a pro rock climber. It also has rounded toe pads that stick to surfaces like suction cups, and its feet produce gluey mucus to help it grip slippery surfaces. It can even cling to the undersides of leaves to hide from predators—Spider-Man-style. That's a sticky surprise.

UNDERSIDE OF FOOT

A RED-EYED TREE FROG IN THE COUNTRY OF COSTA RICA SCALES A PLANT SHOOT.

One of the frog's calls sounds like a baby rattle.

## Shake It Off

When researchers visited the country of Panama to study these frogs, they saw something that gave them a jolt: a male frog shaking the shoot of a plant with his hind legs, similar to a person strumming a guitar string! They realized that males do this when other males come too close to their turf. The shaking creates vibrations, which intruders interpret as a signal to back off.

Why not just croak loudly to ward off intruders? "They don't want to reveal their location to the entire pond, including enemies such as frog-eating bats," biologist Michael Caldwell says. That'd shake things up *way* too much.

NORTH AMERICA
ATLANTIC OCEAN
PACIFIC OCEAN
SOUTH AMERICA

Gulf of Mexico

Caribbean Sea

BELIZE
HONDURAS
MEXICO

GUATEMALA
EL SALVADOR
NICARAGUA

PACIFIC OCEAN
COSTA RICA
PANAMA

COLOMBIA

Where red-eyed tree frogs live

# Meerkat CITY

Meerkats always have something to do. These mongoose relatives live in busy communities, with no time to sit around being bored. In their family groups of up to 40 members, everyone pitches in to get all the jobs done.

## Guards

Meerkats are very territorial. Guards, called sentinels, are always on the lookout for rival meerkats that try to move in on their territory. If a sentinel (left) spots any intruding meerkats, it sends out an alarm call. The whole group gathers together and stands tall to try to scare away the rivals. If that doesn't work, meerkats quickly decide whether to fight or retreat.

Predators such as eagles or jackals rate a different warning call. When the sentinel spots a predator, it lets out an alarm call that sends all the meerkats scurrying into the nearest bolt hole—an underground safety den where the eagle can't follow.

A SENTINEL KEEPS WATCH.

## Diggers

Picture yourself looking for a tasty bug to eat (below) when suddenly you hear the alarm call for "eagle." You dash left, you dash right, and you finally find a bolt hole.

Bolt holes provide fast getaways for meerkats in danger. Members of the group cooperate to make sure bolt holes are properly dug out, that nothing is blocking the entry, and that there are enough bolt holes in every area.

Meerkats are built to be super diggers. All four of their paws have long, sturdy claws that they use like rakes. They dig to find food, such as lizards and other small reptiles, insects and their larvae, and scorpions.

DIGGING FOR FOOD

## Babysitters

Within a meerkat group, the alpha, or leader, female and the alpha male are usually the only ones that have babies. When their babies are too young to follow along while they search for food, meerkat parents have to go without them. So they leave their pups with babysitters—other adult meerkats in the group. The pups stay inside their family's underground burrow for the first three weeks of life, protected and cared for by the babysitters.

HOME SWEET BURROW

# WILD DOGS OF AFRICA

**T**he puppy-dog eyes and pleading squeals of a five-month-old African wild dog named Cici can mean only one thing: dinnertime. An older sister in Cici's pack responds, dragging over a meaty impala bone. In African wild dog society, puppies have all the power. "It's up to the older siblings to take care of the puppies," says Micaela Gunther, a scientist who studies wild dogs, including Cici's family. "The doting grown-ups even deliver toys, such as a strip of impala skin perfect for puppy tug-of-war." Imagine your big brother or sister working hard to hand you snacks and games while you eat, play, and rest all day.

## DOG DAYS

Like wolves, wild dogs live in packs of about 15 dogs. Pups stay in the pack for about two years. Then some may break off to start packs of their own, while others stay with their mom and dad.

When the pups are newborn, every member of the pack works together to provide for them. At first the puppies stay near the den, often under the watch of a babysitter, while the pack hunts. Returning pack members throw up meat for the pups. Sound gross? Puppies love these leftovers.

## PACK ATTACK

By the time the pups are six months old, they join the pack on hunting expeditions. First they learn how to stalk prey, and eventually they participate in the kill. Single 60-pound (27-kg) dogs rarely catch larger prey on their own, but a pack of 20 proves that there really is strength in numbers. Together they can take down a zebra or wildebeest weighing up to 1,000 pounds (454 kg).

Hunting wild dogs often pursue herds of gazelle for miles, fresh dogs trading places with tired ones. Eventually the weakest of the chased animals tires. The dogs surround it and attack from every direction. This teamwork is bred from the pack's intense social bonding, such as puppy play sessions. Team-building is the reason wild dogs spoil the pups, who grow up united and ready to contribute to the strength of the pack.

**35**

# SCALY SUPERHEROES

## Discover the hidden powers of the pangolin.

Clark Kent and Peter Parker—the alter egos of Superman and Spider-Man—don't really stand out. And neither do pangolins in the tropical forests or grasslands of Africa and Asia where they live. But like your favorite movie heroes, this animal has a few hidden superpowers. Check them out here.

ASIA
AFRICA
ATLANTIC OCEAN
INDIAN OCEAN
AUSTRALIA

Where pangolins live

## SPIDER-MAN STICKINESS!

SPIDER-MAN

Spider-Man shoots out sticky strands of webbing from his wrists to swing from one sky-scraper to another. When a pangolin is hungry, it shoots out its sticky tongue, which extends up to 16 inches (40.6 cm) past its mouth. Coated in gluey saliva, the licker scoops up ants and termites, the pangolin's favorite snacks. In all, the mammal can eat some 70 million insects a year. Makes sense that this superhero-like creature would have a super appetite.

## WOLVERINE CLAWS!

WOLVERINE

During fights with villains, Wolverine defends himself with long, sharp claws that pop out of his knuckles. Pangolins have claws on each of their front feet used to rip up ant and termite nests as they search for dinner. Claws also help them clutch onto branches or dig burrows for sleeping. Whether you're a superhero or a pangolin, claws really come in handy.

**Eight species of pangolins exist in all.**

**The animal emits a stinky odor when threatened.**

## IRON-MAN ARMOR!

CLOSE-UP OF SCALES

IRON MAN

Iron Man sports a high-tech suit of armor that shields the superhero from weapons hurled by enemies. Pangolins wear armor, too. Their "suits" consist of rows of overlapping scales that resemble a pinecone. Made out of keratin—the same substance in your fingernails—the pangolin's armor is so tough that predators such as lions can't bite through it. It's too bad that this armor doesn't come with built-in jets!

## ANT-MAN MOVES

ANT MAN

When he senses trouble, Ant-Man shrinks to the size of, well, an ant. Pangolins, which can be almost six feet (1.8 m) long from head to tail tip, have their own way of shrinking. If the mammal notices a nearby predator, it'll curl into a small ball less than half its normal size and shield its stomach and face. Unable to find a vulnerable part of the pangolin to strike, many enemies give up. Tiny can be tough.

## TONGUE TIME

Up to 28 inches (71 cm) in all, a pangolin's tongue can be almost as long as its body (minus the tail)! How does it fit inside the mammal? The tongue runs from its mouth down its sternum (or breastbone). The back end curves around organs in the lower abdomen, arching toward the backbone. At rest, the tongue's front end is coiled inside the pangolin's mouth. The animal flicks out its licker to snag grub.

SHOULDER BLADE

BACKBONE

TONGUE

STERNUM

LOWER ABDOMEN

# The Secret Language of Dolphins

It's no secret that dolphins are able to chat with each other. Using squawks, clicks, and chirps, these smart animals communicate with distinctive dolphin chatter. But what are they saying? Scientists are trying to find out by studying wild and captive dolphins all over the world to decipher their secret language.

## CHATTY Mammals

In many ways, you're just like the more than 30 species of dolphins that swim in the world's oceans and rivers. Dolphins are mammals, like you are, and must swim to the surface to breathe air. Just as you might, they team up in pods, or groups, to accomplish tasks. And they also talk to each other. "Sometimes one dolphin will vocalize and then another will seem to answer," says Sara Waller, who studies bottlenose dolphins off the California coast. "And sometimes members of a pod vocalize in different patterns at the same time, much like many people chattering at a party." And just as you gesture and change facial expressions as you talk, dolphins communicate nonverbally through body postures, jaw claps, bubble blowing, and fin caresses.

Want to have some fun?

Let's chase bubbles!

## THINKING Dolphin

Scientists think dolphins "talk" about everything from basic facts like their age to their emotional state. "I speculate that they say things like 'Good fish are over here,' or 'Watch out for that shark because he's hunting,'" says Denise Herzing, who studies dolphins in the Bahamas. Sometimes, dolphins call for backup. After being bullied by a duo of bottlenose dolphins, one spotted dolphin returned to the scene the next day with a few pals to chase and harass one of the bully bottlenose dolphins. "It's as if the spotted dolphin communicated to his buddies that he needed their help, then led them in search of this guy," says Herzing, who watched the scuffle.

Back off, bud!

If you were a bottlenose dolphin, you could swim at a speed of 20 miles an hour (32 km/h). That's about four times as fast as an Olympic swimmer.

Let's play!

Toss me a treat!

**12 miles (19 km):** distance high-frequency whistles can travel

**2 months:** time before a baby dolphin is born that a mother might start "singing" to her unborn calf

**5 to 20:** individual dolphins in an average pod

**Over 4:** types of vocalizations dolphins use (These include squawks, whistles, clicks, and squeaks.)

**Over 30:** nonverbal behaviors (for instance, tail slapping or rubbing fins) dolphins use to communicate

## LANGUAGE Lessons

Experts use high-tech gear to record and analyze every nuance of the dolphin language. But they're far from speaking "dolphin" yet. Part of the reason is because dolphins are hard to keep up with. Very fast swimmers, they stay underwater for up to 10 minutes between breaths. Also, their language is so dependent on what they're doing, whether they're playing, fighting, or going after tasty fish. It's no different for humans. Think about when you raise a hand to say hello. Under other circumstances, the same gesture can mean goodbye, stop, or that something costs five bucks. It's the same for dolphins. During fights, for example, dolphins clap their jaws to say "Back off!" But they jaw clap while playing too, as if to show who's king of the underwater playground. It's all a bit of a mystery.

So while scientists haven't completely cracked the code on dolphin chatter just yet, they're listening ... and learning.

I'm tougher than I look!

# SEA OTTERS: Super Cute, Super Tough

## ULTIMATE FUR COAT

A sea otter wears a luxurious fur coat made up of about 800 million hairs. A shield from the sea, the coat is covered in natural oils that keep the skin and underfur dry. Because its fur is the only thing protecting a sea otter from the heat-stealing ocean water, the marine mammal spends nearly half of its day cleaning, combing, and fluffing its coat.

Only a female and her pups will hunt in groups or share food.

## FEEDING FRENZY

To stay warm, an otter also relies on a super-revved metabolism. It must eat three times more calories than a kid needs in order to survive. A daily menu might be 7 abalone, 37 cancer crabs, 50 sea urchins, or 157 kelp crabs—that's about equal in calories to 42 scoops of chocolate ice cream! Otters also have to work for their food: To eat 150 kelp crabs, the otter needs to make at least 150 dives!

S ea otters may look like cute, gentle balls of fur, but they're actually rugged, resilient predators that battle prey, the environment, and other otters every day. Here's why they deserve a reputation as the tough guys of the ocean.

## SEA SURVIVOR

A sea otter is about the same size as an 11-year-old kid—but a whole lot tougher. A human would be lucky to last 20 minutes in an otter's home just beyond the breaking waves before hypothermia—a drop in body temperature—set in and their body shut down. Unlike whales and walruses, otters don't even have blubber (a thick layer of fat) to keep them warm. So how do they survive?

Sea otters are related to skunks, weasels, badgers, and river otters.

## SUPER STRENGTH

Sea otters are like superheroes when it comes to strength. A hard clam or mussel shell is no match for an otter's extremely powerful jaws and strong teeth. A person would have to use a special sharp tool to pry a firmly anchored abalone from its rock. An otter has only its paws and an occasional rock. The otter also uses its strong paws to snatch and overpower large crabs while avoiding their dangerous claws.

Super swimmers, super eaters, super divers—sea otters definitely deserve their rep as supertough marine mammals.

# Incredible Powers
## of the OCTOPUS!

### POTIONS AND POISONS

Blue-ringed octopuses make one of the deadliest poisons in the world. They have enough poison in their saliva to kill a human, though these mollusks mostly use their venom to paralyze prey or to defend themselves from enemies.

### TRICK ARMS

When faced with danger, some octopuses will break off an arm and scoot away. The arm keeps wriggling for hours, sometimes crawling all over an attacker and distracting it. The octopus grows a new arm out of the stump.

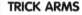

**THE OCTOPUS IS THE TALLER LUMP ON THE RIGHT. THAT'S BRAIN CORAL ON THE LEFT.**

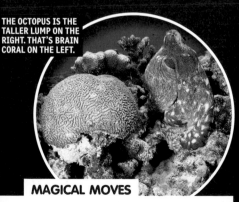

### ESCAPE ARTIST

To confuse attackers, an octopus will squirt a concentrated ink out of its backside that forms a smokelike cloud. This allows enough time for an octopus to escape.

### MAGICAL MOVES

Octopuses can squeeze through tiny holes as if they were moving from room to room through keyholes. Some can even swim through the sand, sticking an eye up like a periscope to see if the coast is clear.

# OCEAN SUPERSTARS

## The fascinating lives of 6 sea turtle species

Think all sea turtles are the same? Think again! Each of these species stands out in its own way.

### 1 GREEN SEA TURTLE: THE NEAT FREAK

In Hawaii, U.S.A., green sea turtles choose a "cleaning station"—a location where groups of cleaner fish groom the turtles by eating ocean gunk, like algae and parasites, off their skin and shells. In Australia, the turtles rub against a favorite sponge or rock to scrub themselves. Neat!

### 2 KEMP'S RIDLEY: THE LITTLE ONE

They may be the smallest sea turtles (babies shown here), but they're not so tiny: Adults weigh as much as many 10-year-old kids, and their shell is about the size of a car tire. They're speedy, too: It takes them less than an hour to dig a nest, then lay and bury their eggs.

## 3 OLIVE RIDLEY: THE ULTRA-MOM

Every year, hundreds of thousands of female olive ridley sea turtles take over beaches to lay their eggs and then bury them before disappearing back into the sea. Call it safety in numbers: With thousands of turtles swarming the shoreline, they're sure to overwhelm any predator.

## 4 LEATHERBACK: THE MEGA-TURTLE

These giants among reptiles have shells about as big as a door and weigh as much as six professional football players! Their size doesn't slow them down, though. A leatherback can swim as fast as a bottlenose dolphin.

## 5 HAWKSBILL: THE HEARTY EATER

What's the hawksbill's favorite snack? Sponges! These turtles gobble about 1,200 pounds (544 kg) of sponges a year. The turtles can safely eat this sea life, which is toxic to other animals. That means there are plenty of sponges to snack on!

## 6 LOGGERHEAD: THE TOUGH GUY

The loggerhead sea turtle's powerful jaws can easily crack open the shells of lobsters, conchs, and snails to get at the meat inside. Some loggerheads swim a third of the way around the world to find food.

# Animal

## Red Fox

A newborn red fox hangs on a small shrub, likely accidentally dropped by his mother as she carried her litter to a new den. Without his mom to keep him warm on this winter night, he won't survive.

The next morning, a couple notices the kit. The woman scoops up the newborn in her hands, and feels him twitch. He's alive, but just barely.

### OUT OF THE WOODS
The fox—now named Albert—is rushed to a wild animal veterinary hospital. Staff place Albert in a toasty incubator, and bottle-feed him formula. They also set a teddy bear beside him for snuggling. Within a few days, Albert perks up and scarfs down his meals.

### FOX FRIENDS
When spring arrives about eight weeks later, Albert joins other rescued kits in a large enclosure next to the sanctuary. The little foxes chase and wrestle one another, practicing their stalking and pouncing skills—two abilities that will help them survive in the wild. Caregivers also hide dead squirrels and mice in their pen so the youngsters can practice hunting.

### HOME STRETCH
Seven months after Albert's rescue, Albert and his fox pals are placed in a pen at the wooded release site, adapting to the sights, smells, and sounds of the wild. One night, Albert and the other foxes quietly slip back into the forest. They are back where they belong.

DINNER IS SERVED.

## Bats

GETTING A BATH

FEEDING TIME

# Rescues

**W**alking along the road at the foot of a hill in China's Sichuan Province, a group of people notice a giant panda on the hillside. Dazed, freezing, and starving, the panda has collapsed and is near death. The humans rush to alert officials—there is not much time left.

## TO THE RESCUE

A rescuer shoots the panda with a tranquilizer dart, and the panda drifts off to sleep. They gently carry her down the hill and race her to a veterinary hospital. The underweight panda is infected with parasites and is suffering from hypothermia—when body temperature drops very low. With just some 1,800 giant pandas left in the wild, the caretakers know just how important it is to save this animal.

## BAMBOO BONANZA

At first, the panda, Wolong II, just lies in her pen. But after a few days of rest and medicine, she sits up and begins munching on bamboo. The animal quickly gains more than 20 pounds (9 kg).

About six weeks after her rescue, Wolong II is healthy enough to return to the wild. She's secured in a metal crate and lifted into a truck. The rescue team carries the crate into the woods, and lays it down in a quiet spot surrounded by bamboo trees. They open its hatch, and Wolong II lumbers off into the forest without looking back.

# Giant Panda

CARETAKERS AT THE HOSPITAL GIVE THE PANDA OXYGEN TO HELP HER BREATHE.

**I**n eastern Australia, hundreds of baby bats were in trouble. The gray-headed flying foxes—who had not yet learned to fly—clung to their mothers, hanging high in a tree. But as a violent storm intensified, the wind knocked the babies from the shelter of their mothers' wings, and they fell to the ground. Wildlife volunteers rushed to the scene and discovered dozens of baby flying foxes lying helpless on the ground, 30 feet (9 m) below the tree.

**The situation was scary,** but after three long days, more than 350 little flying foxes were gently transported to a clinic. Bones were set, and antibiotics were given. Volunteers bottle-fed milk formula to the newborns every three hours. Soon, they graduated from bottles to solid foods, chowing down on chopped apples. They also learned to lap up nectar and finally figured out how to fly. After two and a half months at the clinic, the bats moved into an outside enclosure and eventually began to explore the wild, where they continued to thrive within the forest.

According to an ancient Native American legend, the Raven turned one out of every ten bears white to remind people of a time when Earth was covered by snow and ice.

# Secrets of the Spirit Bear

A rare animal creates a mysterious sight in the forest.

On a cold, rainy October night in the rain forest, a hulking white form with a ghostly glow appears in the distance. No, it's not the ghost of a black bear. It's a spirit bear, also called a Kermode bear, which is a black bear with white hair. Spirit bears live almost exclusively in one place: the Great Bear Rainforest along the coast of British Columbia, Canada. Researchers want to figure out why the bears with white coats have survived here. Fewer than 200 spirit bears call this area home.

## WHITE COAT CLUES

For many animals, unusual white coloration can make it hard to survive because they may have trouble hiding from predators. But the Kermode bear's coloring may actually help it survive and give it an edge while catching salmon.

"A white bear blends into the background during the day and is more successful catching fish," explains biologist Thomas Reimchen. "There is an advantage to one bear in some conditions and the other in different conditions."

## TALE OF TWO ISLANDS

Canada's Gribbell Island has the highest concentration of Kermode bears, followed by neighboring Princess Royal Island. These isolated islands may be another key to the bears' survival, since there's no competition from grizzly bears, and wolves are the only natural threat. The islands' trees provide shelters, and rivers are filled with salmon.

Even though spirit bears have flourished on these islands, new threats such as logging worry scientists and the members of the Native American Gitga'at First Nation, who have lived with and protected spirit bears for centuries. That's why researchers are working hard to understand the biology of the spirit bear. As they do, they can find the best ways to ensure its survival.

# MONKEY TROUBLE
## A YOUNG BABOON TAKES A DANGEROUS SWIM.

It's a chilly winter morning in Botswana's Okavango Delta in Africa. A troop of chacma baboons wades across a narrow stream. But an eight-month-old infant named Chobe is left behind. She frantically paces the shore and calls out. The others ignore her as they move through the cold water without her.

Because the baboons' territory is flooded for half of the year, they must cross water all day. They move from island to island to find food and to escape predators such as lions and leopards.

## 1 DANGEROUS CROSSING

To cross the stream, bigger kid baboons hitch a ride with one of their parents, climbing onto the adult's back. Chobe usually gets a lift across the water with her dad, but today he's gone on ahead. So she has to figure out a way to get across the water and keep up with her troop. A young baboon cannot survive alone in the wild.

## 2 CAUGHT IN THE CURRENT

Chobe begins to wade into the cold stream. The water quickly becomes too deep for her, so she starts to swim clumsily. Midway, the strong current drags her downstream, farther from the shore. Her screams turn to gurgles as she starts to swallow water.

## 3 COMFORT AFTER A CLOSE CALL

Chobe's tiring fast, but just then, her feet find a shallow bank in the stream and she races out of the water. She sits on the shore, shivering. Her mother soon arrives, holds her close, and grooms her. Grooming is a great form of comfort for baboons. In no time, Chobe is running around with the other young baboons.

## 4

## STAYING SAFE WITH DAD

Baboons have to learn to survive on their own, and sometimes that involves dangerous lessons. Chobe got a taste of what it's like to be an independent member of the troop. She decides she isn't quite ready to be a grown-up yet … so she makes sure to find her father and hop onto his back at the next water crossing.

47

# BIZARRE Insects

## Check out some of the strangest bugs on Earth!

The bright-colored head of the puss moth caterpillar warns predators to stay away. This species, one of the most toxic caterpillars in North America, can spray acid from its head when it is attacked.

**puss moth caterpillar**

### walking leaf

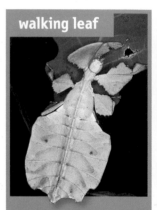

This flat, green insect is a master of disguise: It's common to mistake this bug for an actual leaf, thanks to its large, feathery wings. This clever camouflage provides protection from potential predators.

### giraffe-necked weevil

No surprise, this bug gets its name from its extra-long neck. The males have longer necks than females do, which they use to fight other males for mating rights.

### thorn bugs

One tiny thorn bug may not be a match for a bigger predator, but when grouped together on a branch, these spiky bugs create a prickly pack no bird wants a bite of!

### spiny katydid

This katydid is covered in sharper-than-knives spikes. If a predator attacks, this species springs into action, defending itself by jabbing an enemy with its spiny legs and arms.

## cockchafer beetle

The wild, feathery antennae on the male cockchafer may be cool to look at, but they're also helpful tools. They enable the bug to sniff for food and feel out its surrounding environment.

### acorn weevil

The acorn weevil's hollow nose is longer than its body, and perfect for drilling through the shells of acorns. A female will feast on the nut by sucking up its rich, fatty liquid, and then lay her eggs in the acorn.

## pink grasshopper

Though most grasshoppers are green or brown, some—like this pink nymph—are much brighter. Pink grasshoppers are rare, most likely because they are easy for predators to spot.

### man-faced stinkbug

There are more than 4,500 species of stinkbugs world-wide, including this brilliant yellow species, whose shield-shaped body displays a unique pattern resembling a tribal mask. Like all stinkbugs, this species secretes a foul-smelling liquid from scent glands between its legs when it feels threatened.

## rhinoceros beetle

Ounce for ounce, this insect, which gets its name from the hornlike structure on the male's head, is considered one of the world's strongest creatures. It is capable of carrying up to 850 times its own body weight.

# 5 COOL THINGS ABOUT Butterflies

MONARCH PUPA

## 2
### Butterflies are nature's magicians.
Butterflies begin life as caterpillars. Once grown, the caterpillar becomes a pupa. Protected by a cocoon, the pupa transforms into a butterfly, a process called metamorphosis.

## 1
### Some butterflies start out smelly.
Not all butterflies stink, but the caterpillar of the zebra swallowtail butterfly sure does! Its nasty odor helps keep it safe from hungry animals.

ZEBRA SWALLOWTAIL

## 3 Butterflies taste WITH THEIR "FEET."
Butterflies have chemical receptors on their legs, similar to taste buds, that allow them to taste the sweetness of a peach just by standing on it.

## 4 MANY butterflies ARE poisonous.
The monarch, for example, eats only poisonous milkweed plants, making both the caterpillar and the adult butterfly a dangerous snack for predators.

## 5
OWL BUTTERFLY

### Some are winged tricksters.
Owl butterflies startle predators with huge "eyes" on their wings. The false eyes divert an attacker's attention, giving the butterfly time for a hasty escape.

# Bet You Didn't Know

## 8 surprising facts about spiders

**1** **Golden silk** orb-weaver spiders vibrate their webs to **distract predators.**

**2** **Black widow** spiders are more **venomous** than **rattlesnakes.**

**3** After a **large meal,** a **tarantula** may not **eat** for a **month.**

**4** Crab spiders **change color** to blend in with their surroundings.

**5** There are more than **37,000** species of **spiders.**

**6** A spider **eats** about **2,000 insects** a year.

**7** The **oldest** known **spider fossils** are more than **300 million** years old.

**8** A pound (.45 kg) of **spider silk** could stretch around the Equator.

# Does Your Pet L♥ve You?

**M**ore scientists are beginning to agree with what most pet owners already believe: Pets do love the people in their lives. Decide for yourself!

## Rescue Dog ♡

When two-year-old Daisy Smith wandered from her family's yard one day, she was lucky to have her family's Labrador retriever, Thunder, tagging along. After 13 hours, a search party finally found the little girl (right) sitting by a river a mile and a half (2.4 km) from her home, with Thunder by her side. There's no doubt that this hero dog loves his Daisy!

# Fire Cat

Boo Boo the cat is living proof that animals are capable of unselfish love. One night, as Frances Morris and her husband were asleep in their bed, Boo Boo began meowing and howling. Sleepily, Morris tried to calm Boo Boo, but the cat kept meowing. Fully awake, Morris realized the bedroom was filling with smoke. The kitchen was on fire! Instead of escaping outside, Boo Boo had run upstairs to warn the Morrises, and everyone escaped safely.

# Funny Bunny

Who needs jokes when you have a bunny? That's what 13-year-old Kenny Clessas discovered when his pet rabbit, Killer, got him giggling after a bad day. Noticing Kenny crying, Killer started head-butting and running circles around the boy. Kenny just had to laugh!

## How affectionate is your pet?

**1**
When you arrive at home, your dog ...
- a hides under the couch.
- b barely looks up from its nap.
- c runs to greet you.

**2**
Whenever you sit down on a chair or the floor, your cat ...
- a leaves the room.
- b watches you from afar.
- c cuddles up on your lap, purring.

**3**
If you reach into the cage, your gerbil ...
- a digs into its wood chips to hide.
- b backs away unless coaxed with a treat.
- c jumps onto your hand eagerly.

IF YOUR ANSWER IS a, your pet plays it cool. It decides when it's cuddle time. b, your pet thinks you're its buddy. It likes you to be around. c, your pet is head over heels in love with you. It would do anything to be close to you.

# A PUZZLE FOR YOUR POOCH

## DISCOVER HOW FAST YOUR DOG LEARNS

Your new puppy wants a bit of your pizza. He tries sitting at your feet and whining. No deal. He paws at your knee and gets pushed away. Then he notices that your baby sister dropped some on the floor. Score! Tomorrow night, he'll head straight for the baby's chair. That's learning. You can test your dog's ability to learn by giving him this puzzle and seeing if he can solve it faster with practice.

## YOU NEED

- **9 bite-size treats**
- **3 tennis balls**
- **muffin tin**
- **stopwatch or clock**
- **pencil and paper**

## INSTRUCTIONS

1 Set three treats into different holes in the muffin tin. Show the muffin tin to your dog to get him interested.

2 Place a tennis ball on top of each treat and set the muffin tin on the floor.

3 Start timing. Record how long it takes your dog to uncover all three treats.

4 Repeat the procedure and record how long it takes him to find all the treats a second time.

5 Give him one more round and record the time for his third attempt.

6 Compare the three times. If your dog was faster on his second and third tries, it shows that he learned how to extract the treats quickly.

Whenever a dog does something and gets a reward, he is more likely to do it again. Psychologists call this conditioning. The problem is, dogs are in constant motion. It takes a lot of work to teach them which move is being rewarded. You can almost imagine your dog's thoughts the first time you reward him for a trick, "Oh, I wagged my tail. Is that why I got the treat? I sneezed. Did that do it? Maybe she gave me a treat because I wiggled my ears." Gradually, your dog will realize which action earns the treat.

Treat puzzles work similarly. Spot smells the treat and knows it's there. He may try several ways to get it out: nudging with his nose, pushing with his paw, and looking at you to see if you'll get it for him. With enough practice, he'll figure out the best way to get the treat, and soon he'll be gulping them down.

## clever canines

**TIP**

If the ball sinks all the way into the muffin tin opening, it may be difficult for your dog to move the ball. Try using a muffin tin with slightly narrower openings or a thick treat that will elevate the ball a little.

Check out the book!

# 20 CUTEST ANIMALS OF 2020

From furry bobcats to smiling geckos, there's no shortage of cute creatures on Earth. Here's NG Kids' roundup of cuddly critters that are sure to make you say *awww*.

## 1 GET UP, STAND UP

A group of meerkats stands at attention by its burrow. Extremely family-oriented, meerkat "mobs" spend a lot of time playing together in a tight-knit group. The furry family may look sweet, but if confronted, they will stand together, arching their backs, raising their hair, and hissing.

## 2 CLOSE-UP

This young wombat is definitely not camera shy! Native to Australia, these marsupials are about the size of a jelly bean at birth and stay in their mom's pouch for several months before venturing out, where they'll spend most of their days burrowing underground tunnels.

# 3 TRUNK SHOW

Get out of these elephants' way! African elephants can weigh some 200 pounds (91 kg) at birth; by adulthood, they can top the scales at more than seven tons (6.4 t). The world's largest land mammal also has a big appetite, eating more than 300 pounds (136 kg) of grass, fruit, and leaves a day.

# 5 THINK PINK

Adult greater flamingos may be famous for their coral-colored hue, but their chicks look a lot different—at first. Born with gray or white feathers, it takes two to three years for a young flamingo's pink feathers to show.

# 4 SPOT ON

This cuddly-looking bobcat may have one of the finest fur coats in the animal world, but it's not all about looking good. The spotted fur helps North America's most common wild cat blend in with many habitats. Those ear tufts? Bobcats may twitch them to communicate with other bobcats.

# 6

## BEAR-Y HUNGRY

In the fall, this brown bear cub will start packing on about three pounds (1.4 kg) a day to prepare for its deep winter sleep. Those pounds of fat are what the bear will live on while snoozing. Luckily, Mom is an expert at sniffing out a meal in their northwestern U.S. habitat and can detect food from 18 miles (29 km) away.

# 7

## HANGING OUT

This young raccoon might be an expert climber—many raccoons spend their first few months living in a nest in a tree hole. As adults, raccoons rely more on their sense of touch than on their senses of sight and smell to find meals such as frogs, bird eggs, insects, and even snakes.

# 8

## UP A TREE

This baby orangutan may have figured out the best part of life in the trees: just hanging out! Orangutans spend up to 95 percent of their time high up in trees on the Southeast Asia islands of Borneo and Sumatra. They sleep, eat, and play in nests that are big enough for a 10-year-old kid to stretch out in.

## 9

### RAD REPTILE

The gentle leopard gecko is famous for its spots as well as for its urine, which comes out as tiny crystals. Its calm nature and long life span—it can live up to 20 years if treated well—make this gecko a very popular pet.

## 10

### ALL EARS

Nobody sports a birthday suit better than a baby aardvark. Born pink and wrinkly, this big baby slurps milk but will gobble thousands of ants a night when it's older. An African native, the aardvark's name means "earth pig" in one South African language. It has donkey ears, a kangaroo tail, and a piggy nose, but it's actually a distant relation to the elephant.

**11**

**FLYING LEAP**
Caracals may not have wings, but they can sure fly! This small wild cat, native to Africa and the Middle East, has strong hind legs that allow it to jump more than six feet (2 m) in the air—the height of a tall adult human.

## 12

### HANGING ON

This 10-month-old gorilla keeps a tight hold on a bamboo pole in Volcanoes National Park in Rwanda, Africa. Gorillas are born with a powerful grip, which allows them to hang on to their moms for transport—and, of course, to climb.

## 13

### BLENDING IN

Hares, beware! This critter may look adorable, but it could be your enemy. Silent and sneaky, the ermine can pounce on prey that's larger than it is, such as an arctic hare. The stealthy stalker gets help from its changing coat, which is white during winter and brown in spring and summer—perfect camouflage.

## 14

### STARTING SMALL

Coyote pups may be tiny at first, but they eventually grow to be the size of medium dogs. They're cared for from birth by both parents, who give their offspring an early start on hunting by bringing live mice to their den for stalking practice.

## 15

### WHAT A HOOT!

Why, hello there! A Eurasian pygmy owl peers out of a tree in a forest in Sweden. These tiny owls—which grow to be about the size of a robin—are small enough to squeeze into tree holes made by woodpeckers, where they build their nests.

## SMILEY SQUID

Say cheese? It may look like this piglet squid is smiling, but in reality this deepwater dweller isn't quite hamming for the camera. Rather, the squid's friendly "face" is the result of tentacles and unusual skin patterns, which form the shape of an adorable mug topped by a mop of curly hair.

**16**

**18**

## TALL TALE

Talk about a grand entrance: A baby giraffe falls about six feet (1.8 m) from its mom during birth before hitting the ground. But the bumpy landing doesn't stop the little guys from getting a jump start on life—they're usually up on their hooves and walking at just an hour old.

**17**

## JUST LION AROUND

A mother Galápagos sea lion lounges around with her pup. These animals share a tight bond: Although baby sea lions usually learn to swim by the time they're two weeks old, they stick to their mothers' sides for a few years before venturing out on their own.

## BADGE OF HONOR

What's black and white and striped all over? An American badger, of course! This species is easily recognized by the telltale white stripe, which runs from the tip of their noses all the way to the back of their heads. But it's the badgers' black cheek patches—called "badges"— that give them their name.

**19**

## HOP TO IT

Native to tropical Amazon forests, this frog's see-through skin helps it hide high in the trees. Sunlight shines right through the frog and provides camouflage. When it's time to lay its eggs, a glass frog deposits tiny white eggs onto a leaf above a stream. When the tadpoles emerge, they slip off the leaf and splash into the water below.

**20**

# Prehistoric TIMELINE

**HUMANS HAVE WALKED** on Earth for some 200,000 years, a mere blip in the planet's 4.5-billion-year history. A lot has happened during that time. Earth formed, and oxygen levels rose in the millions of years of the Precambrian time. The productive Paleozoic era gave rise to hard-shelled organisms, vertebrates, amphibians, and reptiles.

Dinosaurs ruled Earth in the mighty Mesozoic. And 65 million years after dinosaurs became extinct, modern humans emerged in the Cenozoic era. From the first tiny mollusks to the dinosaur giants of the Jurassic and beyond, Earth has seen a lot of transformation.

## THE PRECAMBRIAN TIME

### 4.5 billion to 542 million years ago

- Earth (and other planets) formed from gas and dust left over from a giant cloud that collapsed to form the sun. The giant cloud's collapse was triggered when nearby stars exploded.
- Low levels of oxygen made Earth a suffocating place.
- Early life-forms appeared.

## THE PALEOZOIC ERA

### 542 million to 252 million years ago

- The first insects and other animals appeared on land.
- 450 million years ago (m.y.a.), the ancestors of sharks began to swim in the oceans.
- 430 m.y.a., plants began to take root on land.
- More than 360 m.y.a., amphibians emerged from the water.
- Slowly, the major landmasses began to come together, creating Pangaea, a single supercontinent.
- By 300 m.y.a., reptiles had begun to dominate the land.

## What Killed the Dinosaurs?

It's a mystery that's boggled the minds of scientists for centuries: What happened to the dinosaurs? While various theories have bounced around, a recent study confirms that the most likely culprit is an asteroid or comet that created a giant crater. Researchers say that the impact set off a series of natural disasters like tsunamis, earthquakes, and temperature swings that plagued the dinosaurs' ecosystem and disrupted their food chain. This, paired with intense volcanic eruptions that caused drastic climate changes, is thought to be why half of the world's species—including the dinosaurs—died in a mass extinction.

# DINO TIMES

## THE MESOZOIC ERA

**251 million to 65 million years ago**

The Mesozoic era, or the age of the reptiles, consisted of three consecutive time periods (shown below). This is when the first dinosaurs began to appear. They would reign supreme for more than 150 million years.

## TRIASSIC PERIOD

**251 million to 201 million years ago**

- Appearance of the first mammals. They were rodent-size.
- The first dinosaur appeared.
- Ferns were the dominant plants on land.
- The giant supercontinent of Pangaea began breaking up toward the end of the Triassic.

## JURASSIC PERIOD

**201 million to 145 million years ago**

- Giant dinosaurs dominated the land.
- Pangaea continued its breakup, and oceans formed in the spaces between the drifting landmasses, allowing sea life, including sharks and marine crocodiles, to thrive.
- Conifer trees spread across the land.

## CRETACEOUS PERIOD

**145 million to 66 million years ago**

- The modern continents developed.
- The largest dinosaurs developed.
- Flowering plants spread across the landscape.
- Mammals flourished, and giant pterosaurs ruled the skies over small birds.
- Temperatures grew more extreme. Dinosaurs lived in deserts, swamps, and forests from the Antarctic to the Arctic.

## THE CENOZOIC ERA—TERTIARY PERIOD

**65 million to 2.6 million years ago**

- Following the dinosaur extinction, mammals rose as the dominant species.
- Birds continued to flourish.
- Volcanic activity was widespread.
- Temperatures began to cool, eventually ending in an ice age.
- The period ended with land bridges forming, which allowed plants and animals to spread to new areas.

# DINO Classification

Classifying dinosaurs and all other living things can be a complicated matter, so scientists have devised a system to help with the process. Dinosaurs are put into groups based on a very large range of characteristics.

Scientists put dinosaurs into two major groups: the bird-hipped ornithischians and the lizard-hipped saurischians.

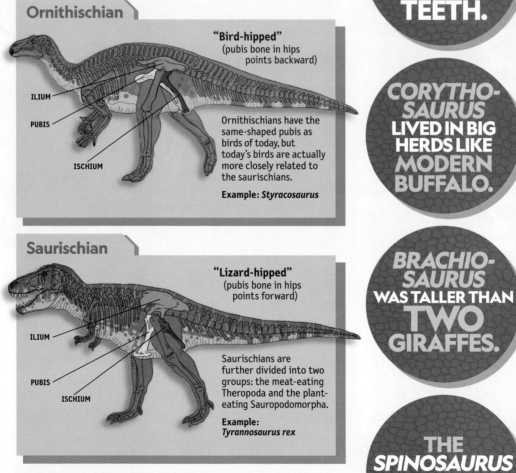

## Ornithischian

ILIUM

PUBIS

ISCHIUM

**"Bird-hipped"**
(pubis bone in hips points backward)

Ornithischians have the same-shaped pubis as birds of today, but today's birds are actually more closely related to the saurischians.

**Example: *Styracosaurus***

## Saurischian

ILIUM

PUBIS

ISCHIUM

**"Lizard-hipped"**
(pubis bone in hips points forward)

Saurischians are further divided into two groups: the meat-eating Theropoda and the plant-eating Sauropodomorpha.

**Example: *Tyrannosaurus rex***

**Within these two main divisions,** dinosaurs are then separated into orders and then families, such as Stegosauria. Like other members of the Stegosauria, *Stegosaurus* had spines and plates along the back, neck, and tail.

THE FIERCE *ALLOSAURUS* HAD NEARLY **70** TEETH.

*CORYTHO-SAURUS* LIVED IN BIG HERDS LIKE MODERN BUFFALO.

*BRACHIO-SAURUS* WAS TALLER THAN TWO GIRAFFES.

THE *SPINOSAURUS* ATE SHARKS.

# ③ NEWLY DISCOVERED DINOS

**H**umans have been searching for—and discovering—dinosaur remains for hundreds of years. In that time, at least 1,000 species of dinos have been found all over the world, and thousands more may still be out there waiting to be unearthed. Recent discoveries include *Borealopelta markmitchelli*. Found in western Canada, the plant-eating armored dinosaur is so well preserved that paleontologists have discovered remnants of its skin.

**① *Borealopelta markmitchelli*** (Ornithischian)

**Named After:** Mark Mitchell, the man who chipped the rock away from the fossil

**Length:** 18 feet (5.5 m)

**Time Range:** Cretaceous

**Where:** Alberta, Canada

**② *Mansourasaurus shahinae*** (Saurischian)

**Named After:** Mansoura University in Egypt

**Length:** 33 feet (10 m)

**Time Range:** Late Cretaceous

**Where:** Egypt

**③ *Diluvicursor pickeringi*** (Ornithischian)

**Named After:** Australian paleontologist David Pickering

**Length:** 7.5 feet (2.3 m)

**Time Range:** Cretaceous

**Where:** Australian-Antarctic rift valley

# DINO DEFENSES

Scientists don't know for sure whether plant-eating dinos used their amazing attributes to battle their carnivorous cousins, but these herbivores were armed with some pretty wicked ways they could have used to defend themselves.

## ARMOR: GASTONIA
## (GAS-TONE-EE-AH)

Prickly *Gastonia* was covered in heavy, defensive armor. To protect it from the strong jaws of meat-eaters it had four horns on its head, thick layers of bone shielding its brain, rows of spikes sticking out from its back, and a tail with triangular blades running along each side.

## SPIKES: KENTROSAURUS
## (KEN-TROH-SORE-US)

Stand back! This cousin of *Stegosaurus* had paired spikes along its tail, which it could swing at attackers with great speed. One paleontologist estimated that *Kentrosaurus* could have swung its treacherous tail fast enough to shatter bones!

## CLUB TAILZ:
### *ANKYLOSAURUS*
## (AN-KYE-LOH-SORE-US)

Steer clear! *Ankylosaurus* possessed a heavy, knobby tail that it could have used to whack attackers. It may not have totally protected the tanklike late Cretaceous dino from a determined *T. rex*, but a serious swing could have generated enough force to do some real damage to its rival reptile.

## WHIP TAIL:
### *DIPLODOCUS*
## (DIH-PLOD-UH-KUS)

Some scientists think this late Jurassic giant's tail—about half the length of its 90-foot (27-m) body—could have been used like a whip and swished at high speeds, creating a loud noise that would send potential predators running.

## HORNS:
### *TRICERATOPS*
## (TRI-SER-UH-TOPS)

There's no evidence *Triceratops* ever used its horns to combat late Cretaceous snack-craving carnivores. But scientists do believe the famous three-horned creature used its frills and horns in battle with other members of its species.

# Dynamite DINO AWARDS

**Spiky body armor. Razor-sharp teeth. Unimaginable strength.** No doubt, all dinos are cool. But whether they were the biggest, the fiercest, or the biggest-brained of the bunch, some stand out more than others. Here are seven of the most amazing dinos ever discovered.

**Supersize Appetite**

**Big Brain**

**Cool Camo**

Scientists think that *Tyrannosaurus rex* could gulp down 500 pounds (227 kg) of meat at a time—that's like eating 2,000 hamburger patties in one bite!

*Troodon*, a meat-eater the size of a man, had a brain as big as an avocado pit—relatively large for a dinosaur of its small stature. Because of its big brain, scientists think *Troodon* may have been the smartest dino and as intelligent as modern birds.

The birdlike *Sinornithosaurus* had feathers similar to those of modern birds. It may have also had reddish brown, yellow, and black coloring that kept this turkey-size raptor camouflaged as it hunted in the forest.

**Heavy-weight**

The heaviest of all dinosaurs, *Argentinosaurus* is believed to have weighed 220,000 pounds (99,790 kg)—more than 15 elephants.

**Built for Speed**

**Ornithomimids,** a group of dinosaurs that resembled ostriches, would have given the world's fastest man a run for his money. Some of these long-limbed, toothless meat-eaters are thought to have clocked speeds of 50 miles an hour (80 km/h).

**Pint-Size Predator**

*Microraptor zhaoianus,* the smallest meat-eating dinosaur, measured just 16 inches (40 cm) tall. With long toe tips for grasping branches, it's thought to be closely related to today's birds.

**Super Spines**

Known as the "spine lizard," *Spinosaurus* had huge spines sticking out of its back, some taller than a fourth grader! Weighing up to 22 tons (20 t), it may have been the biggest meat-eating dinosaur.

# QUIZ WHIZ

**Explore just how much you know about animals with this quiz!**

Write your answers on a piece of paper. Then check them below.

**1** Sea otters are related to _____.
a. skunks
b. dolphins
c. sloths
d. narwhals

**2** One of the red-eyed tree frog's calls sounds like a _____.
a. car horn
b. baby rattle
c. guitar
d. cricket

**3** **True or false?** A margay's ankle can rotate all the way around to face backward.

**4** Which dinosaur feature is believed to have been used for defense?
a. knobby tail
b. horns and frills
c. thick layer of bone
d. all of the above

**5** Which is not a characteristic of birds?
a. They lay eggs.
b. They breathe with lungs.
c. They are cold-blooded.
d. They have feathers and wings.

Not **STUMPED** yet? Check out the *NATIONAL GEOGRAPHIC KIDS QUIZ WHIZ* collection for more crazy **ANIMAL** questions!

ANSWERS: 1. a; 2. b; 3. True; 4. d; 5. c

72

## HOMEWORK HELP

# Wildly Good Animal Reports

Seahorse

**Your teacher wants** a written report on the seahorse. Not to worry. Use these organizational tools so you can stay afloat while writing a report.

**STEPS TO SUCCESS:** Your report will follow the format of a descriptive or expository essay (see p. 199 for "How to Write a Perfect Essay") and should consist of a main idea, followed by supporting details and a conclusion. Use this basic structure for each paragraph as well as the whole report, and you'll be on the right track.

### 1. Introduction
State your **main idea.**
*Seahorses are fascinating fishes with many unique characteristics.*

### 2. Body
Provide **supporting points** for your main idea.
*Seahorses are very small fishes.*
*Seahorses are named for their head shape.*
*Seahorses display behavior that is rare among almost all other animals on Earth.*

Then **expand** on those points with further description, explanation, or discussion.
*Seahorses are very small fishes.*
*Seahorses are about the size of an M&M at birth, and most adult seahorses would fit in a teacup.*
*Seahorses are named for their head shape.*
*With long, tubelike snouts, seahorses are named for their resemblance to horses.*
*A group of seahorses is called a herd.*
*Seahorses display behavior that is rare among almost all other animals on Earth.*
*Unlike most other fish, seahorses stay with one mate their entire lives. They are also among the only species in which dads, not moms, give birth to the babies.*

### 3. Conclusion
Wrap it up with a **summary** of your whole paper.
*Because of their unique shape and unusual behavior, seahorses are among the most fascinating and easily distinguishable animals in the ocean.*

## KEY INFORMATION

**Here are some things you should consider including in your report:**
What does your animal look like?
**To what other species is it related?**
How does it move?
**Where does it live?**
What does it eat?
**What are its predators?**
How long does it live?
**Is it endangered?**
Why do you find it interesting?

**SEPARATE FACT FROM FICTION:** Your animal may have been featured in a movie or in myths and legends. Compare and contrast how the animal has been portrayed with how it behaves in reality. For example, penguins can't dance the way they do in *Happy Feet*.

**PROOFREAD AND REVISE:** As with any great essay, when you're finished, check for misspellings, grammatical mistakes, and punctuation errors. It often helps to have someone else proofread your work, too, as he or she may catch things you have missed. Also, look for ways to make your sentences and paragraphs even better. Add more descriptive language, choosing just the right verbs, adverbs, and adjectives to make your writing come alive.

**BE CREATIVE:** Use visual aids to make your report come to life. Include an animal photo file with interesting images found in magazines or printed from websites. Or draw your own! You can also build a miniature animal habitat diorama. Use creativity to help communicate your passion for the subject.

**THE FINAL RESULT:** Put it all together in one final, polished draft. Make it neat and clean, and remember to cite your references.

# SCIENCE and TECHNOLOGY

It's a bird, it's a plane, it's a ... driverless air taxi? Volocopter 2X, still in the prototype stage, can transport two passengers. The 18-rotor drone aircraft is being tested in Dubai.

# EARTH EXPLORER
## Meet Kakani Katija!

**This National Geographic emerging explorer blends biology and math to create cool tools.**

Kakani Katija loved science and math growing up, so she thought she would be an astronaut one day. But after discovering she had a passion for bio-engineering—the combination of engineering and biology—she decided to dive into an even deeper area: the ocean.

Today, Kakani develops instruments to enable exploration of previously hard-to-reach areas, like far below the ocean's surface. At the Monterey Bay Aquarium Research Institute (MBARI), Kakani created a tool called DeepPIV (short for Particle Image Velocimetry) that measures tiny plastic particles called microplastics thousands of meters underwater—and the animals that eat them.

"The tool uses laser illumination to see how these animals consume plastics," she says of DeepPIV, which is attached to a submersible robot that can travel 2.5 miles

(4,000 m) below the ocean's surface. "Many people assume that the plastic problem is constrained to the surface of the ocean. What we discovered is that there are microplastics in the deepest parts, even on the ocean floor, and there are animals ingesting them."

By continuing to develop better observational tools and techniques, Kakani can arm biologists and other experts with more knowledge about what's going on in the deep sea. She hopes this will trigger change that can ultimately improve the condition of our oceans—and the entire planet.

"It's hard to come up with the best solutions if you don't know what the problem is," says Kakani. "As bio-engineers, we use technology to find new ways to approach a problem, and help others fix it."

8 million tons (7.2 million t) of trash wind up in the ocean each year.

MICROPLASTICS

> I was always enamored by the search for life in outer planets. And then I realized that there is a lot of life in our oceans that we knew almost nothing about. That story is just beginning.

KAKANI OPERATING DEEPPIV

It took about four years for Kakani and her team to design, build, and finally use the DeepPIV tool.

## CALL TO ACTION!

Want to get into bioengineering? Better start crunching some numbers. "Math is the foundation of any bioengineering career," says Kakani. "Our focus is on finding solutions." To do your part in reducing the amount of plastics that DeepPIV finds in the ocean, a good place to start is by using reusable straws instead of plastic ones. Encourage your friends and family to do the same!

INSPECTING A FISHING NET FOUND IN THE OCEAN

# COOL INVENTIONS

## FLOATING ISLAND

You'd *want* to be stranded on this island. Modeled after a large species of lily pad that drifts down the Amazon River, the Lilypad floating ecopolis is designed to float on the ocean. This human-made habitat would feature homes and shops structured around a lagoon that could collect rain for drinking water. Fueled in part by wind and solar power, the island concept could provide up to 50,000 residents with an eco-friendly home—and the ultimate oceanfront view.

PART OF THE ISLAND HABITAT DIPS UNDERWATER.

## GLOVES GIVE CONCERT

These gloves hit the right notes. Sensors inside the fingertips detect when you press on a hard surface and send a signal to a speaker to produce the same musical notes created by hitting piano keys. Tap out a tune with your hands side by side. Then move your mitts away from each other and drum your fingers again. The sensors can tell that your digits have moved, and they signal the speaker to play different notes—same as if you moved your hands in different directions on an actual piano. That rocks!

## ROBOT FOLDS LAUNDRY

Doing laundry is no longer such a chore with FoldiMate, a robot that folds clean clothes. All you have to do is clip garments to hangers on the machine's exterior. The hangers, attached to a conveyor belt, rotate downward, pulling articles of clothing one at a time into a slot. Inside the robot, an electronic arm plucks each garment from its hanger and lays it on a platform. Here, more arms fold and dispense the item. Soon your laundry's done—case *clothed.*

BEFORE

AFTER

TAP YOUR FINGERS!

BATTER GOES HERE.

THE MACHINE MADE THESE PANCAKES!

RAIN ALERT!

9:41

## UMBRELLA PREDICTS WEATHER

Getting caught in the rain is no fun. That's where the Oombrella comes in. This umbrella's handle contains a device that measures temperature, air pressure, and humidity to predict exactly when it's going to rain. Connecting wirelessly to your phone, it alerts you about 15 minutes before the first drops fall. And don't worry about accidentally leaving this gear at a friend's house once the skies clear. The Oombrella pings your phone if you're more than 130 feet (40 m) away from it. That's one unforgettable umbrella.

## PANCAKE ART

Create art with pancake mix! The PancakeBot produces flapjacks shaped as the Eiffel Tower, George Washington, Scooby-Doo, and more. First, use the PancakeBot computer program to trace over a design with the drawing tool. The movements are translated into step-by-step instructions for the PancakeBot to follow. Now just pour batter into the machine. The bot's electronic nozzle will squeeze the mixture onto a heated griddle below, shifting as it follows the directions to create the flapjack formation. The result? Pancakes that look *almost* too good to eat.

## SPACE GLIDER

The Perlan 2 plane will sweep you 17 miles (27 km) off the ground to the edge of space—and it doesn't even have an engine, jets, or propellers. What the two-passenger glider *does* have is an 84-foot (26-m) wingspan, about the length of two school buses. To take off, this lightweight craft is connected by cable to another plane and towed 10,000 feet (3,050 m) into the air. Then it's released over mountainous regions where extra-strong air currents buoy the plane under its large wings and carry the craft 90,000 feet (27,500 m) high. Here, data is collected on the atmosphere before pilots use the glider's air brakes to descend. Glide on!

PILOT

AIRBUS

# FUTURE WORLD:

The year is 2070 and it's time to get dressed for school. You step in front of a large video mirror that projects different clothes on you. After you decide on your favorite T-shirt, a robot fetches your outfit. No time is lost trying to find matching socks! Chores? What chores? Get ready for a whole new home life.

## STAY CONNECTED

Whether your future home is an urban skyscraper or an underwater pod, all buildings will one day be connected via a central communications hub. Want to check out a *T. rex* skeleton at a faraway museum? You can virtually connect to it just as though you were checking it out in person. But you're not just seeing something miles away. Connect to a beach house's balcony and smell the salt water and feel the breeze. Buildings might also share information about incoming weather and emergencies to keep you safe.

## CUSTOM COMFORT

Soon, your house may give you a personal welcome home. No need for keys—sensors scan your body and open the door. Walk into the living room, and the lighting adjusts to your preferred setting. Thirsty? A glass of water pops up on the counter. Before bed, you enter the bathroom and say, "Shower, please." The water starts flowing at exactly the temperature you want.

## ON LOCATION

Your room has a spectacular view of the ocean ... because your house is suspended above it. New technologies will allow us to build our homes in unusual spots. In the future, "floating" structures elevated by supporting poles above water or other hard-to-access spots (think mountain peaks) will be more common as cities become more crowded. And this won't be limited to dry land on Earth. That means one day, your family could even live in space!

# Homes

## ON THE GO

Homes of the future will always be on the move. Walls will be capable of expanding and contracting, and houses will rotate with the sun's movements to conserve energy. Buildings will also be capable of changing size depending on who's inside. Grandparents could "move in" by attaching a modular section to the front, back, or top of the house.

## BRING ON THE BOTS

While you were outside playing with your friends, your house robot did the laundry, vacuumed, and cleaned the bathroom. Meanwhile a drone just delivered groceries for the home-bot to put away. Minutes later, lunch is ready. The service is great ... but how will you earn your allowance? Instead of taking out the garbage or setting the table, you'll earn money by helping clean and maintain the robots.

81

# FUTURE WORLD:

**H**ow do you get to the store in the year 2060? It's raining, so you decide not to take the drone. Instead you ride in your driverless cube car.

"The sky's no longer the limit in terms of where transportation is headed," says Tom Kurfess, a mechanical engineering professor at the Georgia Institute of Technology. Take a peek at these wild rides of the future.

## GOING UP ... WAY UP!

The space elevator doors open—welcome to the space station lobby. It's possible that people will one day ride a space elevator from Earth to a space station that orbits our planet from 22,370 miles (36,000 km) above. The elevator will carry passengers and cargo into space without burning huge amounts of fuel, unlike today's rockets. Aboard the station, travelers might stay in a hotel room with a truly out-of-this-world view. Then those heading to, say, Mars, can transfer to a spaceship to continue their journey.

## NO DRIVER NEEDED

You exit your high-rise apartment balcony into your own private glass elevator, take a seat, and say your destination. The elevator car descends 205 floors to street level before detaching from the building and moving to the street. It's now a cube-shaped car. Another cube carrying your friends is nearby; the vehicles connect while in motion, transforming into one bigger car. The cube drops you off at school and parks itself. According to Tommaso Gecchelin, founder of NEXT Future Transportation, driverless cars will work together to end traffic jams and improve safety.

# Transportation

## POWER PLANE

Passenger planes will still be around in the future—they'll just travel *much* faster. Today flying 6,850 miles (11,025 km) from New York City to Beijing, China, takes about 14 hours. But thanks to future technological advancements such as sleeker, more lightweight aircraft, a passenger plane could make the same trip in just under two hours.

## FLOWN BY DRONE

"One day soon drones and robots will deliver our meals," Gecchelin says. But further into the future, helicopter-size drones could also deliver *people*. Some experts even think that cargo drones will be able to lift small houses from a city and carry them to scenic vacation spots.

## TOTALLY TUBULAR

Your friend invites you to her birthday party. It's today—and across the country. No prob. You can tube it from the West Coast to the East Coast in just two hours. You sit in a capsule that looks like a train without rails. *Whoosh!* The capsule's sucked into a vacuum tube. Like a bullet train, the capsule uses magnets to fly forward in the tube without friction or resistance. The result: a smooth, fast ride that never slows down below 750 miles an hour (1,200 km/h).

# WHAT IS LIFE?

This seems like such an easy question to answer. Everybody knows that singing birds are alive and rocks are not. But when we start studying bacteria and other microscopic creatures, things get more complicated.

## SO WHAT EXACTLY IS LIFE?

Most scientists agree that something is alive if it can do the following: reproduce; grow in size to become more complex in structure; take in nutrients to survive; give off waste products; and respond to external stimuli, such as increased sunlight or changes in temperature.

## KINDS OF LIFE

Biologists classify living organisms by how they get their energy. Organisms such as algae, green plants, and some bacteria use sunlight as an energy source. Animals (like humans), fungi, and some Archaea use chemicals to provide energy. When we eat food, chemical reactions within our digestive system turn our food into fuel.

Living things inhabit land, sea, and air. In fact, life also thrives deep beneath the oceans, embedded in rocks miles below Earth's crust, in ice, and in other extreme environments. The life-forms that thrive in these challenging environments are called extremophiles. Some of these draw directly upon the chemicals surrounding them for energy. Since these are very different forms of life than what we're used to, we may not think of them as alive, but they are.

## HOW IT ALL WORKS

To try and understand how a living organism works, it helps to look at one example of its simplest form—the single-celled bacterium called *Streptococcus*. There are many kinds of these tiny organisms, and some are responsible for human illnesses. What makes us sick or uncomfortable are the toxins the bacteria give off in our bodies.

A single *Streptococcus* bacterium is so small that at least 500 of them could fit on the dot above this letter *i*. These bacteria are some of the simplest forms of life we know. They have no moving parts, no lungs, no brain, no heart, no liver, and no leaves or fruit. Yet this life-form reproduces. It grows in size by producing long chain structures, takes in nutrients, and gives off waste products. This tiny life-form is alive, just as you are alive.

What makes something alive is a question scientists grapple with when they study viruses, such as the ones that cause the common cold and smallpox. They can grow and reproduce within host cells, such as those that make up your body. Because viruses lack cells and cannot metabolize nutrients for energy or reproduce without a host, scientists ask if they are indeed alive. And don't go looking for them without a strong microscope— viruses are a hundred times smaller than bacteria.

Scientists think life began on Earth some 4.1 to 3.9 billion years ago, but no fossils exist from that time. The earliest fossils ever found are from the primitive life that existed 3.6 billion years ago. Other life-forms, some of which are shown below, soon followed. Scientists continue to study how life evolved on Earth and whether it is possible that life exists on other planets.

## MICROSCOPIC ORGANISMS

# The Three Domains of Life

Biologists divide all living organisms into three domains: Bacteria, Archaea, and Eukarya. Archaean and Bacterial cells do not have nuclei, but they are so different from each other that they belong to different domains. Since human cells have a nucleus, humans belong to the Eukarya domain.

**1** BACTERIA

**DOMAIN BACTERIA:** These single-celled microorganisms are found almost everywhere in the world. Bacteria are small and do not have nuclei. They can be shaped like rods, spirals, or spheres. Some of them are helpful to humans, and some are harmful.

**2** ARCHAEA

**DOMAIN ARCHAEA:** These single-celled micro-organisms are often found in extremely hostile environments. Like Bacteria, Archaea do not have nuclei, but they have some genes in common with Eukarya. For this reason, scientists think the Archaea living today most closely resemble the earliest forms of life on Earth.

**3** EUKARYA

**DOMAIN EUKARYA:** This diverse group of life-forms is more complicated than Bacteria and Archaea, as Eukarya have one or more cells with nuclei. These are the tiny cells that make up your whole body. Eukarya are divided into four groups: fungi, protists, plants, and animals.

**FYI** WHAT IS A DOMAIN? Scientifically speaking, a domain is a major taxonomic division into which natural objects are classified (see p. 26 for "What Is Taxonomy?").

FUNGI

KINGDOM FUNGI (about 100,000 species): Mainly multicellular organisms, fungi cannot make their own food. Mushrooms and yeast are fungi.

PROTISTS

PROTISTS (about 250,000 species): Once considered a kingdom, this group is a "grab bag" that includes unicellular and multicellular organisms of great variety.

PLANTS

KINGDOM PLANTAE (about 400,000 species): Plants are multicellular, and many can make their own food using photosynthesis (see p. 86 for "Photosynthesis").

ANIMALS

KINGDOM ANIMALIA (about 1,000,000 species): Most animals, which are multi-cellular, have their own organ systems. Animals do not make their own food.

# HOW DOES YOUR GARDEN GR🌻W?

The plant kingdom is about 400,000 species strong, growing all over the world: on top of mountains, in the sea, in frigid temperatures—everywhere. Without plants, life on Earth would not be able to survive. Plants provide food and oxygen for animals and humans.

**Three characteristics make plants distinct:**

1. Most have chlorophyll (a green pigment that makes photosynthesis work and turns sunlight into energy), while some are parasitic. These plants don't make their own food—they take it from other plants.
2. They cannot change their location on their own.
3. Their cell walls are made from a stiff material called cellulose.

## Photosynthesis

Plants are lucky—most don't have to hunt or shop for food. Most use the sun to produce their own food. In a process called photosynthesis, a plant's chloroplast (the part of the plant where the chemical chlorophyll is located) captures the sun's energy and combines it with carbon dioxide from the air and nutrient-rich water from the ground to produce a sugar called glucose. Plants burn the glucose for energy to help them grow. As a waste product, plants emit oxygen, which humans and other animals need to breathe. When we breathe, we exhale carbon dioxide, which the plants then use for more photosynthesis—it's all a big, finely tuned system. So the next time you pass a lonely houseplant, give it thanks for helping you live.

# Make a TERRARIUM

## COLLECT MATERIALS FROM THE GREAT OUTDOORS

so you can enjoy nature when you're back inside. A terrarium is a great way to experiment with plants on a miniature level.

### SUPPLY LIST

- Fishbowl or jar
- Activated charcoal
- Potting soil
- A variety of plants (miniature ferns or spider moss) or seeds (such as sweet alyssum or wheatgrass)
- Bits of nature from the outdoors, such as leaves, twigs, and mosses

### STEPS

1. Wash and dry a large glass bowl or jar. (An old fishbowl works well.)
2. Fill the bottom—about 1 inch (2.5 cm) high—with stones you have collected from your nature hikes.
3. Using a shovel or spoon, add several inches of potting soil mixed with activated charcoal bits.
4. If you are using potted plants, dig a little hole in the soil for the roots and place the plants in. Pack extra soil around the plants. Add water until the soil is moist. (If you're using seeds, press them into the soil and moisten.)
5. Add sheet moss on top of the soil around the plants.
6. Now the fun part! Add a few decorative bits of nature—a small pinecone, a special rock, or a little figurine. Keep your terrarium in a well-lit place, and don't forget to add a little water when the soil looks dry.

**Time:** about 30 minutes

## fun fact

Mosses grow in damp environments and are home to a little creature called a moss piglet! Moss piglets, also known as water bears, have eight legs and grow up to about .06 inch (1.5 mm) in length.

**Bet You Didn't Know!**

# 10 facts about the

**1** **Brain cells** live longer than all of the other cells in your body.

**2** The more you **concentrate,** the less you blink.

**3** Your **teeth** are **harder** than your **bones.**

**4** Some people can **hear their eyeballs** moving.

**5** It is **not possible** to tickle yourself.

**6** You can buy **fake eyebrows** and **eyelashes** made out of **real hair.**

# human body

**7** Fingernails grow **faster** than **toenails.**

**8** Your heart beats about **100,000 times** each day.

**9** Your foot is about the **same length** as the distance between your **elbow and wrist.**

**10** The saliva you produce in your lifetime could fill nearly **30,000** water bottles.

# MUSCLE POWER

## With its strong bones and flexible joints, your skeleton is built to be on the go.

But without muscles, it won't go anywhere! You need muscle power to make your body walk, run, skip, rub your nose, or even just sit up without toppling over.

The muscles that do these jobs are called skeletal muscles. You have about 650 of them, and you can control what they do. Sometimes, it takes a lot of skeletal muscles to make even a simple move. Your tongue alone contains eight muscles!

You also have muscles that work without your having to do a thing. Most of these muscles are called smooth muscles. Sheets of smooth muscle line your blood vessels, throat, stomach, intestines, lungs, and other organs. They are hard at work keeping your blood circulating and your food digesting while you're busy doing other things. And there's also that mighty muscle, your heart. It pumps thanks to cardiac muscles, which are found only in the heart.

## THE HIBERNATION MYSTERY

Very sick people often lie in bed for a long time as they recover. This lack of exercise weakens muscles—a process called "muscle atrophy." Preventing atrophy may be possible someday thanks to researchers who study hibernating animals.

Bears, for example, spend winter sleeping but do not suffer severe atrophy. When they wake up in spring, they're as strong as—well, bears! Scientists are studying the muscles and blood of bears, ground squirrels, and other hibernators to find out how they stay in shape while sleeping. The answers may one day help people suffering from muscle atrophy when they're sick or in the hospital for a long time.

**Bet You Didn't Know!**

Some of your body's strongest muscles aren't in your arms or legs. They're in your jaws! These strong muscles are called the masseters. They help you chew by closing your lower jaw. Clenching your teeth will make your masseters bulge so you can feel them.

# BODY ELECTRIC

The nerve signal that tells your muscles to move is super fast! It zooms at 250 miles an hour (402 km/h), as fast as the fastest race car.

## Your body is just humming with electricity.

Nerve cells from head to toe speak to each other through electrical signals. The electrical signals zap down each nerve cell and, when they get to the end, jump across a tiny gap called a synapse (see photo, right). How does the signal jump across the gap?

The nerve produces special chemicals that can flow across the gap to the next cell. There, a new electrical charge travels down the next nerve. Messages jump from neuron to neuron in a chain of electrical-chemical-electrical-chemical signals until they reach their destination.

Because nerves don't actually touch, they can change the path of their signals easily. They can make new connections and break old ones. This is how your brain learns and stores new information.

## Bet You Didn't Know!

A reflex is a nerve message that doesn't go through your brain. When you touch a hot stove, for example, a sensory neuron picks up the message ("Hot!") and passes it to a motor neuron in your spinal cord. The motor neuron then sends a message to your hand, telling it to move ("Quick!").

## BUNDLE OF NERVES

A 1.2-inch (3-cm) section of your brain stem (called the medulla oblongata) controls some of your body's most important functions, such as breathing and heart rate. Amazingly, it also contains your body's motor and sensory nerves and is where nerves from the left and right sides of your body cross each other on their journey toward your cerebrum.

SENSORY NERVES pull in information from nerve endings in your eyes, ears, skin, hands, and other parts of your body and then send this information to your brain.

MOTOR NERVES send messages from your brain to your muscles, telling them to contract, to run, or to walk.

# LOOK OUT!

blood vessels

sclera

eyelash

retina

optic nerve

lens

pupil

conjunctiva

cornea

On a dark, clear night, it would be possible for you to see a car's headlights from about two miles (3.2 km) away.

## Your eyes are two of the most amazing organs in your body.

These small, squishy, fluid-filled balls have almost three-quarters of your body's sensory receptors. They're like two supersmart cameras, but more complex.

So how do you see the world around you? It begins when you open the protective cover of your eyelid and let in the light. Light enters your eye through the window of your cornea and passes through the aqueous humor, a watery fluid that nourishes the eye tissue. It enters the black circle in the iris (the colored part of your eye), called the pupil. Because people need to be able to see in both bright and low light, muscles in the iris automatically make the pupil smaller when the light is strong and wider when the light is dim. Light then travels to the lens, whose muscles adjust it to be able to see objects both near and far. Then the light goes through the vitreous humor (a clear jellylike substance) to the retina. The retina, a layer of about 126 million light-sensitive cells, lines the back of your eyeball. When these cells absorb the light, they transform it into electrical signals that are sent along the optic nerve to the brain. The brain then makes sense of what you are seeing.

## A TOPSY-TURVY WORLD

Turn this over in your mind: You're looking at the world topsy-turvy, and you don't even know it. Like a camera lens, your lens focuses light, creates an image, and turns it upside down. Yep, when your lens focuses light inside your eye, it flips the image so it lands on your retina upside down. But, your brain knows to flip the image automatically to match your reality. But what if your reality suddenly

CAMERA LENS

changed? A well-known experiment in the mid-20th century in which a person wore special light-inverting goggles showed that his brain actually adjusted to the new, inverted world by eventually seeing the reversed view as normal! It is thought that newborns see the world upside down for a short while, until their brains learn how to turn things right-side up.

# AWESOME
# OPTICAL ILLUSIONS

**Ready to work your brain and show your visual alertness?
Ponder these puzzling pictures to see what you see!**

## WHICH CIRCLE IS BIGGER?

Both of these circle clusters have an orange circle surrounded by purple ones. But which orange circle is bigger? The answer may surprise you: neither! The two orange circles are the same size. The one on the right may appear bigger because it's surrounded by purple circles that are smaller than it is. The one on the left seems smaller because it's surrounded by purple circles that are larger than it is.

## RABBIT OR DUCK?

It's a duck! Or is it a rabbit? Can you see it both ways? A recent study using this illusion suggests that the more easily people can switch back and forth between the two images, the more creative they are.

## SPINNING CIRCLES

Do you see all the spinning circles? Don't look too long, or you might get dizzy! This illusion plays with your peripheral vision (vision from the sides of your eyes, not the middle). Sometimes when you look out the sides of your eyes, you see movement where really there are only patterns.

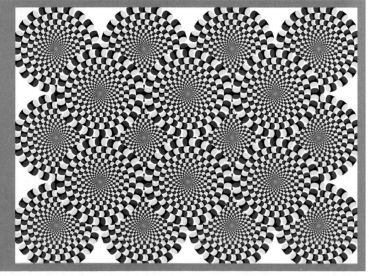

93

# THE INVADERS ARE COMING!

BACTERIA

FUNGUS

VIRUS

Every square inch (6.5 sq cm) of your skin hosts about **six million bacteria.**

PROTOZOA (CAN BE TRANSMITTED BY MOSQUITOES)

**Some microorganisms (tiny living things) can make your body sick.** They are too small to see with the naked eye. These creatures—bacteria, viruses, fungi, and protozoa—are what you may know as germs.

Bacteria are microscopic organisms that live nearly everywhere on Earth, including on and in the human body. "Good" bacteria help sour digestive systems work properly. Harmful bacteria can cause ailments, including ear infections and strep throat.

A virus, like a cold or the flu, needs to live inside another living thing (a host) to survive; then it can grow and multiply throughout the host's body.

Fungi get their food from the plants, animals, or people they live on. Some fungi can get on your body and cause skin diseases such as ringworm.

Protozoa are single-celled organisms that can spread disease to humans through contaminated water and dirty living conditions. Protozoa can cause infections such as malaria, which occurs when a person is bitten by an infected mosquito.

## ADD IT UP

So you know that you have bacteria on your skin and in your body. But do you know how many? One hundred trillion— that's 100,000,000,000,000! Most are harmless and some are pretty friendly, keeping more dangerous bacteria at bay, protecting you from some skin infections, and helping your cuts heal.

# GERM **SHOWDOWN**

Scientists in Wales studied three greeting styles to determine which was the cleanest. Find out which one has the upper hand.

## HANDSHAKE

AN AVERAGE HANDSHAKE TRANSFERRED **MORE THAN 5 TIMES AS MUCH BACTERIA** AS A FIST BUMP. (A STRONG HANDSHAKE TRANSFERRED **10 TIMES** AS MUCH.)

## HIGH FIVE

A HIGH FIVE PASSED **TWICE AS MANY** GERMS AS A FIST BUMP.

## FIST BUMP

WINNER:

FIST BUMPS HAVE THE **LEAST SKIN-TO-SKIN CONTACT** OF THE GREETINGS, WHICH MAKES IT LESS LIKELY FOR MICROBES TO JUMP **FROM ONE HAND TO ANOTHER.**

# WHAT DIED?

## CONCEPTS
decomposition, microbiology, decay, organic materials, bacteria, insects, corpse fauna

## HOW LONG IT TAKES
two to four days, possibly longer in cold weather

## WHAT YOU NEED
food samples
containers
outdoor thermometer
magnifying lens
dissecting microscope
bug identification guides
optional: camera, smartphone, or video camera

f you leave food out, SOMETHING will come to live on it or lay eggs on it. In this observation, discover what arrives to make the most of your leftovers.

What comes to get food that's left out?

## WHAT TO DO

### DAY ONE:

**1 WORK IN AN OPEN-AIR** area, compost heap, or compost bin—a place that is open to bugs but not birds or other animals. Ask an adult to help you choose a location.

**2 SET UP FOUR** containers with a small sample of food inside each. If you want, these samples can represent the four food groups: vegetable/fruit, meat/fish, bread/grains, and milk/dairy.

### DAYS TWO TO FOUR:

**3 KEEP A CAREFUL** record of what you observe through your senses. Each day, record the temperature in the area where your samples are. Note whether you can see signs that bugs or other creatures have been attracted to your samples, including any film or mold that forms. You may want to photograph the samples every day to compare them.

**4 EVERY ONE OR TWO** days (decide which interval you want to study), remove the samples from the containers to examine them with a magnifying lens and microscope. Count, try to identify, and sketch the bugs and other life-forms that colonize each sample. Add descriptions to your notes, including sensory observations: texture, color, and smell—but not taste!

**WHAT TO EXPECT?**
You may see mold, biofilm or scum, bugs, worms, flies, and so on.

**WHAT'S GOING ON?**
Nature abhors a vacuum. If there is food, something will come to eat it.

## OUR TRY

We put out duplicate food—chicken broth, blackberry jam, and cat food—every other day for six days. We set out the food in the yard, in a cat carrier with a brick on top, but that didn't stop coyotes from pulling it apart and getting the food on the second night. After that we replaced the food and kept the cat carrier in the garage, where flies could still get to it. After we opened it to see what we had and examine it with the microscope, we dumped the cat carrier near the compost heap—and later, we had a glorious infestation of beetles.

### QUESTION THIS!

- What would happen to this food if nothing were able to reach it?
- What would happen to this food if you let more time pass?

# QUIZ WHIZ

## Discover your tech-savvy smarts by taking this quiz!

Write your answers on a piece of paper. Then check them below.

**1** How many plant species are there on Earth?

a. 400,000     c. 4,000
b. 40,000      d. 400

**2** **True or false?** Some of your body's strongest muscles are in your jaw.

**3** Microscopic organisms that live in moss are also known as _____ .

a. moss monsters
b. moss piglets
c. moss monkeys
d. moss cows

**4** **True or false?** Scientists think life began on Earth about 1 million years ago.

**5** An architect has designed a conceptual floating island shaped like which object?

a. a lotus flower
b. a UFO
c. a lily pad
d. a roller coaster

Not **STUMPED** yet? Check out the *NATIONAL GEOGRAPHIC KIDS QUIZ WHIZ* collection for more crazy **TECHNOLOGY** questions!

**ANSWERS:**
1. a; 2. True; 3. b; 4. False. Experts think life began about four billion years ago; 5. c.

# This Is How It's Done!

Sometimes, the most complicated problems are solved with step-by-step directions. These "how-to" instructions are also known as a process analysis essay. While scientists and engineers use this tool to program robots and write computer code, you also use process analysis every day, from following a recipe to putting together a new toy or gadget. Here's how to write a basic process analysis essay.

## Step 1: Choose Your Topic Sentence

Pick a clear and concise topic sentence that describes what you're writing about. Be sure to explain to the reader why the task is important—and how many steps there are to complete it.

## Step 2: List Materials

Do you need specific ingredients or equipment to complete your process? Mention these right away so the readers will have all they need to do this activity.

## Step 3: Write Your Directions

Your directions should be clear and easy to follow. Assume that you are explaining the process for the first time, and define any unfamiliar terms. List your steps in the exact order the reader will need to follow to complete the activity. Try to keep your essay limited to no more than six steps.

## Step 4: Restate Your Main Idea

Your closing idea should revisit your topic sentence, drawing a conclusion relating to the importance of the subject.

## EXAMPLE OF A PROCESS ANALYSIS ESSAY

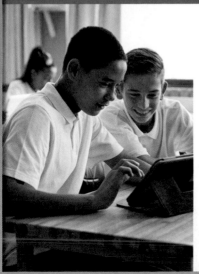

Downloading an app is a simple way to enhance your tablet. Today, I'd like to show you how to search for and add an app to your tablet. First, you will need a tablet with the ability to access the internet. You'll also want to ask a parent for permission before you download anything onto your tablet. Next, select the specific app you're seeking by going to the app store on your tablet and entering the app's name into the search bar. Once you find the app you're seeking, select "download" and wait for the app to load. When you see that the app has fully loaded, tap on the icon and you will be able to access it. Now you can enjoy your app and have more fun with your tablet.

# GOING GREEN

# EARTH EXPLORER

## Meet **Katey Walter Anthony!**

**This aquatic ecologist and National Geographic explorer is tapping into new research on global warming.**

Katey Walter Anthony remembers the first time she saw the bubbles. One day, while walking across a frozen lake in Siberia, she looked down and saw clusters of gas trapped beneath the thick, dark ice. "It looked like the starry night sky," Katey recalls.

But these weren't your average air bubbles. As Katey soon discovered, the bubbles were actually methane, a potent greenhouse gas that contributes to global warming. So how does the methane get under the ice? It comes from permafrost, the frozen ground that once covered the entire Arctic, including the bottom of ancient lakes that Katey studies. As the permafrost thaws from solid, frozen ground to looser soil and mud with Earth's rising temperatures, it can release carbon. Microbes in the soil turn the carbon into methane. In the summer, the gas rises up from the bottom of the lake, through the lake's surface, and enters the atmosphere. In the winter, it gets stuck under the frozen surface, creating those beautiful bubbles.

The way Katey determines whether the bubbles are methane is, well, pretty lit. "We tap holes into the ice and light a match," she says. "If there's methane and it mixes with oxygen, you'll get fireballs up to the trees."

As she's looked for methane in some 250 ancient lakes throughout Alaska and Russia, Katey has uncovered preserved woolly mammoth tusks and rhino bones. And she's also dug up proof that the methane being released from the melting permafrost is a source of climate change that many experts haven't recognized.

"Right now, if you look at the models of climate change, none of them include methane from thawing permafrost at the bottom of lakes as a source," says Katey. "We believe that the release of these gases intensifies global warming. It's a big part of the climate change story."

Siberian lakes have the potential to release an estimated 50 billion tons (45.4 billion t) of methane—10 times more methane than the atmosphere holds right now.

FROZEN METHANE BUBBLES

"All that carbon was locked up safely in the permafrost freezer for tens of thousands of years. Now the freezer door is opening, releasing the carbon into Arctic lake bottoms, where microbes convert it to methane."

Katey's team has studied 42,000-year-old methane gas.

## CALL TO ACTION!

"My wish for all kids is that you go out and explore nature," says Katey. "Be curious, study the world around you. And maybe that will help you one day make decisions that will help save the planet." You can also do your part to fight climate change through simple steps at home like recycling, powering down your electronics when you're not using them, and trying not to waste food.

KATEY CHECKING BUBBLES FOR METHANE

# Trapped by TRASH!

**VICTIM: SKUNK**
**TRASH: YOGURT CONTAINER**
**PROBLEM: HEAD STUCK**

A HOMEOWNER finds a writhing baby skunk in her recycling bin. The skunk has a plastic yogurt container over his head. When the animal tries to push the container off, it won't budge. He claws at his head, struggling to free himself, then tumbles out of the uncovered bin. The panicked little skunk can't see a thing and begins to suffocate.

A PHONE CALL to Wildlife in Crisis, an animal rescue organization in nearby Weston, Connecticut, brings help. Director Dara Reid dispatches caretaker Anna Clark to the woman's home. She wraps the skunk in a towel and then gently tugs the container until the exhausted creature is finally free.

BUT HE'S NOT SAFE. There is no sign of the animal's mother, and this baby skunk is far too young to survive on his own. Wildlife in Crisis feeds him milk and wet cat food until his teeth grow in, and then adds natural foods like berries and worms to his diet. About four months later he's released into the wild.

**Animals get trapped every day by the things people carelessly discard. Here are stories of lucky animals that have tangled with trash—and escaped.**

**VICTIM: SEA LION**
**TRASH: FISHING LINE**
**PROBLEM: MOUTH TRAPPED**

The sea lion prowls for food off the California shore, sticking his nose in places where fish might hide. When his whiskers snag on some fishing line, he tries to shake it off. But the strong material tangles, wraps around his snout and neck, and eventually traps his mouth shut.

Someone notices the distressed animal and informs the Marine Mammal Center in nearby Sausalito. When the sea lion reappears in a bay, the center's rescue team speeds to the scene. The feisty sea lion eludes them for nearly three weeks.

The worried rescue team sedates him with darts while he rests on a dock. After he becomes sleepy, the team rushes the 260-pound (118-kg) mammal to the center to cut the fishing line, treat his wounds, and feed him. The sea lion eats 100 pounds (45 kg) of herring and is then set free. Hopefully now he steers clear of trash.

FISHING LINE

**VICTIM: BALD EAGLE**
**TRASH: STRING**
**PROBLEM: WING TANGLED**

A young bald eagle is in trouble. When her parents searched for sticks to build the nest, they also found balloon string, fishing line, and other trash. Now the young eagle is tangled in the debris and falls from the nest. The bird hangs four feet (1.2 m) above the ground, breaking her wing in the process.

Dara Reid of Wildlife in Crisis comes to the rescue. She cuts down the suspended eagle and rushes her to the rescue facility. After removing the trash, Reid aligns the bird's broken wing and immobilizes it by bandaging the wing against the eagle's body.

Following 14 months of TLC, the bald eagle is ta__ to a field. With a helpful heave from Reid, the eagle flaps hard, circles above, and then re-enters the wild—with a perfectly healed wing.

GETTING BETTER

FLYING AGAIN

105

# A GLOBAL RACE TO ZERO WASTE

BOTH SWEDEN (MAIN PHOTO) AND SINGAPORE (INSET) ARE WORLDWIDE LEADERS IN RECYCLING AND WASTE REDUCTION.

It's an ambitious goal, but one that some countries hope to achieve in less than 10 years. The aim? Zero waste, meaning every single piece of trash will be reused or composted. The idea may seem impossible, but several spots are coming close.

Take Sweden, for example. Less than one percent of the country's household garbage ends up in landfills. Rather, the Swedes recycle nearly everything—some 1.5 billion bottles and cans annually—and the rest winds up at waste-to-energy plants to produce electricity. The program is so successful that Sweden actually imports trash from other places, such as the United Kingdom, Norway, and Ireland, to keep up the rapid pace of its incinerators.

Other places narrowing in on zero waste? The Himalayan country of Bhutan is shooting for that status by 2030, while Singapore and Dubai have announced similar timelines. In the United States, individual cities like San Francisco and New York have also declared their dedication to going zero waste. The U.S. National Park Service, as well as major corporations like Lego and Nike, are also making big moves toward creating zero waste—all in an effort to make this world a cleaner place.

So what's the secret to zero waste? It's all about enforcing the rules of reducing, reusing, and recycling. In Sweden, for example, recycling stations must be no more than 984 feet (300 m) from any residential area. And in Bhutan—which is aspiring to become the world's first nation to have an all-organic farming system—composting from food scraps is the norm. Simple practices like these, as well as educating the public on the problems stemming from too much trash, can lead to major changes. And, perhaps, zero waste around the world one day.

DUBAI—HOME TO THE FAMOUS PALM JUMEIRAH ISLAND—IS AIMING TO GO WASTE-FREE BY 2030.

# FROM FILTH **TO** FASHION

**Order up!** One creative company called Garbage Gone Glam made this dress out of diner menus. Other things they've made? A cocktail dress out of playing cards and a ball gown out of old magazines!

**HOW SOME TRASH TRAVELS FROM THE RECYCLING CENTER TO THE RUNWAYS—AND EVEN TO YOUR CLOSET.**

A hat made out of an old soccer ball brings new meaning to the term "header."

This eco-friendly bag is made from 365 recycled computer keyboard keys.

This head-piece, made from recycled corrugated cardboard, is hard to top!

LEVI STRAUSS & CO. MAKES JEANS OUT OF OLD COTTON T-SHIRTS.

This bow tie made out of an old aluminum can is both fashion-forward and eco-friendly.

# Pollution

## Cleaning Up Our Act

**So what's the big deal** about a little dirt on the planet? Pollution can affect animals, plants, and people. In fact, some studies show that more people die every year from diseases linked to air pollution than from car accidents. And right now nearly one billion of the world's people don't have access to clean drinking water.

### A LITTLE POLLUTION = BIG PROBLEMS

You can probably clean your room in a couple of hours. (At least we hope you can!) But you can't shove air and water pollution under your bed or cram them into the closet. Once released into the environment, pollution—whether it's oil leaking from a boat or chemicals spewing from a factory's smokestack—can have a lasting environmental impact.

### KEEP IT CLEAN

It's easy to blame things like big factories for pollution problems. But some of the mess comes from everyday activities. Exhaust fumes from cars and garbage in landfills can seriously trash Earth's health. We all need to pitch in and do some housecleaning. It may mean bicycling more and riding in cars less. Or not dumping water-polluting oil or household cleaners down the drain. Look at it this way: Just as with your room, it's always better not to let Earth get messed up in the first place.

## kids VS. PLASTIC

Part of the PLANET OR PLASTIC? initiative

A straw stuck in a sea turtle's nostril. A seahorse swimming along with its tail curled around a cotton swab. Sea birds washing up on sandy shores, entangled in plastic bags. Sadly, we do not have to look too far to see how animals are directly impacted by the staggering amount of plastic piling up on our planet. We've created more than 6.9 billion tons (6.3 billion t) of plastic waste, with only a small percentage landing in recycling bins. The rest of it lingers in landfills and winds up in our oceans. In fact, 700 species of animals are threatened because of ocean waste—and among seabirds, a whopping 90 percent eat plastic trash, according to a study. But as scary as these stats are, we can do something about them. Experts say it all starts with reducing the amount of plastic we use, including options for reusable containers or those made with marine biodegradable components. You can also pledge to do your part to reduce the plastic problem by visiting kids.nationalgeographic.com/explore/nature/kids-vs-plastic. Together, we can work to cut back on plastic and protect our planet—and everything on it.

# Declining Biodiversity

## Saving All Creatures, Great and Small

Earth is home to a huge mix of plants and animals—millions and possibly billions of species—and scientists have officially identified and named only about 1.9 million so far! Scientists call this healthy mix biodiversity.

### THE BALANCING ACT

The bad news is that half of the planet's plant and animal species may be on the path to extinction, mainly because of human activity. People cut down trees, build roads and houses, pollute rivers, overfish, and overhunt. The good news is that many people care. Scientists and volunteers race against the clock every day, working to save wildlife before time runs out. By building birdhouses, planting trees, and following the rules for hunting and fishing, you can be a positive force for preserving biodiversity, too. Every time you do something to help a species survive, you help our planet to thrive.

Green sea turtle

# Habitats Threatened

## Living on the Edge

Even though tropical rain forests cover only about 7 percent of the planet's total land surface, they are home to half of all known species of plants and animals. Because people cut down so many trees for lumber and firewood and clear so much land for farms, hundreds of thousands of acres of rain forest disappear every year.

### SHARING THE LAND

Wetlands are also important feeding and breeding grounds. People have drained many wetlands, turning them into farm fields or sites for industries. More than half the world's wetlands have disappeared within the past century, squeezing wildlife out. Balancing the needs of humans and animals is the key to lessening habitat destruction.

Jaguar

**109**

# WORLD ENERGY & MINERALS

**A**lmost everything people do—from cooking to powering the International Space Station—requires energy. But energy comes in different forms. Traditional energy sources, still used by many people in the developing world, include burning dried animal dung and wood. Industrialized countries and urban centers around the world rely on coal, oil, and natural gas—called fossil fuels because they formed from decayed plant and animal material accumulated from long ago. Fossil fuel deposits, either in the ground or under the ocean floor, are unevenly distributed on Earth, and only some countries can afford to buy them. Fossil fuels are also not renewable, meaning they will run out one day. And unless we find other ways to create energy, we'll be stuck. Without energy we won't be able to drive cars, use lights, or send emails to friends.

## TAKING A TOLL

Environmentally speaking, burning fossil fuels isn't necessarily the best choice, either: Carbon dioxide from the burning of fossil fuels, as well as other emissions, are contributing to global warming. Concerned scientists are looking at new ways to harness renewable, alternative sources of energy, such as water, wind, and sun.

## HIGH VOLTAGE

It seems like we use electricity for everything—from TVs and cell phones to air conditioners and computers. In fact, power plants generate 3.7 times more electrical power than they did just 40 years ago. How they do this can differ around the world. Is it from burning coal or taming the energy in moving water? Here's the global breakdown.

**5%** OTHER, SUCH AS GEOTHERMAL, SOLAR, WIND, HEAT, ETC.

**5%** OIL

**10.9%** NUCLEAR

**16.2%** HYDRO POWER

**40.4%** COAL

**22.5%** NATURAL GAS

Electricity travels at the speed of light—about 186,000 miles a second (299,340 km/s).

# Climate CHANGE

POLAR BEAR ON A PIECE OF MELTING ICEBERG

# Rising Temperatures, Explained

## Fact: The world is getting warmer.

Earth's surface temperature has been increasing. In the past 50 years, our planet has warmed twice as fast as in the 50 years before that. This is the direct effect of climate change, which refers not only to the increase in Earth's average temperature (known as global warming), but also to the long-term effects on winds, rain, and ocean currents. Global warming is the reason glaciers and polar ice sheets are melting—resulting in rising sea levels and shrinking habitats. This makes survival for some animals a big challenge. Warming also means more flooding along the coasts and drought for inland areas.

## Why are temperatures climbing?

Some of the recent climate changes can be tied to natural causes—such as changes in the sun's intensity, the unusually warm ocean currents

SCIENTISTS ARE CONCERNED THAT GREENLAND'S ICE SHEET HAS BEGUN TO MELT IN SUMMER. BIRTHDAY CANYON, SHOWN HERE, WAS CARVED BY MELTWATER.

of El Niño, and volcanic activity—but human activities are a major factor as well.

Everyday activities that require burning fossil fuels, such as driving gasoline-powered cars, contribute to global warming. These activities produce greenhouse gases, which enter the atmosphere and trap heat. At the current rate, Earth's global average temperature is projected to rise between 1.8 and 11.5°F (1 and 6.4°C) by the year 2100, and it will get even warmer after that. And as the climate continues to warm, it will unfortunately continue to affect the environment and our society in many ways.

# FUNKY JUNK ART

## Try This!

Who knew recycling could be so much fun? Check out these ideas for turning junk into awesome art.

ASK FOR A PARENT'S HELP AND PERMISSION BEFORE YOU START THESE PROJECTS.

## Bottle Cap Snake

### YOU WILL NEED
- 30–50 BOTTLE CAPS
- HAMMER
- AWL
- BOARD (TO HAMMER ON)
- PLASTIC-COATED WIRE
- CRAFT GLUE
- SELF-HARDENING CLAY
- 1 CORK
- 2 PUSHPINS

### Create a College

Cut up magazines or the Sunday comics and glue the pictures onto construction paper to make a funny collage.

### WHAT TO DO

Work with a parent to punch a hole in the center of each bottle cap using a hammer and awl. Do this on a board that is resting on a sturdy surface. Cut a piece of wire that is slightly longer than you want your snake to be. Tie a knot at one end of the wire. String all the bottle caps on the wire with the tops facing the open end of the wire. Knot the other end of the wire and cut off the excess. Glue a piece of clay to the snake's tail end and twist it into a tail shape. Glue a piece of clay to the opposite end of the snake. Create an indentation with the cork. Let the clay dry. Glue the cork into the clay. Once dry, press pushpins into the cork for eyes and some wire into the end of the cork for the tongue. Glue a piece of clay to the cork tip.

# Toy Mosaic

## YOU WILL NEED
- OLD TOYS, COLORED GLASS, STONES, BUTTONS, SHELLS, OR OTHER SMALL ITEMS
- THICK WHITE POSTER BOARD
- CRAFT GLUE
- THICK BLACK POSTER BOARD

## WHAT TO DO
Collect small decorative items (see suggestions above) from around your house. Sketch a pattern for your collage on a piece of white poster board. Glue all of the pieces on top of the pattern. Let the glue dry. Cut a piece of heavy black poster board that is two inches (5 cm) wider on all sides than the white poster board. Center the white piece on the black one and glue it in place. Let the glue dry, then put your masterpiece on display for everyone to see.

# Hang Your Name

Find the letters of your name in old posters or catalogs and cut them out. Glue the letters to cardboard that's covered with paper. Tape your nameplate to your bedroom door.

# 10 WAYS YOU CAN GO GREEN!

**WANT TO DO YOUR PART TO SAVE THE PLANET? HERE ARE 10 THINGS TO TRY TODAY!**

**1** **Use rechargeable batteries,** and recycle them when they die to keep harmful metals from entering the environment.

**2** **Never litter.** Trash tossed carelessly outside often winds up in storm drains, which empty into rivers and streams that eventually flow to the oceans.

**3** **Plant a deciduous (leafy) tree** that loses its leaves in the fall on the south side of your home. When it grows tall, its shade will cool your house in the summer. After its leaves fall, sunlight will help warm your house in winter.

**4** **Reuse or recycle plastic bags.** When one ton (0.9 t) of plastic bags is reused or recycled, the energy equivalent of 11 barrels of oil is saved!

**5** **Donate your old clothes** and toys to reduce waste.

**6** **Take shorter showers** to save water.

**7** **Switch off the light** every time you leave a room.

**8** **Participate in cleanup days** at your school or at a park—or organize one on your own.

**9** **Place your desk next to a window** and use natural light instead of a lamp.

**10** **Have a drippy faucet at home?** Ask your parents to replace the washer inside it to save water.

# QUIZ WHIZ

## What's your eco-friendly IQ? Find out with this quiz!

Write your answers on a piece of paper. Then check them below.

**1** **True or false?** The country of Sweden recycles some 1.5 billion bottles and cans annually.

**2** **What does global warming cause?**
a. rising sea levels
b. shrinking animal habitats
c. melting glaciers
d. all of the above

**3** **Electricity travels at about the same rate as what?**
a. sound
b. light
c. Wi-Fi
d. a sloth

**4** **True or false?** Hundreds of thousands of acres of rain forest disappear every year.

**5** **700 species of animals are severely threatened because of _____ waste.**
a. ocean
b. food
c. electronic
d. paper

Not **STUMPED** yet? Check out the *NATIONAL GEOGRAPHIC KIDS QUIZ WHIZ* collection for more crazy **ENVIRONMENT** questions

**ANSWERS:** 1. True : 2. d; 3. b; 4. True 5. a

# HOMEWORK HELP

# Write a Letter That Gets Results

**Knowing how to write** a good letter is a useful skill. It will come in handy anytime you want to persuade someone to understand your point of view. Whether you're emailing your congressperson or writing a letter for a school project or to your grandma, a great letter will help you get your message across. Most important, a well-written letter leaves a good impression.

**CHECK OUT THE EXAMPLE BELOW FOR THE ELEMENTS OF A GOOD LETTER.**

**Your address**

**Date**

**Salutation**
Always use "Dear" followed by the person's name; use Mr., Mrs., Ms., or Dr. as appropriate.

**Introductory paragraph**
Give the reason you're writing the letter.

**Body**
The longest part of the letter, which provides evidence that supports your position. Be persuasive!

**Closing paragraph**
Sum up your argument.

**Complimentary closing**
Sign off with "Sincerely" or "Thank you."

**Your signature**

Abby Jones
1204 Green Street
Los Angeles, CA 90045

April 22, 2020

Dear Ms. School Superintendent,

I am writing to you about how much excess energy our school uses and to offer a solution.

Every day, we leave the computers on in the classroom. The TVs are plugged in all the time, and the lights are on all day. All of this adds up to a lot of wasted energy, which is not only harmful for the Earth, as it increases the amount of harmful greenhouse gas emissions into the environment, but is also costly to the school. In fact, I read that schools spend more on energy bills than on computers and textbooks combined!

I am suggesting that we start an Energy Patrol to monitor the use of lighting, air-conditioning, heating, and other energy systems within our school. My idea is to have a group of students dedicated to figuring out ways we can cut back on our energy use in the school. We can do room checks, provide reminders to students and teachers to turn off lights and computers, replace old lightbulbs with energy-efficient products, and even reward the classrooms that do the most to save energy.

Above all, I think our school could help the environment tremendously by cutting back on how much energy we use. Let's see an Energy Patrol at our school soon. Thank you.

Sincerely,

*Abby Jones*

Abby Jones

---

**COMPLIMENTARY CLOSINGS**

**Sincerely, Sincerely yours, Thank you, Regards, Best wishes, Respectfully,**

Inca dancers perform in traditional dress in the Cusco region of Peru.

# CULTURE
# CONNECTION

# EARTH EXPLORER
## Meet **Elizabeth Kapu'uwailani Lindsey!**

**This National Geographic explorer-in-residence makes it her mission to tell the stories of different cultures around the world.**

As a little girl growing up in Hawaii, Elizabeth Kapu'uwailani Lindsey watched her elders—the older women who looked after her—pay close attention to signs in nature to gain a better understanding of the world around them. "They didn't rely on their smartphones to tell them the weather forecast," she explains. "Instead, they watched the clouds, felt the winds, and looked at the color of the sky. The simple task of observing what's going on around you can teach you so much."

Today, Elizabeth is an anthropologist who travels the world to study indigenous—or native—people who still follow ancient traditions, like the adults she grew up with. Her purpose? To keep these cultures from vanishing.

"Their cultures are often misunderstood and forced to blend into mainstream society," she says. "Instead, why not learn more about them and understand that they are just a part of our planet?"

Elizabeth has spent time with Southeast Asian sea nomads and with native people of New Zealand, Peru, China, Micronesia, and India, among others. She has also studied wayfinding—or the native science of navigating without tools, most recently featured in the movie *Moana*.

"Wayfinders don't use maps," Elizabeth explains. "They look at everything from ocean waves to the flight patterns of birds to get to where they need to go. Their approach is that if you gather enough information from the world around you, you essentially find your way home."

Elizabeth is hoping to discover a complete story of the peoples of the world, with each culture representing a chapter.

"We are alive at an age when there are still elders whose wisdom is available," she says. "I look for the lessons we can learn from their ancient wisdom and knowledge. This way, we can be sure their voices are heard for many more years to come. If one voice is missing, the story is incomplete."

There are at least 8 different languages spoken in Micronesia, a country in the Pacific Ocean.

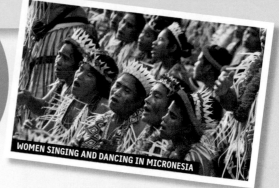

WOMEN SINGING AND DANCING IN MICRONESIA

> "Wayfinders look at nature to know where they are. The underbellies of the clouds are like mirrors and reflect colors. When you're on the ocean and you can see the palest color of green in the clouds, you know you're getting close to land. Little clues help them find their way."

BOATS OF THE MOKEN TRIBE IN SOUTHERN THAILAND

Maui, the famous demigod from the movie *Moana*, is based on a legend from traditional Polynesian stories passed down from generation to generation.

## CALL TO ACTION!

Be curious! Seek out information about traditions in your own family and learn their importance. Talk to your parents, grandparents, aunts, and uncles about what makes your family's history unique. Gather as many details as you can and share them. That way you can carry on traditions from one generation to another.

# CELEBRATIONS

## 1 CHINESE NEW YEAR
**January 25**
Also called Lunar New Year, this holiday marks the new year according to the lunar calendar. Families celebrate with parades, feasts, and fireworks. Young people may receive gifts of money in red envelopes.

## 2 HOLI
**March 9**
This festival in India celebrates spring and marks the triumph of good over evil. People cover one another with powdered paint, called *gulal*, and douse one another with buckets of colored water.

## 3 NYEPI
**March 25**
A national day of silence, this Hindu holiday marks Lunar New Year in Bali, Indonesia, and encourages meditation and reflection. Those who follow traditional customs do not talk, use electricity, travel, or eat for 24 hours.

## 4 QINGMING FESTIVAL
**April 4**
Also known as Grave Sweeping Day, this Chinese celebration calls on people to return to the graves of their deceased loved ones. There, they tidy up the graves, as well as light firecrackers, burn fake money, and leave food as an offering to the spirits.

## 5 EASTER
**April 12**
A Christian holiday that honors the resurrection of Jesus Christ, Easter is celebrated by giving baskets filled with gifts, decorated eggs, or candy to children.

## 6 VESAK DAY
**April or May, date varies by country**
Buddhists around the world observe Buddha's birthday with rituals including chanting and prayer, candlelight processions, and meditation.

## 7 RAMADAN AND EID AL-FITR
**April 23\*–May 24\*\***
A Muslim holiday, Ramadan is a month long, ending in the Eid al-Fitr celebration. Observers fast during this month— eating only after sunset. People pray for forgiveness and hope to purify themselves through observance.

## 8 BERMUDA DAY
**May 29**
The first day of the year that Bermudians take a dip in the ocean. It is also traditionally the first day on which Bermuda shorts are worn as business attire. To celebrate the holiday, there is a parade in Hamilton, and a road race from the west end of the island into Hamilton.

## 9 ST. JOHN'S NIGHT
**June 23**
In Poland, people celebrate the longest day of the year—also known as the summer solstice—with rituals including bonfires, floating flower wreaths down a stream, and releasing thousands of paper lanterns into the night sky.

## 10 BORYEONG MUD FESTIVAL
**July**
During the Boryeong Mud Festival in South Korea, people swim, slide, and wrestle in the mud, then kick back and relax to music and fireworks.

\*Begins at sundown.
\*\*Dates may vary slightly by location.

# Around the World

## 11 LA TOMATINA
**August 26**

Close to 250,000 pounds (113,000 kg) of tomatoes are hurled during this annual event in the Spanish town of Buñol. The festivities involve more than 20,000 people, making this one of the world's largest food fights.

## 12 MASSKARA FESTIVAL
**October**

Celebrated in Bacolod, Philippines, this relatively young holiday was established in 1980 to promote happiness. People dance in the streets wearing colorful costumes and smiley-face masks.

## 13 ROSH HASHANAH
**September 18*–20**

A Jewish holiday marking the beginning of a new year on the Hebrew calendar. Celebrations include prayer, ritual foods, and a day of rest.

## 14 HANUKKAH
**December 10*–18**

This Jewish holiday is eight days long. It commemorates the rededication of the Temple in Jerusalem. Hanukkah celebrations include the lighting of menorah candles for eight days and the exchange of gifts.

## 15 CHRISTMAS DAY
**December 25**

A Christian holiday marking the birth of Jesus Christ, Christmas is usually celebrated by decorating trees, exchanging presents, and having festive gatherings.

---

# 2020 CALENDAR

### JANUARY

| S | M | T | W | T | F | S |
|---|---|---|---|---|---|---|
|   |   |   | 1 | 2 | 3 | 4 |
| 5 | 6 | 7 | 8 | 9 | 10 | 11 |
| 12 | 13 | 14 | 15 | 16 | 17 | 18 |
| 19 | 20 | 21 | 22 | 23 | 24 | 25 |
| 26 | 27 | 28 | 29 | 30 | 31 |   |

### FEBRUARY

| S | M | T | W | T | F | S |
|---|---|---|---|---|---|---|
|   |   |   |   |   |   | 1 |
| 2 | 3 | 4 | 5 | 6 | 7 | 8 |
| 9 | 10 | 11 | 12 | 13 | 14 | 15 |
| 16 | 17 | 18 | 19 | 20 | 21 | 22 |
| 23 | 24 | 25 | 26 | 27 | 28 | 29 |

### MARCH

| S | M | T | W | T | F | S |
|---|---|---|---|---|---|---|
| 1 | 2 | 3 | 4 | 5 | 6 | 7 |
| 8 | 9 | 10 | 11 | 12 | 13 | 14 |
| 15 | 16 | 17 | 18 | 19 | 20 | 21 |
| 22 | 23 | 24 | 25 | 26 | 27 | 28 |
| 29 | 30 | 31 |   |   |   |   |

### APRIL

| S | M | T | W | T | F | S |
|---|---|---|---|---|---|---|
|   |   |   | 1 | 2 | 3 | 4 |
| 5 | 6 | 7 | 8 | 9 | 10 | 11 |
| 12 | 13 | 14 | 15 | 16 | 17 | 18 |
| 19 | 20 | 21 | 22 | 23 | 24 | 25 |
| 26 | 27 | 28 | 29 | 30 |   |   |

### MAY

| S | M | T | W | T | F | S |
|---|---|---|---|---|---|---|
|   |   |   |   |   | 1 | 2 |
| 3 | 4 | 5 | 6 | 7 | 8 | 9 |
| 10 | 11 | 12 | 13 | 14 | 15 | 16 |
| 17 | 18 | 19 | 20 | 21 | 22 | 23 |
| 24 | 25 | 26 | 27 | 28 | 29 | 30 |
| 31 |   |   |   |   |   |   |

### JUNE

| S | M | T | W | T | F | S |
|---|---|---|---|---|---|---|
|   | 1 | 2 | 3 | 4 | 5 | 6 |
| 7 | 8 | 9 | 10 | 11 | 12 | 13 |
| 14 | 15 | 16 | 17 | 18 | 19 | 20 |
| 21 | 22 | 23 | 24 | 25 | 26 | 27 |
| 28 | 29 | 30 |   |   |   |   |

### JULY

| S | M | T | W | T | F | S |
|---|---|---|---|---|---|---|
|   |   |   | 1 | 2 | 3 | 4 |
| 5 | 6 | 7 | 8 | 9 | 10 | 11 |
| 12 | 13 | 14 | 15 | 16 | 17 | 18 |
| 19 | 20 | 21 | 22 | 23 | 24 | 25 |
| 26 | 27 | 28 | 29 | 30 | 31 |   |

### AUGUST

| S | M | T | W | T | F | S |
|---|---|---|---|---|---|---|
|   |   |   |   |   |   | 1 |
| 2 | 3 | 4 | 5 | 6 | 7 | 8 |
| 9 | 10 | 11 | 12 | 13 | 14 | 15 |
| 16 | 17 | 18 | 19 | 20 | 21 | 22 |
| 23 | 24 | 25 | 26 | 27 | 28 | 29 |
| 30 | 31 |   |   |   |   |   |

### SEPTEMBER

| S | M | T | W | T | F | S |
|---|---|---|---|---|---|---|
|   |   | 1 | 2 | 3 | 4 | 5 |
| 6 | 7 | 8 | 9 | 10 | 11 | 12 |
| 13 | 14 | 15 | 16 | 17 | 18 | 19 |
| 20 | 21 | 22 | 23 | 24 | 25 | 26 |
| 27 | 28 | 29 | 30 |   |   |   |

### OCTOBER

| S | M | T | W | T | F | S |
|---|---|---|---|---|---|---|
|   |   |   |   | 1 | 2 | 3 |
| 4 | 5 | 6 | 7 | 8 | 9 | 10 |
| 11 | 12 | 13 | 14 | 15 | 16 | 17 |
| 18 | 19 | 20 | 21 | 22 | 23 | 24 |
| 25 | 26 | 27 | 28 | 29 | 30 | 31 |

### NOVEMBER

| S | M | T | W | T | F | S |
|---|---|---|---|---|---|---|
| 1 | 2 | 3 | 4 | 5 | 6 | 7 |
| 8 | 9 | 10 | 11 | 12 | 13 | 14 |
| 15 | 16 | 17 | 18 | 19 | 20 | 21 |
| 22 | 23 | 24 | 25 | 26 | 27 | 28 |
| 29 | 30 |   |   |   |   |   |

### DECEMBER

| S | M | T | W | T | F | S |
|---|---|---|---|---|---|---|
|   |   | 1 | 2 | 3 | 4 | 5 |
| 6 | 7 | 8 | 9 | 10 | 11 | 12 |
| 13 | 14 | 15 | 16 | 17 | 18 | 19 |
| 20 | 21 | 22 | 23 | 24 | 25 | 26 |
| 27 | 28 | 29 | 30 | 31 |   |   |

# DIWALI

**FLAMES FROM OIL LAMPS** flicker as families gather together to share music, food, and gifts in the spirit of Diwali, often called the Festival of Lights. This Hindu holiday, celebrating the triumph of good over evil and the lifting of spiritual darkness, is actually a series of festivals: Each of the five days of Diwali honors a different tradition. Diwali customs include cleaning and decorating houses and wearing new clothes.

Women in Chandigarh, India, light lamps on the eve of Diwali.

Carnival celebration in Salvador, Brazil

# CARNIVAL

**COLORFUL COSTUMES,** festive music, parades, and parties for days—sounds fun, huh? One of the biggest bashes around the world, Carnival originated as a way for Catholics to mark the last days before Lent, the period of fasting before Easter. Thousands of partyers also take to the streets each spring, especially in the Caribbean country of Trinidad and Tobago and throughout South America. The hottest place to celebrate at Carnival time? Salvador, Brazil, considered one of the biggest street parties on the planet!

# What's Your Chinese Horoscope?
## Locate your birth year to find out.

In Chinese astrology the zodiac runs on a 12-year cycle, based on the lunar calendar. Each year corresponds to one of 12 animals, each representing one of 12 personality types. Read on to find out which animal year you were born in and what that might say about you.

## RAT
**1972, '84, '96, 2008, '20**
Say cheese! You're attractive, charming, and creative. When you get mad, you can have really sharp teeth!

## HORSE
**1966, '78, '90, 2002, '14**
Being happy is your "mane" goal. And while you're smart and hardworking, your teacher may ride you for talking too much.

## OX
**1973, '85, '97, 2009, '21**
You're smart, patient, and as strong as an ... well, you know what. Though you're a leader, you never brag.

## SHEEP
**1967, '79, '91, 2003, '15**
Gentle as a lamb, you're also artistic, compassionate, and wise. You're often shy.

## TIGER
**1974, '86, '98, 2010**
You may be a nice person, but no one should ever enter your room without asking—you might attack!

## MONKEY
**1968, '80, '92, 2004, '16**
No "monkey see, monkey do" for you. You're a clever problem-solver with an excellent memory.

## RABBIT
**1975, '87, '99, 2011**
Your ambition and talent make you jump at opportunity. You also keep your ears open for gossip.

## ROOSTER
**1969, '81, '93, 2005, '17**
You crow about your adventures, but inside you're really shy. You're thoughtful, capable, brave, and talented.

## DRAGON
**1976, '88, 2000, '12**
You're on fire! Health, energy, honesty, and bravery make you a living legend.

## DOG
**1970, '82, '94, 2006, '18**
Often the leader of the pack, you're loyal and honest. You can also keep a secret.

## SNAKE
**1977, '89, 2001, '13**
You may not speak often, but you're very smart. You always seem to have a stash of cash.

## PIG
**1971, '83, '95, 2007, '19**
Even though you're courageous, honest, and kind, you never hog all the attention.

# HALLOWEEN PET PARADE

What spell can I cast to get some oats and hay?

DISGUISED AS HARRY POTTER, RAMSEY THE HORSE MAKES MAGIC.

Stop in the name of the paw, er, law!

COREY THE DACHSHUND IS ARRESTING IN HIS WILD WEST SHERIFF GARB.

I am one classy kitty.

ELROY THE CAT SHOWS SOME STYLE DRESSED AS THE MAD HATTER FROM *ALICE'S ADVENTURES IN WONDERLAND*.

I'm ready to say "I do" to a chew toy and a belly rub.

TANK THE ENGLISH BULLDOG ROCKS A BRIDAL COSTUME.

# Cool Carvings

Show your pumpkin's true personality with these wacky designs. Use a child-safe carving tool or ask an adult for help.

## Express Yourself!

Let your jack-o'-lantern tell the world how it feels with emoticon smileys. It'll make your friends LOL!

## Ahoy, Matey!

Pumpkins can wear costumes, too. Hats, inexpensive jewelry, and other accessories can create a pirate, cowboy, or even a baseball player.

## Spell It Out

Who says a jack-o'-lantern needs a face? Carve spooky messages into your pumpkins instead.

## Stack 'Em Up

Build a snowman by placing the biggest pumpkin at the bottom and the smallest one on top. Slant the knife when you cut off the tops, creating a ledge to support another pumpkin.

## CREATE THE **PERFECT** DESIGN

Before you start cutting, sketch your design on white paper. Tape the paper to your pumpkin where you want the design to be. Punch along the lines of the sketch with a pin, poking through the paper and into the pumpkin. Then carve along the dotted lines you've made on the pumpkin.

# CHEW ON THIS

## TACOS!

The word "taco" hasn't always been on restaurant menus. In the 18th century, "tacos" were charges of gunpowder wrapped in paper used by Mexican miners. The wrap concept stuck when cooks started calling tortillas stuffed with meat and beans "tacos." Chow down on more filling facts.

People in the United States spend more money on **SALSA** than on ketchup.

Made from avocado, **GUACAMOLE** comes from the Aztec word *ahuacamolli* (ah-wah-kah-MOH-lee), or avocado sauce.

Natural **CHEDDAR CHEESE** has an almost white color. The bright orange color you see in grocery store cheddar comes from food coloring.

One type of **BLACK BEAN** tastes like mushrooms.

Crunchy corn **TACO** shells have been in U.S. cookbooks only since 1939. But soft tortillas have been around since the 13th century.

## MAKE YOUR OWN TACOS

Tacos are crunchy sandwiches—the tortilla is like the bread, which you can stuff with anything you want! **Get a parent's help to create a yummy taco.**

**1** Warm a skillet over medium heat. Cook 1½ pounds (680 g) ground beef or turkey for 6 to 8 minutes.

**2** Add 1 teaspoon (2 g) cumin and ¾ teaspoon (4 g) salt. Stir occasionally for 2 to 3 minutes.

**3** Fill 8 taco shells with the meat and top with diced avocado, sour cream, black beans, and salsa.

**4** Sprinkle with cheddar cheese.

# PIZZA!

Pizza may have originated 2,000 years ago when the ancient Greeks prepared round, flat breads covered with oil, herbs, and spices. In 1830, chefs in Naples, Italy, cooked their crust in an oven lined with rocks from a nearby volcano. Some say that could have been the first pizzeria. The restaurant is still open today. Gobble up these other tasty tidbits.

**MUSHROOMS** are some seriously freaky fungi. They've been grown in caves and buried in, um, excrement, and some even glow in the dark.

People in the United States eat about 250 million pounds (113 million kg) of **PEPPERONI** a year, more than any other pizza topping.

**BELL PEPPERS** are fruits, not vegetables.

Most **CHEESE** is made from cow's, goat's, or sheep's milk. The traditional way to make mozzarella is from water buffalo's milk.

**TOMATOES** can be red, orange, yellow, green, purple, and even striped.

13x.5in

# MAKE YOUR OWN PIZZA

Created in Naples, Italy, the Margherita pizza represents the colors in the Italian flag: red tomatoes, green basil, and white cheese. Get a parent's help to make your own Margherita pizza, or use toppings like mushrooms and bell peppers to make a new tasty creation!

**1** Bake premade pizza dough at 450°F (232°C) for about 5 minutes. Brush the crust lightly with olive oil.

**2** Top dough with 4 or 5 thin tomato slices, and a pinch each of dried oregano, salt, and pepper. Sprinkle 1 cup (125 g) shredded mozzarella on top.

**3** Bake until golden for 10 to 12 minutes. Sprinkle ½ cup (20 g) chopped fresh basil over the top.

# MONEY AROUND THE WORLD!

**Jordan's** HALF-DINAR COIN has seven sides.

ACCORDING to some **PEOPLE, CANADA'S $100 BANKNOTE** gives off the scent of **MAPLE SYRUP.**

A British businessman created his own currency —named the **PUFFIN**— for an island he owned off of England.

IN FEBRUARY 2015 SCUBA DIVERS OFF ISRAEL FOUND OVER 2,600 GOLD COINS DATING BACK AS FAR AS THE 9TH CENTURY.

BANCO CENTRAL DE CHILE
FA6876603
20 MIL PESOS
FA6876603
2006
20000 VEINTE MIL PESOS

A **20,000**-PESO BANKNOTE FROM CHILE CONTAINS INK THAT CHANGES **COLOR WHEN TILTED.**

The INCA called gold "THE SWEAT OF THE SUN" and silver "THE TEARS OF THE MOON."

**3-CENT COINS** CIRCULATED IN THE **UNITED STATES** FROM **1851** TO **1889.**

*I knew I should've tried a fake ATM instead.*

IN 2002, A MAN OPENED A FAKE BANK AND TOOK IN **$650,000** BEFORE HE WAS CAUGHT.

COINS CREATED IN **1616** FOR WHAT IS NOW **BERMUDA** WERE NICKNAMED **"HOGGIES"** BECAUSE THEY PICTURED **HOGS.**

A 1913 U.S. LIBERTY HEAD NICKEL—ONE OF THE ONLY FIVE IN EXISTENCE— **SOLD AT** AUCTION FOR MORE THAN $3.1 MILLION.

THE PHRASE **"BRING HOME THE BACON"** STARTED AFTER A 12TH-CENTURY PRIEST REWARDED A MARRIED COUPLE WITH A SIDE OF BACON.

**A BRITISH ARTIST** MADE A DRESS OUT OF USED **BANKNOTES** FROM AROUND THE **WORLD.**

**MONEY TIP!** WHEN YOU GET YOUR ALLOWANCE OR A CASH GIFT, BREAK IT INTO **SMALLER BILLS.** ONLY SPEND HALF AND STASH THE REST IN YOUR **PIGGY BANK.**

# CRAFTS AROUND THE GLOBE

**Try This!**

## Try these fun activities inspired by different cultures

Ask for a parent's help and permission before you start these projects.

**FUN FACT**
Trolls are part of Norway's folklore. Legend has it that these creatures of the dark turn to stone if they're caught in the sun.

## TROLL DOLLS

### YOU WILL NEED
- GLUE
- FELT AND/OR FABRIC
- SMALL PLASTIC BOTTLE SUCH AS A SPICE JAR
- FAKE FUR
- GOOGLY EYES
- DECORATIONS SUCH AS YARN, STICKERS, AND PAPER CUTOUTS

### WHAT TO DO
Decide what characters you want to make and pick out the materials you need at a craft store. Glue felt around the bottle where the face will go. Glue the fake fur along the top edge of the felt so it stands up straight. Then glue on the fabric "clothing," googly eyes, and your choice of decorations and accessories. Be sure to let each layer dry before adding the next layer of material.

# SANDPAINTING

## YOU WILL NEED
- CANVAS BOARD OR FOAM BOARD
- GLUE
- COLORED SAND (AVAILABLE IN CRAFT STORES)
- PENCIL AND BLACK MARKER

## WHAT TO DO
Sketch your design on the board in pencil. When you are happy with the sketch, outline it with the marker. Starting at the top, cover a small area with glue and then one color of sand. Make sure you don't get glue and sand on the marker lines. Shake excess sand back into the container and let the glue dry. Repeat using different colors for different areas. Dry overnight.

# TIE-DYED T-SHIRT

## YOU WILL NEED
- WHITE, 100% COTTON T-SHIRT (PREWASHED)
- RUBBER BANDS
- LARGE POT
- HOT WATER
- FABRIC DYE (ANY COLOR)
- LARGE BUCKET
- TONGS
- WATER- AND HEAT-SAFE RUBBER GLOVES

**CAUTION!** Dye can stain anything, even the sink. Cover your work area with plastic and read the cleaning instructions on the dye package. Always wear rubber gloves.

## WHAT TO DO
1. Dampen the T-shirt. For a random pattern, twist and scrunch the fabric, using rubber bands to hold the T-shirt in that position. For a circular pattern like the one at right, grab part of the T-shirt and squeeze it into a long, skinny shape. Tie several equally spaced rubber bands around the fabric. Each rubber band will form a circle.

2. Ask a parent to boil water in the large pot. Using the measurements on the dye package, ask your parent to pour the hot water into a bucket and stir in the dye.

3. Dunk the shirt into the water with the tongs and stir constantly for about 10 to 15 minutes. (The T-shirt appears slightly darker when it's wet.)

4. Rinse the shirt under cold water. Then remove the rubber bands and rinse until the water runs clear. Dry in a clothes dryer to help set the color.

# 15 Ways to Say Hello

1. ARMENIAN: **Barev**
2. DUTCH: **Goedendag**
3. FINNISH: **Hei**
4. FRENCH: **Bonjour**
5. GREEK: **Yia sou**
6. HEBREW: **Shalom**
7. HINDI: **Namaste**
8. ICELANDIC: **Halló**
9. ITALIAN: **Ciao**
10. MANDARIN: **Ni hao**
11. RUSSIAN: **Privyet**
12. SPANISH: **Hola**
13. SWAHILI: **Jambo**
14. TURKISH: **Merhaba**
15. WELSH: **Helô**

# LANGUAGES IN PERIL

**TODAY,** there are more than 7,000 languages spoken on Earth. But by 2100, more than half of those may disappear. In fact, experts say one language dies every two weeks, due to the increasing dominance of larger languages, such as English, Spanish, and Mandarin. So what can be done to keep dialects from disappearing? Efforts like National Geographic's Enduring Voices Project have been created to track and document the world's most threatened indigenous languages, such as Tofa, spoken only by people in Siberia, and Magati Ke, from Aboriginal Australia. The hope is to preserve these languages—and the cultures they belong to.

# 10 LEADING LANGUAGES

Approximate population of first-language speakers (in millions)

| Language | Speakers |
|---|---|
| 1. Chinese* | 1,299 |
| 2. Spanish | 442 |
| 3. English | 378 |
| 4. Arabic | 315 |
| 5. Hindi | 260 |
| 6. Bengali | 243 |
| 7. Portuguese | 223 |
| 8. Russian | 154 |
| 9. Japanese | 122 |
| 10. Punjabi | 93 |

Some languages have only a few hundred speakers, while Chinese has nearly 1.3 billion native speakers worldwide. That's about triple the next largest group of language speakers. Colonial expansion, trade, and migration account for the spread of the other most widely spoken languages. With growing use of the internet, English is becoming the language of the technology age.

*Includes all forms of the language.

# Bet You Didn't Know!

# 6 fun language facts

**1** The **most commonly** used letters in the English language are **E, T, A,** and **O.**

**2** The **Russian** word for **"RED"** also means **"beautiful."**

**3** The **longest** word in English is **pneumonoultramicroscopic-silicovolcanoconiosis,** a lung disease.

**4** **Babies' cries** can sound **different** in various **languages.**

**5** People in **Papua New Guinea** speak more than **840** languages.

**6** The word **"taxi"** means the same thing in English, German, French, Swedish, Spanish, and Portuguese.

# MYTHOLOGY

## GREEK

## EGYPTIAN

The ancient Greeks believed that many gods and goddesses ruled the universe. According to this mythology, the Olympians lived high atop Greece's Mount Olympus. Each of these 12 principal gods and goddesses had a unique personality that corresponded to particular aspects of life, such as love or death.

Egyptian mythology is based on a creation myth that tells of an egg that appeared on the ocean. When the egg hatched, out came Ra, the sun god. As a result, ancient Egyptians became worshippers of the sun and of the nine original deities, most of whom were the children and grandchildren of Ra.

### THE OLYMPIANS

**Aphrodite** was the goddess of love and beauty.

**Apollo,** Zeus's son, was the god of the sun, music, and healing. Artemis was his twin.

**Ares,** Zeus's son, was the god of war.

**Artemis,** Zeus's daughter and Apollo's twin, was the goddess of the hunt and of childbirth.

**Athena,** born from the forehead of Zeus, was the goddess of wisdom and crafts.

**Demeter** was the goddess of fertility and nature.

**Hades,** Zeus's brother, was the god of the underworld and the dead.

**Hephaestus,** the son of Hera, was the god of fire.

**Hera,** the wife and older sister of Zeus, was the goddess of women and marriage.

**Hermes,** Zeus's son, was the messenger of the gods.

**Poseidon,** the brother of Zeus, was the god of the sea and earthquakes.

**Zeus** was the most powerful of the gods and the top Olympian. He wielded a thunderbolt and was the god of the sky and thunder.

### THE NINE DEITIES

**Geb,** son of Shu and Tefnut, was the god of the earth.

**Isis (Ast),** daughter of Geb and Nut, was the goddess of fertility and motherhood.

**Nephthys (Nebet-Hut),** daughter of Geb and Nut, was protector of the dead.

**Nut,** daughter of Shu and Tefnut, was the goddess of the sky.

**Osiris (Usir),** son of Geb and Nut, was the god of the afterlife.

**Ra (Re),** the sun god, is generally viewed as the creator. He represents life and health.

**Seth (Set),** son of Geb and Nut, was the god of the desert and chaos.

**Shu,** son of Ra, was the god of air.

**Tefnut,** daughter of Ra, was the goddess of rain.

**A**ll cultures around the world have unique legends and traditions that have been passed down over generations. Many myths refer to gods or supernatural heroes who are responsible for occurrences in the world. For example, Norse mythology tells of the red-bearded Thor, the god of thunder, who is responsible for creating lightning and thunderstorms. And many creation myths, especially those from some of North America's native cultures, tell of an earth-diver represented as an animal that brings a piece of sand or mud up from the deep sea. From this tiny piece of earth, the entire world takes shape.

# NORSE

# ROMAN

Norse mythology originated in Scandinavia, in northern Europe. It was complete with gods and goddesses who lived in a heavenly place called Asgard that could be reached only by crossing a rainbow bridge.

While Norse mythology is lesser known, we use it every day. Most days of the week are named after Norse gods, including some of these major deities.

## NORSE GODS

**Balder** was the god of light and beauty.

**Freya** was the goddess of love, beauty, and fertility.

**Frigg,** for whom Friday was named, was the queen of Asgard. She was the goddess of marriage, motherhood, and the home.

**Heimdall** was the watchman of the rainbow bridge and the guardian of the gods.

**Hel,** the daughter of Loki, was the goddess of death.

**Loki,** a shape-shifter, was a trickster who helped the gods—and caused them problems.

**Skadi** was the goddess of winter and of the hunt. She is often represented as "The Snow Queen."

**Thor,** for whom Thursday was named, was the god of thunder and lightning.

**Tyr,** for whom Tuesday was named, was the god of the sky and war.

**Wodan,** for whom Wednesday was named, was the god of war, wisdom, death, and magic.

Much of Roman mythology was adopted from Greek mythology, but the Romans also developed a lot of original myths as well. The gods of Roman mythology lived everywhere, and each had a role to play. There were thousands of Roman gods, but here are a few of the stars of Roman myths.

## ANCIENT ROMAN GODS

**Ceres** was the goddess of the harvest and motherly love.

**Diana,** daughter of Jupiter, was the goddess of hunting and the moon.

**Juno,** Jupiter's wife, was the goddess of women and fertility.

**Jupiter,** the patron of Rome and master of the gods, was the god of the sky.

**Mars,** the son of Jupiter and Juno, was the god of war.

**Mercury,** the son of Jupiter, was the messenger of the gods and the god of travelers.

**Minerva** was the goddess of wisdom, learning, and the arts and crafts.

**Neptune,** the brother of Jupiter, was the god of the sea.

**Venus** was the goddess of love and beauty.

**Vesta** was the goddess of fire and the hearth. She was one of the most important of the Roman deities.

# World Religions

A round the world, religion takes many forms. Some belief systems, such as Christianity, Islam, and Judaism, are monotheistic, meaning that followers believe in just one supreme being. Others, like Hinduism, Shintoism, and most native belief systems, are polytheistic, meaning that many of their followers believe in multiple gods.

All of the major religions have their origins in Asia, but they have spread around the world. Christianity, with the largest number of followers, has three divisions—Roman Catholic, Eastern Orthodox, and Protestant. Islam, with about one-fifth of all believers, has two main divisions—Sunni and Shiite. Hinduism and Buddhism account for almost another one-fifth of believers. Judaism, dating back some 4,000 years, has more than 13 million followers, less than one percent of all believers.

## CHRISTIANITY

Based on the teachings of Jesus Christ, a Jew born some 2,000 years ago in the area of modern-day Israel, Christianity has spread worldwide and actively seeks converts. Followers in Switzerland (above) participate in an Easter season procession with lanterns and crosses.

## BUDDHISM

Founded about 2,400 years ago in northern India by the Hindu prince Gautama Buddha, Buddhism spread throughout East and Southeast Asia. Buddhist temples have statues, such as the Mihintale Buddha (above) in Sri Lanka.

## HINDUISM

Dating back more than 4,000 years, Hinduism is practiced mainly in India. Hindus follow sacred texts known as the Vedas and believe in reincarnation. During the festival of Navratri, which honors the goddess Durga, the Garba dance is performed (above).

## Technology Meets Tradition

It has been 1,200 years since the bishop of Rome became known as the pope. Pope Francis became the head of the Roman Catholic Church in 2013 and has embraced technology as a way to reach Catholics around the globe. He's the first pope to pose for a selfie and has more than 34 million Twitter followers.

## ISLAM

Muslims believe that the Koran, Islam's sacred book, records the words of Allah (God) as revealed to the Prophet Muhammad beginning around A.D. 610. Believers (above) circle the Kaaba in the Haram Mosque in Mecca, Saudi Arabia, the spiritual center of the faith.

## JUDAISM

The traditions, laws, and beliefs of Judaism date back to Abraham (the Patriarch) and the Torah (the first five books of the Old Testament). Followers pray before the Western Wall (above), which stands below Islam's Dome of the Rock in Jerusalem.

# QUIZ WHIZ

**How vast is your knowledge about the world around you? Quiz yourself!**

Write your answers on a piece of paper. Then check them below.

**1** The word _____ means the same thing in English, German, French, Swedish, Spanish, and Portuguese.
a. "hello"     c. "taxi"
b. "goodbye"     d. "banana"

**2** Today, there are more than _____ languages spoken on Earth.
a. 70
b. 700
c. 7,000
d. 70,000

**3** A British artist made a dress out of _____ from around the world.
a. gum wrappers
b. postcards
c. newspapers
d. banknotes

**4** _____ is a Hindu holiday often called the Festival of Lights.

**5** True or false? Bell peppers are fruits, not vegetables.

Not **STUMPED** yet? Check out the *NATIONAL GEOGRAPHIC KIDS QUIZ WHIZ* collection for more crazy **CULTURE** questions!

**ANSWERS:** 1. c; 2. c; 3. d; 4. Diwali; 5. True

138

# Explore a New Culture

STAMPS OF BRAZIL

**YOU'RE A STUDENT,** but you're also a citizen of the world. Writing a report on a foreign nation or your own country is a great way to better understand and appreciate how different people live. Pick the country of your ancestors, one that's been in the news, or one that you'd like to visit someday.

CURRENCY AND COINS OF BRAZIL

## Passport to Success
A country report follows the format of an expository essay because you're "exposing" information about the country you choose.

**The following step-by-step tips will help you with this monumental task.**

THE FLAG OF BRAZIL

**1** **RESEARCH.** Gathering information is the most important step in writing a good country report. Look to internet sources, encyclopedias, books, magazine and newspaper articles, and other sources to find important and interesting details about your subject.

**2** **ORGANIZE YOUR NOTES.** Put the information you gathered into a rough outline. For example, sort everything you found about the country's system of government, climate, etc.

**3** **WRITE IT UP.** Follow the basic structure of good writing: introduction, body, and conclusion. Remember that each paragraph should have a topic sentence that is then supported by facts and details. Incorporate the information from your notes, but make sure it's in your own words. And make your writing flow with good transitions and descriptive language.

**4** **ADD VISUALS.** Include maps, diagrams, photos, and other visual aids.

**5** **PROOFREAD AND REVISE.** Correct any mistakes, and polish your language. Do your best!

**6** **CITE YOUR SOURCES.** Be sure to keep a record of your sources.

# SPACE and EARTH

A Tesla roadster launched from a Falcon Heavy rocket heads around Mars with a dummy driver named "Starman" at the wheel. The Falcon Heavy—considered the world's most powerful rocket—is being tested by the company SpaceX.

# EARTH EXPLORER
## Meet **Christine Chen!**

**This National Geographic young explorer studies ancient lakes to predict future climate change.**

Just call Christine Chen a climate detective! As a geologist and climate scientist, she is on the hunt for clues about ancient climate change to piece together a puzzle that may reveal what Earth's future may look like.

So where do Christine's clues come from? She heads to ancient lake basins in places such as the Mojave Desert in California, U.S.A., and the Andes Mountains in South America. Because these specific locations are landlocked, their ancient lakes were once filled exclusively by rainfall. Over time, as the climate shifted and these landscapes went from lush and green to dry and arid, the lakes dried up—leaving behind a rocky landscape and fossilized remains of algae reefs called tufa, which Christine collects samples of and studies.

"My goal is to determine the ages of many tufa samples so that I can begin to build a broad picture of the history of lake level changes in the western United States and the central Andes," she says. "Perhaps we'll be able to see how rainfall patterns shifted in response to past abrupt climate changes thousands of years ago."

This bigger picture, says Christine, can teach us about current climate change, including how rainfall patterns may shift as Earth's temperature rises.

"One of the biggest questions climate scientists still have is how rainfall patterns will change and reorganize in response to our rapidly warming planet," says Christine. "Will places that are already dry continue to get drier? Since water availability plays a big role in determining where people and animals can live, knowing how rainfall will change now and in the future is important."

Christine has collected tufa samples dating back to 25,000 years ago.

THE CENTRAL ANDES MOUNTAINS WHERE CHRISTINE DOES RESEARCH

" Like an archaeologist recovering artifacts from ancient human civilizations to reconstruct their history, I hunt for clues left behind by these ancient climates and try to piece together a picture of what these old climates were like. "

A CLOSE-UP LOOK AT TUFA

Some tufa towers are as a high as a three-story building.

## CALL TO ACTION!

To follow Christine's rockin' career path, head to a museum to check out geology exhibits, read about local geology at your library, or simply go outside and research the rocks in your neighborhood. "Learn more about what story they capture about the history of Earth," Christine says. "Each rock on Earth has an interesting story to tell."

CHRISTINE WORKING IN THE AUSTRALIAN OUTBACK

# A Universe of Galaxies

## 5 COOL FACTS TO RECORD

When astronauts first journeyed beyond Earth's orbit in 1968, they looked back to their home planet. The big-picture view of our place in space changed the astronauts' lives—and perhaps humanity. If you could leave the universe and similarly look back, what would you see? Remarkably, scientists are mapping this massive area. They see ... bubbles. Not literal soap bubbles, of course, but a structure that looks like of a pan full of them. Like bubble walls, thin surfaces curve around empty spaces in an elegantly simple structure. Zoom in to see that these surfaces are groups of galaxies. Zoom in further to find one galaxy, with an ordinary star—our sun—orbited by an ordinary planet—Earth. How extraordinary.

### DIGITAL TRAVELER!

Take a simulated flight through our universe, thanks to the data collected by the Sloan Digital Sky Survey. Search the internet for "APOD flight through universe sdss." Sit back and enjoy the ride!

## 2 DARK MATTER

The universe holds a mysterious source of gravity that cannot be properly explained. This unseen matter—the ghostly dark ring in this composite Hubble telescope photo—seems to pull on galaxy clusters, drawing galaxies toward it. But what is this strange stuff? It's not giant black holes, planets, stars, or anti-matter. These would show themselves indirectly. For now, astronomers call this source of gravity "dark matter."

## 1 GALAXY CLUSTERS AND SUPERCLUSTERS

Gravity pulls things together—gas in stars, stars in galaxies. Galaxies gather, too, sometimes by the thousands, form-ing galaxy clusters and superclusters with tremendously superheated gas. This gas can be as hot as 180 million degrees Fahrenheit (100 million degrees Celsius), filling space between them. These clusters hide a secret. The grav-ity among the galaxies isn't enough to bring them together. The source of the extra gravity is a dark secret.

# 3 IT STARTED WHEN ...
## The Big Bang

Long ago, the universe was compressed: It was hotter, smaller, denser than now, and completely uniform—almost. Extremely minor unevenness led to a powerful energy release that astronomers call the big bang. In a blip of time, the universe expanded tremendously. The first particles formed. Atoms, galaxies, forces, and light ... all developed from this. Today's great filaments (see fact 4) may be organized where those first uneven patches existed.

# 4 FILAMENTS AND SHEETS
## Bubbles of space

What is the universe like at its grandest scale? The biggest big-picture view is jaw-dropping. Clusters and superclusters of galaxies—red and yellow areas in this illustration—along with dark matter, string together to form structures that are millions and billions of light-years long. These so-called walls, sheets, or filaments surround vast voids, or "bubbles," of nearly empty space—the blue areas. The universe has a structure, non-random and unexpected.

# 5 COLLISION ZONE

Saying that galaxies form clusters and superclusters is like saying two soccer teams simply meet. During a game, there's a lot of action and energy. Similarly, as clusters and superclusters form, there's lots going on—as evidenced by the super-high-energy x-rays that are detected (pink in this colorized image).

# PLANETS

CERES

MARS

EARTH

VENUS

MERCURY

JUPITER

SUN

## MERCURY

Average distance from the sun:
  35,980,000 miles (57,900,000 km)
Position from the sun in orbit: 1st
Equatorial diameter: 3,030 miles (4,878 km)
Length of day: 59 Earth days
Length of year: 88 Earth days
Surface temperatures: -300°F (-184°C)
  to 800°F (427°C)
Known moons: 0
**Fun fact: Mercury is shrinking.**

## VENUS

Average distance from the sun:
  67,230,000 miles (108,200,000 km)
Position from the sun in orbit: 2nd
Equatorial diameter: 7,520 miles (12,100 km)
Length of day: 243 Earth days
Length of year: 224.7 Earth days
Average surface temperature: 864°F (462°C)
Known moons: 0
**Fun fact: Venus is covered in thick
  clouds that reflect a lot of
  light, making it the brightest
  planet in the night sky.**

## EARTH

Average distance from the sun:
  93,000,000 miles (149,600,000 km)
Position from the sun in orbit: 3rd
Equatorial diameter: 7,900 miles (12,750 km)
Length of day: 24 hours
Length of year: 365 days
Surface temperatures: -126°F (-88°C)
  to 134°F (57°C)
Known moons: 1
**Fun fact: Earth is the only planet in
  our solar system with liquid water.**

## MARS

Average distance from the sun:
  141,633,000 miles (227,936,000 km)
Position from the sun in orbit: 4th
Equatorial diameter: 4,221 miles (6,794 km)
Length of day: 25 Earth hours
Length of year: 1.9 Earth years
Surface temperatures: -270°F (-168°C)
  to 80°F (27°C)
Known moons: 2
**Fun fact: Deserts have been
  discovered on Mars.**

This artwork shows the eight planets and five dwarf planets in our solar system. The relative sizes and positions of the planets are shown but not the relative distances between them.

SATURN

URANUS

NEPTUNE

PLUTO
· HAUMEA
· MAKEMAKE
ERIS

## JUPITER
Average distance from the sun:
 483,682,000 miles (778,412,000 km)
Position from the sun in orbit: 6th
Equatorial diameter: 88,840 miles (142,980 km)
Length of day: 9.9 Earth hours
Length of year: 11.9 Earth years
Average surface temperature: -235°F (-148°C)
Known moons: 79*
**Fun fact: Jupiter has a magnetic field that's 19,000 stronger than Earth's.**

## SATURN
Average distance from the sun:
 890,800,000 miles (1,433,600,000 km)
Position from the sun in orbit: 7th
Equatorial diameter: 74,900 miles (120,540 km)
Length of day: 10.7 Earth hours
Length of year: 29.5 Earth years
Average surface temperature: -218°F (-139°C)
Known moons: 62*
**Fun fact: You can't walk on Saturn because it doesn't have a solid surface.**

## URANUS
Average distance from the sun:
 1,784,000,000 miles (2,871,000,000 km)
Position from the sun in orbit: 8th
Equatorial diameter: 31,760 miles (51,120 km)
Length of day: 17.2 Earth hours
Length of year: 84 Earth years
Average surface temperature: -323°F (-197°C)
Known moons: 27
**Fun fact: It may rain diamonds on Uranus.**

## NEPTUNE
Average distance from the sun:
 2,795,000,000 miles (4,498,000,000 km)
Position from the sun in orbit: 9th
Equatorial diameter: 30,775 miles (49,528 km)
Length of day: 16 Earth hours
Length of year: 164.8 Earth years
Average surface temperature: -353°F (-214°C)
Known moons: 14*

*Includes provisional moons, which await confirmation and naming from the International Astronomical Union.

For information about dwarf planets—Ceres, Pluto, Haumea, Makemake, and Eris—see p. 148.

# DWARF PLANETS

Haumea

Eris

Pluto

**Thanks to advanced technology,** astronomers have been spotting many never-before-seen celestial bodies with their telescopes. One new discovery? A population of icy objects orbiting the sun beyond Pluto. The largest, like Pluto itself, are classified as dwarf planets. Smaller than the moon but still massive enough to pull themselves into a ball, dwarf planets nevertheless lack the gravitational "oomph" to clear their neighborhood of other sizable objects. So, while larger, more massive planets pretty much have their orbits to themselves, dwarf planets orbit the sun in swarms that include other dwarf planets as well as smaller chunks of rock or ice.

So far, astronomers have identified five dwarf planets: Ceres, Pluto, Haumea, Makemake, and Eris. There are also three newly discovered dwarf planets that will need additional study before they are named. Astronomers are observing hundreds of newly found objects in the frigid outer solar system. As time and technology advance, the family of known dwarf planets will surely continue to grow.

### CERES
Position from the sun in orbit: 5th
Length of day: 9.1 Earth hours
Length of year: 4.6 Earth years
Known moons: 0

### PLUTO
Position from the sun in orbit: 10th
Length of day: 6.4 Earth days
Length of year: 248 Earth years
Known moons: 5

### HAUMEA
Position from the sun in orbit: 11th
Length of day: 3.9 Earth hours
Length of year: 282 Earth years
Known moons: 2

### MAKEMAKE
Position from the sun in orbit: 12th
Length of day: 22.5 Earth hours
Length of year: 305 Earth years
Known moons: 1*

### ERIS
Position from the sun in orbit: 13th
Length of day: 25.9 Earth hours
Length of year: 561 Earth years
Known moons: 1

*Includes provisional moons, which await confirmation and naming from the International Astronomical Union.

# THE SEARCH FOR
# PLANET NINE

## IS A NEPTUNE-SIZE WORLD HIDDEN IN OUR SOLAR SYSTEM?

Way out in the farthest reaches of the solar system, a mysterious undiscovered planet could be orbiting through space. It's gigantic—almost four times the size of Earth. And it's so far away that it takes up to 20,000 years to orbit the sun. Astronomers have dubbed it Planet Nine, and they're searching the skies to find it.

## FAR OUT

Scientists used to think the area beyond Neptune, known as the Kuiper (sounds like KY-pur) belt, was empty. But it turns out the Kuiper belt is home to icy, rocky objects; billions of comets; and a few dwarf planets such as Pluto. While observing the belt in 2014, astronomer Mike Brown and his research partner, Konstantin Batygin, saw something strange: The orbits of many of the smaller objects in the Kuiper belt were aligned. Weirder still, they never came closer to the sun than twice the distance to Neptune. It was like something was pulling them away. But what?

## STRANGE SPACE

Brown and Batygin spent over a year trying to figure out the objects' odd behavior and could only come to one conclusion. "We were convinced another planet was out there," Brown says.

To find out if they were right, the pair created a computer model illustrating the objects. Then they plugged an imaginary planet into the model. The model showed that the planet's gravity would pull on these icy objects, making them move in exactly the way they had moved in space. The pair also inferred that the planet would be roughly the size of Neptune. Like Neptune, it would likely be made of gas, and the temperature there would be a frigid minus 374.8°F (-226°C).

"It's hard to believe that we could miss something as big as Neptune!" Brown says. But the planet is really far away, about 56 billion miles (90 billion km) from Earth. If it exists, only two telescopes in the world are powerful enough to search vast areas of the sky for it efficiently—and until now, they haven't been looking for the planet.

## THE HUNT IS ON

Brown and Batygin are convinced that their evidence proves that Planet Nine is hidden somewhere beyond the Kuiper belt. But Brown predicts the search will take at least a few years.

"There's this huge part of the solar system that we're only just beginning to learn about," says Brown.

**OUR NEW SOLAR SYSTEM?** Scientists aren't sure of Planet Nine's exact location, but they think it might lurk in the outer edges of our solar system, somewhere beyond Neptune. SUN▶

PLANET NINE  NEPTUNE  URANUS  SATURN  JUPITER  MARS EARTH VENUS MERCURY

# Sky Calendar
## 2020

Jupiter

Leonid meteor shower

Supermoon

- **JANUARY 3–4**
QUADRANTIDS METEOR SHOWER PEAK. Featuring up to 40 meteors an hour, it is the first meteor shower of every new year.

- **JANUARY 10**
PENUMBRAL LUNAR ECLIPSE. Look for the moon to darken as it passes through Earth's penumbra—or partial shadow. Visible throughout most of Europe, western Australia, Asia, Africa, and the Indian Ocean. View three more eclipses on June 5 (most of Europe, Australia, Asia, Africa, and the Indian Ocean), July 5 (North and South America), and November 30 (North America, northeastern Asia, and the Pacific Ocean).

- **FEBRUARY 9**
SUPERMOON, FULL MOON. The moon will be full and at a close approach to Earth, likely appearing bigger and brighter than usual. Look for three more supermoons on March 9, April 8, and May 7.

- **FEBRUARY 10**
MERCURY AT GREATEST EASTERN ELONGATION. Visible low in the western sky just after sunset, Mercury will be at its highest point above the horizon.

- **MAY 6–7**
ETA AQUARIDS METEOR SHOWER PEAK. View about 30 to 60 meteors an hour.

- **AUGUST 12–13**
PERSEID METEOR SHOWER PEAK. One of the best! Up to 60 meteors an hour. Best viewing is in the direction of the constellation Perseus.

- **OCTOBER 13**
MARS AT OPPOSITION. Grab a friend ... and your camera! This is your best chance to view the red planet in 2020. Mars will appear bright in the sky and be visible throughout the night.

- **OCTOBER 21–22**
ORIONID METEOR SHOWER PEAK. View up to 20 meteors an hour. Look toward the constellation Orion for the best show.

- **NOVEMBER 17–18**
LEONID METEOR SHOWER PEAK. View up to 15 meteors an hour.

- **DECEMBER 13–14**
GEMINID METEOR SHOWER PEAK. A spectacular show! Up to 120 multicolored meteors an hour.

- **DECEMBER 21**
RARE CONJUNCTION OF JUPITER AND SATURN. Look for two bright planets in the western sky just after sunset. They will be so close they could appear as a double planet! The last time this rare event occurred was 2000.

**VARIOUS DATES THROUGHOUT 2020**
VIEW THE INTERNATIONAL SPACE STATION. Visit spotthestation.nasa.gov to find out when the ISS will be flying over your neighborhood.

Dates may vary slightly depending on your location. Check with a local planetarium for the best viewing time in your area.

# SUPER SUN!

THE SUN IS 99.8 PERCENT OF ALL THE MASS IN OUR SOLAR SYSTEM.

The SUN'S surface is about 10,000°F! (5500°C)

E ven from 93 million miles (150 million km) away, the sun's rays are powerful enough to provide the energy needed for life to flourish on Earth. This 4.6-billion-year-old star is the anchor of our solar system and accounts for more than 99 percent of the mass in the solar system. What else makes the sun so special? For starters, it's larger than one million Earths and is the biggest object in our solar system. The sun also converts about four million tons (3,628,739 t) of matter to energy every second, helping to make life possible here on Earth. Now that's sun-sational!

The SUN has HOLES in it.

## Storms on the Sun!

Solar flares are 10 million times more powerful than a volcanic eruption on Earth.

With the help of specialized equipment, scientists have observed solar flares—or bursts of magnetic energy that explode from the sun's surface as a result of storms on the sun. Solar storms occur about 2,000 times every 11 years, or once every two days. Most solar storms are minor and do not impact Earth. But the fiercer the flare, the more we may potentially feel its effects, as it could disrupt power grids or interfere with GPS navigation systems. Solar storms can also trigger stronger-than-usual auroras, light shows that can be seen on Earth.

Solar storm

Some solar storms travel at speeds of **THREE MILLION MILES AN HOUR** (4.8 million km/h).

# ROCK STARS

The world is full of rocks—some big, some small, some formed deep within the Earth, and some formed at the surface. While they may look similar, not all rocks are created equal. Look closely, and you'll see differences between every boulder, stone, and pebble. Here's more about the three top varieties of rocks.

## Igneous

Named for the Greek word meaning "from fire," igneous rocks form when hot, molten liquid called magma cools. Pools of magma form deep underground and slowly work their way to the Earth's surface. If they make it all the way, the liquid rock erupts and is called lava. As the layers of lava build up, they form a mountain called a volcano. Typical igneous rocks include obsidian, basalt, and pumice, which is so chock-full of gas bubbles that it actually floats in water.

ANDESITE

GRANITE PORPHYRY

## Metamorphic

Metamorphic rocks are the masters of change! These rocks were once igneous or sedimentary, but thanks to intense heat and pressure deep within the Earth, they have undergone a total transformation from their original form. These rocks never truly melt; instead, the heat twists and bends them until their shapes substantially change. Metamorphic rocks include slate as well as marble, which is used for buildings, monuments, and sculptures.

MICA SCHIST

BANDED GNEISS

## Sedimentary

When wind, water, and ice constantly wear away and weather rocks, smaller pieces called sediment are left behind. These are sedimentary rocks, also known as gravel, sand, silt, and clay. As water flows down-hill, it carries the sedimentary grains into lakes and oceans, where they get deposited. As the loose sediment piles up, the grains eventually get compacted or cemented back together again. The result is new sedimentary rock. Sandstone, gypsum, limestone, and shale are sedimentary rocks that have formed this way.

LIMESTONE

HALITE

# A LOOK INSIDE

The **CRUST** includes tectonic plates, landmasses, and the ocean. Its average thickness varies from 5 to 25 miles (8 to 40 km).

The **MANTLE** is about 1,800 miles (2,897 km) of hot, thick, solid rock.

The **OUTER CORE** is liquid molten lava made mostly of iron and nickel.

The **INNER CORE** is a solid center made mostly of iron and nickel.

The distance from Earth's surface to its center is 3,963 miles (6,378 km) at the Equator. There are four layers: a thin, rigid crust; the rocky mantle; the outer core, which is a layer of molten iron; and finally the inner core, which is believed to be solid iron.

## What would happen if Earth had rings like Saturn?

It's good that Earth *doesn't* have rings. Saturn's rings are made of countless pieces of rock and ice that can be as tiny as a grain of sand or as big as a house. If Earth had similar rings, they'd be positioned in a way that would block sunlight and cast a shadow over the Northern and Southern Hemispheres during each region's winter. (That's when the hemispheres are tilted away from the sun.) Both areas would be darker and colder at these times. With less light coming in, crops and plants that depend on the sun to survive the season might die out. No thanks!

# It's a Rocky World!

**ROCKS AND MINERALS** can be found in a wide range of different environments. In addition to being useful materials, they also give scientists clues to how our world has changed over time.

**GYPSUM** Sedimentary rock that forms from the evaporation of mineral-rich water.

**GRANITE** Plutonic igneous rock rich in quartz and feldspar. It is a hard rock used as a building stone and for monuments.

**FOSSILS IN SHALE** Shale is a fine-grained sedimentary rock made from compacted mud. It often contains fossils of extinct organisms or plants, such as the fern at right.

**SANDSTONE** Sedimentary rock that forms when sand grains get cemented back together again.

**BASALT** The most common type of igneous rock, basalts form most of the Earth's crust under the ocean.

**OLIVINE** This group of greenish minerals is found mainly in dark-colored igneous rocks such as basalt, peridotite, and gabbro.

**BERYL** Commonly found in pegmatite and schist. Well-formed green beryl crystals are also known as emeralds.

**TOURMALINE** Commonly found in both igneous and metamorphic rocks.

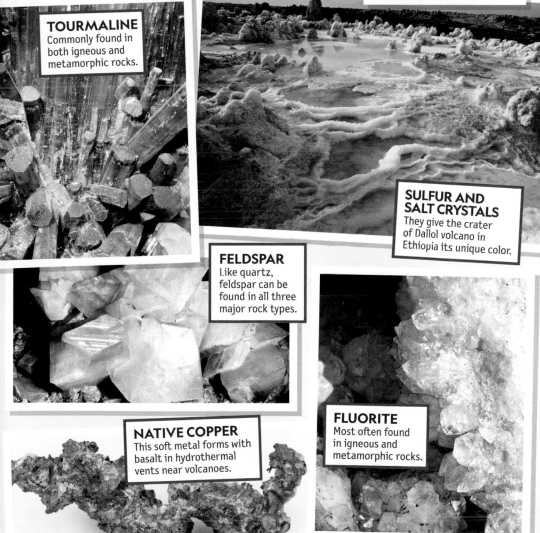

**SULFUR AND SALT CRYSTALS** They give the crater of Dallol volcano in Ethiopia its unique color.

**FELDSPAR** Like quartz, feldspar can be found in all three major rock types.

**FLUORITE** Most often found in igneous and metamorphic rocks.

**NATIVE COPPER** This soft metal forms with basalt in hydrothermal vents near volcanoes.

# A HOT TOPIC

## WHAT GOES ON
### INSIDE A STEAMING, BREWING VOLCANO?

If you could look inside a volcano, you'd see something that looks like a long pipe, called a conduit. It leads from inside the magma chamber under the crust up to a vent, or opening, at the top of the mountain. Some conduits have branches that shoot off to the side, called fissures.

When pressure builds from gases inside the volcano, the gases must find an escape, and they head up toward the surface! An eruption occurs when lava, gases, ash, and rocks explode out of the vent.

Vent

Conduit

Fissures

Magma Chamber

# TYPES OF VOLCANOES

## CINDER CONE VOLCANO
### Eve's Cone, Canada

Cinder cone volcanoes look like an upside-down ice-cream cone. They spew out cinder and hot ash. Some of these volcanoes smoke and erupt for years at a time.

## COMPOSITE VOLCANO
### Licancábur, Chile

Composite volcanoes, or stratovolcanoes, form as lava, ash, and cinder from previous eruptions harden and build up over time. These volcanoes spit out pyroclastic flows, or thick explosions of hot ash that travel at hundreds of miles an hour.

## SHIELD VOLCANO
### Mauna Loa, Hawaii, U.S.A.

The gentle, broad slopes of a shield volcano look like an ancient warrior's shield. Its eruptions are often slower. Lava splatters and bubbles rather than shooting forcefully into the air.

## LAVA DOME VOLCANO
### Mount St. Helens, Washington, U.S.A.

Dome volcanoes have steep sides. Hardened lava often plugs the vent at the top of a dome volcano. Pressure builds beneath the surface until the top blows.

**HOT SPOTS** Some volcanoes form at hot spots, or holes beneath Earth's crust in the middle of a tectonic plate. As lava pushes up through the hole and forms a volcanic island, the plate keeps moving. More volcanoes form as it moves. Some hot spots are big enough to create a chain of volcanic islands, such as the Hawaiian Islands.

**COLLAPSE!** An erupting volcano can cause damage to itself! A caldera is a large bowl-like depression caused by the collapse of a magma chamber during an eruption. Crater Lake in Oregon, U.S.A., is a caldera that has filled with rainwater and snowfall.

# FROZEN

## A COLORFUL ICE CAVE LIES HIDDEN BENEATH A REMOTE RUSSIAN GLACIER.

RUSSIA

Kamchatka Peninsula

Bering Sea

Sea of Okhotsk

KAMCHATKA CAVE

PACIFIC OCEAN

RUSSIA

ASIA

NORTH AMERICA

PACIFIC OCEAN

The inside of Kamchatka (Kam-CHAT-kuh) Cave is full of cool shades of white and gray. That's because it's an ice cave—a 20-foot (6-m)-high, 30-foot (9-m)-wide passage that tunnels half a mile (0.8 km) through a glacier. But sometimes the cave's scenery is transformed. Its icy interior occasionally glows with a dazzling display of blue and violet lights. So what gives this cave its unique colors?

## COLD HARD FACTS

The icy tunnel is tucked away in a remote valley on the Kamchatka Peninsula in Russia. But because it's a three-hour off-road drive from the nearest community, the cave was hidden from the world until 2012. That's when local hiking guide Denis Budkov and some fellow adventurers discovered the site.

The magical-looking cave is in a region known for a weird mix of volcanoes and glaciers.

That's why Kamchatka is sometimes called "the land of fire and ice." It's a combination of these two forces that created the cavern.

The first force in action: ice. Regular winter blizzards in the area created gigantic snow piles, which eventually became the many glaciers found on Kamchatka. "The weight of the snow from above squeezes ice crystals together," says Daniel McGrath, a glacier scientist with the U.S. Geological Survey. "Over long periods of time, these crystals combine to produce a glacier." Or, in this case, hundreds of glaciers.

But how did one of these glaciers become an ice cave? Blame the second force, fire—sort of. A nearby volcano-heated spring sends a steady stream of hot water down a mountainside that the glacier runs up against. Steam from this water seeped under the glacier and hollowed it out from the ground up, carving out the ice cave.

# WORLD

Russia is the world's largest country. It covers about 11 percent of Earth's land.

THE ENTRANCE TO THE CAVE IS ONLY ACCESSIBLE TO EXPERIENCED HIKERS.

The Ural Mountains split Russia between two continents, Europe and Asia.

The country's Trans-Siberian Railway, the world's longest railroad, stretches from Europe to the Sea of Japan.

THIS IS A PERSON!

THE RED COLOR OF A FLARE REFLECTS OFF THE CAVE'S INTERIOR, GIVING AN EXPLORER A BETTER VIEW.

## RAINBOW ROOF

The colors visible in the cave's ceiling are a result of sunlight streaming in through the cave's thin walls—or, at least, trying to. Snow and ice have something called a high albedo, meaning they reflect much of the sunlight that reaches their surface. But some shades of light are able to filter through water better than others. Red and yellow hues don't make it very far through the cave's icy ceiling, but blue and violet shades do.

## MAJOR MELTDOWN

Some melting is natural for glaciers. Budkov has witnessed this meltdown in Kamchatka, where the area of the peninsula's visible glaciers has shrunk

TAKE A PEEK INTO KAMCHATKA CAVE'S ICY INTERIOR. The water in the cave's stream comes from a hot spring gushing from the nearby Mutnovsky volcano and winds about a half mile (0.8 km) until it dries up at the cave's end. Sunlight streaming into the cavern through the glacial ice that forms the "roof" of the cave creates spectacular light shows on the inside.

VOLCANO
ENTRANCE
OUTSIDE / ROOF
INSIDE
CAVE EXIT THIS WAY!
STREAM

by about 24 percent since 2000. But even though Kamchatka Cave has melted a couple of times, it always reforms. "If it melts, it reappears the next year," Budkov says. Guess you could call it the comeback cave.

# QUIZ WHIZ

**Are your space and Earth smarts out of this world? Take this quiz!**

Write your answers on a piece of paper. Then check them below.

**1** **True or false?** There will be 14 supermoon sightings in 2020.

**2** **What is Earth's outer core made of?**
a. mud
b. molten lava
c. minerals
d. marshmallows

**3** **True or false?** The sun has holes in it.

**4** **Which of the following is NOT a volcano?**
a. lava dome
b. composite
c. shield
d. sedimentary

**5** _____ **is an example of metamorphic rock.**
a. Marble
b. Pumice
c. Brick
d. Limestone

Not **STUMPED** yet? Check out the *NATIONAL GEOGRAPHIC KIDS QUIZ WHIZ* collection for more crazy **SPACE AND EARTH** questions!

**ANSWERS:**
1. False. There will be four supermoons in 2020; 2. b; 3. True; 4. d; 5. a

## HOMEWORK HELP

# ACE YOUR SCIENCE FAIR

**You can learn a lot about** science from books, but to really experience it firsthand, you need to get into the lab and "do" some science. Whether you're entering a science fair or just want to learn more on your own, there are many scientific projects you can do. So put on your goggles and lab coat, and start experimenting.

Most likely, the topic of the project will be up to you. So remember to choose something that is interesting to you.

**THE BASIS OF ALL SCIENTIFIC INVESTIGATION AND DISCOVERY IS THE SCIENTIFIC METHOD. CONDUCT YOUR EXPERIMENT USING THESE STEPS:**

**Observation/Research—**Ask a question or identify a problem.

**Hypothesis—**Once you've asked a question, do some thinking and come up with some possible answers.

**Experimentation—**How can you determine if your hypothesis is correct? You test it. You perform an experiment. Make sure the experiment you design will produce an answer to your question.

**Analysis—**Gather your results, and use a consistent process to carefully measure the results.

**Conclusion—**Do the results support your hypothesis?

**Report Your Findings—** Communicate your results in the form of a paper that summarizes your entire experiment.

## Bonus!

Take your project one step further. Your school may have an annual science fair, but there are also local, state, regional, and national science fair competitions. Compete with other students for awards, prizes, and scholarships!

## EXPERIMENT DESIGN
There are three types of experiments you can do.

**MODEL KIT—**a display, such as an "erupting volcano" model. Simple and to the point.

**DEMONSTRATION—**shows the scientific principles in action, such as a tornado in a wind tunnel.

**INVESTIGATION—**the home run of science projects, and just the type of project for science fairs. This kind demonstrates proper scientific experimentation and uses the scientific method to reveal answers to questions.

**KNOCK, KNOCK.**

*Who's there?*
*T. rex*
*T. rex who?*
**There's a *T. rex* at your door and you want to know its name?**

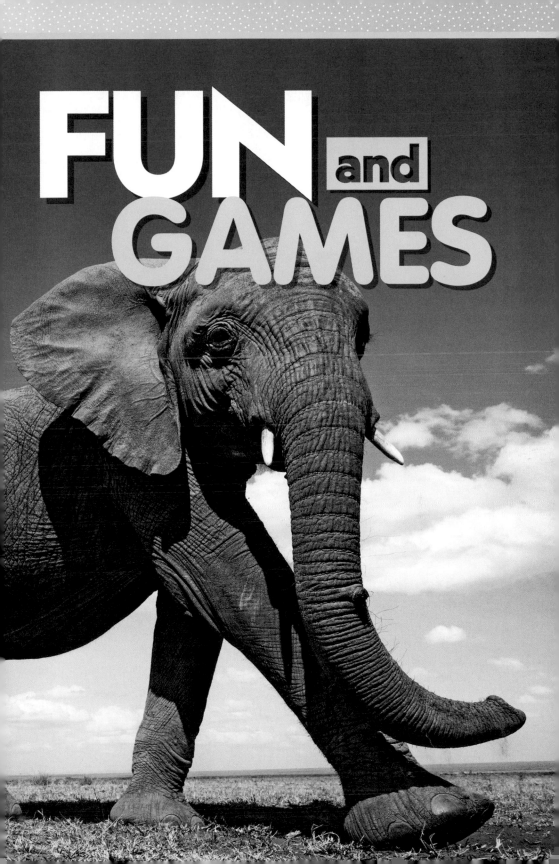

# FUN and GAMES

# WHAT IN THE WORLD?

## BACK TO NATURE

These photographs are close-up and faraway views of different textures in nature. On a separate sheet of paper, unscramble the letters to identify what's in each picture.

**ANSWERS ON PAGE 338**

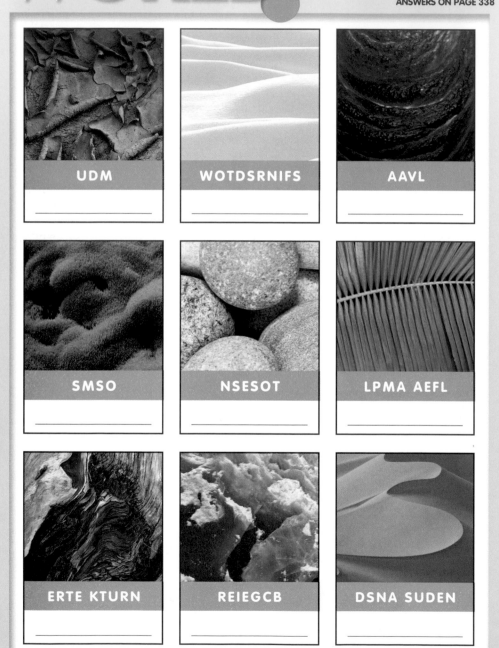

**UDM**

**WOTDSRNIFS**

**AAVL**

**SMSO**

**NSESOT**

**LPMA AEFL**

**ERTE KTURN**

**REIEGCB**

**DSNA SUDEN**

# FIND THE HIDDEN ANIMALS

Animals often blend in with their environments for protection. Find the animals listed below in the photographs. Write the letter of the correct photo on a separate sheet of paper.

**ANSWERS ON PAGE 338**

| 1. spider | |
|---|---|
| 2. frog | |
| 3. bald eagle | |
| 4. fox | |
| 5. jaguar | |
| 6. viscacha* | |

*HINT: A viscacha is a type of rodent that lives in South America.

A

B

C

D

E

F

# SIGNS OF THE TIMES

Seeing isn't always believing. Two of these funny signs are not real. Can you figure out which two are fake?

ANSWER ON PAGE 338

**1** 212 Boring ↗

**2** SURFER X-ING

**3** DUMP CLEAN DIRT HERE → SEE 910

**4** 45TH PARALLEL — HALFWAY BETWEEN THE EQUATOR AND THE NORTH POLE — PASS WITH CARE

**5** W 37 St

**6** NO NAME ST

**7** SIGN NOT IN USE

**8** SLIDE AREA

**9** SMILE PLEASE

# FUNNY FILL-IN

Ask a friend to give you words to fill in the blanks in this story and write them on a separate sheet of paper. Then read the story out loud and fill in the words for a laugh.

I was deep in the rain forest of _____ with my friend _____ , searching for
_____country_____famous person

an ancient ruin called the Lost _____ of the _____ . But just _____ minutes
_____noun_____animal_____number

into the journey, we realized we'd forgotten our _____ spray! A swarm of bugs were
_____type of insect

_____ us! We _____ _____ through the trees and soon smacked
verb ending in -ing_____adverb ending in -ly____past-tense verb

into a(n) _____ . I pulled back some _____ and couldn't believe my
_____something hard_____type of plant, plural

_____ . It was a part of the ruin—and we could hear _____ coming
body part, plural_____sound ending in -ing

from inside! We peeked through a hole in the wall and saw a group of _____ . They
_____animal, plural

were lounging on stone _____ , snacking on _____ , and even
_____type of furniture, plural_____favorite food, plural

swimming in a pool filled with _____ . I guess this ruin isn't really lost at all!
_____liquid

**Play more Funny Fill-In!**
natgeokids.com/ffi

FROM THE PAGES OF *QUIZ WHIZ:*

# STUMP
## YOUR PARENTS

Answer the questions on a separate sheet of paper. If your parents can't answer these questions, maybe they should go to school instead of you!

**ANSWERS ON PAGE 338**

**1** Where is the world's tallest building?
A. New York, New York
B. Chicago, Illinois
C. Moscow, Russia
D. Dubai, United Arab Emirates

**2** More _____ live in New Zealand than people.
A. river otters
B. sheep
C. koalas
D. unicorns

**3** Which rain forest animal is attracted to the gross-smelling flowers of the kapok tree?
A. snake
B. monkey
C. toucan
D. bat

**4** About how many teeth will a shark lose in its lifetime?
A. 4,000
B. 23,000
C. 30,000
D. 120,000

**5** In the virtual world of *Animal Jam,* which land is most similar to the Arctic on Earth?
A. Appondale
B. Mount Shiveer
C. Lost Temple of Zios
D. Crystal Sands

**6** A dog's eye has how many eyelids?
A. 1
B. 2
C. 3
D. 422

**7** The first space tourist to visit the International Space Station paid how much for a 10-day trip?
A. $20 million
B. $100 million
C. $1 billion
D. nothing

**8** Match these Harry Potter characters with their pets.
A. Ron Weasley
B. Hermione Granger
C. Neville Longbottom
D. Hagrid
E. Dumbledore

1. Fawkes the phoenix
2. Trevor the toad
3. Fang the dog
4. Crookshanks the cat
5. Pigwidgeon the owl

**9** What type of bat can eat 600 mosquitoes in an hour?
A. little brown bat
B. big brown bat
C. leaf-nosed bat
D. fruit bat

**10** The most poisonous frog in the world is _____.
A. the blue poison dart frog
B. the golden poison frog
C. the red-eyed tree frog
D. the American bullfrog

# LAUGH OUT LOUD

"JOEY AND TEDDY
LOVE MY NEW HOODIE."

"HE CAN ONLY FIND
SEVEN OF HIS SHOES."

"PULL OVER, SPEEDY."

"IF YOU DON'T STOP PLAYING POSSUM,
YOU'RE GOING TO MISS THE SCHOOL BUS!"

"YOU SAY YOU'VE BEEN FEELING
RATHER JUMPY LATELY?"

"I WISH YOU WOULD EAT LIKE OTHER SEA OTTERS."

# WHAT IN THE WORLD?

## TRUE BLUE

These photographs show close-up and faraway views of things that are blue. On a separate sheet of paper, unscramble the letters to identify what's in each picture. Feeling blue? **ANSWERS ON PAGE 338**

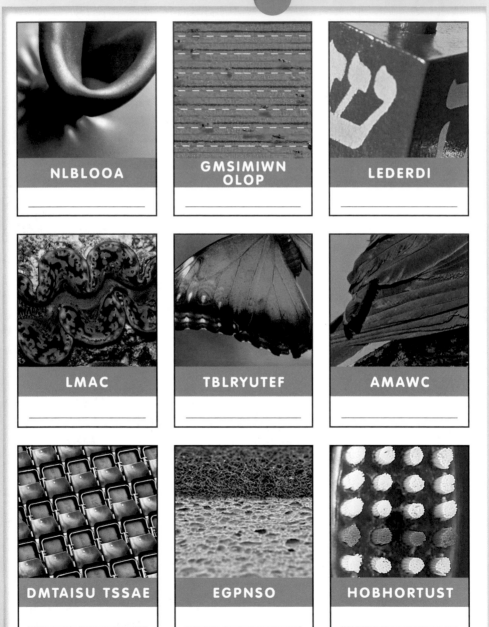

NLBLOOA

GMSIMIWN OLOP

LEDERDI

LMAC

TBLRYUTEF

AMAWC

DMTAISU TSSAE

EGPNSO

HOBHORTUST

# Just Joking

BLUE-WEBBED GLIDING FROG

**KNOCK, KNOCK.**
*Who's there?*
Cash.
*Cash who?*
No thanks.
I prefer peanuts.

How did **the lion** greet **the impala?** **Q**

**A** "Pleased to eat you!"

**Q** What do you call a shy lamb?

**A** Baaash-ful.

**Q** What protects a **clown** from the **sun?**

**A** The bozone layer.

171

# ARE YOU A GARBAGE GENIUS?

Hey! Don't throw away that doggie bag!

How much do you know about trash? Take this quiz and write your answers on a separate sheet of paper, to find out if you're a waste whiz. **ANSWERS ON PAGE 338**

## 1 TRUE OR FALSE?

Before the days of trash collectors and dumps, people used to throw their trash on the streets for animals to eat.

## 3 PICK ONE

What makes up the bulk of waste around the world?
A. newspapers
B. plastic
C. food scraps
D. yard trimmings

## 4 FILL IN THE BLANK

Some _____ zip(s) around at 20 times the speed of sound.
A. garbage trucks
B. motorized trash cans
C. space trash
D. trash robots

## 5 PICK ONE

Which creepy crawlers can help compost your food?
A. crickets
B. centipedes
C. spiders
D. worms

## 2 TRUE OR FALSE?

Old landfills are often turned into parks or green spaces.

## Trash isn't just filthy—it's funny!

Here are some rubbish-themed riddles and jokes to try on your friends and family.

**Q** What has four wheels and flies?

**A** A garbage truck.

**Q** What did the waste collector say while digging through the trash?

**A** I'm down in the dumps today!

THIS BOOK STINKS!

Check out this book!

172

# FIND THE HIDDEN ANIMALS

Animals often blend in with their environments for protection. Find each animal listed below in one of the pictures. Write the letter of the correct picture next to each animal's name.

**ANSWERS ON PAGE 338**

1. sea star _____
2. crab _____
3. arctic hare _____
4. owl _____
5. antelope _____
6. chameleon _____

A

B

C

D

E

F

173

# FUNNY FILL-IN

Ask a friend to give you words to fill in the blanks in this story and write them on a separate sheet of paper. Then read the story out loud and fill in the words for a laugh.

My band, the Three _____ (animal, plural), finally got our big break. _____ (male celebrity) was looking for kids to star in his new show, "_____ (your hometown)'s Got Talent." We grabbed our musical _____ (noun, plural) and filed into the auditorium, where _____ (large number) people were waiting to audition. Finally it was my band's turn to perform. I took a(n) _____ (adjective) breath, then we started to play a rock 'n' _____ (verb) tune. _____ (relative's name) jammed on the _____ (adjective) keyboard and _____ (friend's name) _____ (past-tense verb) on the drums. Then it was time for my _____ (adjective) solo. I went to hit a(n) _____ (adjective) chord when my guitar flew out of my hands. I _____ (past-tense verb) backward and grabbed it in midair, but I lost my balance, crashed into the drum set, and broke the keyboard. I _____ (past-tense verb) off the stage and landed in the front row. Everyone was silent until _____ (same celebrity) jumped to his feet and gave us a(n) _____ (verb ending in -ing) ovation. "_____ (silly word)!" he yelled. "That was the best comedy routine I've seen so far. You're in!"

FROM THE PAGES OF *QUIZ WHIZ:*

# STUMP
# YOUR PARENTS

Answer the questions on a separate sheet of paper. If your parents can't answer these questions, maybe they should go to school instead of you!

**ANSWERS ON PAGE 338**

**1** How many years can a macaw, a kind of parrot, live in the wild?
A. 5          C. 60
B. 20         D. 100

**2** Each year, almost a million people travel to the Andes Mountains in Peru to see which cultural site?
A. Angkor Wat      C. Machu Picchu
B. Chichén Itzá    D. Stonehenge

**3** Paper can be made from which of these materials?
A. panda droppings
B. hemp
C. wood
D. all of the above

**4** A company developed what new kind of item after studying the way butterfly wings produce colors?
A. color screens for electronic devices
B. color-changing helmets
C. tie-dyed sunglasses
D. holiday lights

**5** The tropical forest around the Lost Temple of Zios in the virtual world of *Animal Jam* would need long days and plenty of rain. If it were on Earth, where would it be found?
A. Arctic Circle    C. Great Barrier
B. Equator              Reef
                    D. South Pole

**6** On the Indonesian island of Komodo, which large animals do Komodo dragons eat?
A. water buffalo    C. polar bear
B. blue whale       D. hippopotamus

**7** If you were to make a rain forest ice cream, which flavors could you use?
A. lemon
B. banana
C. mango
D. all of the above

**8** Which type of animal is Rikki-Tikki-Tavi from *The Jungle Book?*
A. goat
B. bear
C. mongoose
D. meerkat

**9** In the Sagano Forest in Japan, bamboo grows at a rate of _____ a day.
A. 1 inch
B. 12 inches
C. 40 inches
D. 60 inches

**10** Spider monkeys have a prehensile tail, meaning they can _____ with their tails.
A. shoot venom
B. grab branches
C. peel bananas
D. scratch their backs

# MOVIE MADNESS

It's chaos on this crazy movie set in Hollywood. Eleven things beginning with the letter *C* have gone missing. Find and write down on a separate sheet of paper the missing items in the scene so the show can go on.

ANSWERS ON PAGE 338

# CRITTER CHAT

If wild animals used social media, what would they say? Follow this Galápagos tortoise's day as it updates its feed.

## GALÁPAGOS TORTOISE

**LIVES IN:** Galápagos Islands, off the coast of Ecuador   **SCREEN NAME:** SwellShell
**FRIENDS:**

**TealToes**
BLUE-FOOTED BOOBY

**FrostyFur**
HOARY BAT

**LionAround**
GALÁPAGOS SEA LION

**START**

### 11 a.m.

**SwellShell:** Boy, it's hot! Time to head up the "Tortoise Highway" to cooler ground for a few months. Thousands of tortoises made these tracks!

**LionAround:** You weigh, what, 500 pounds? How fast can you cruise with that big backpack?

**SwellShell:** My shell's actually pretty light—it's my legs that weigh so much! And it's not like I need to hustle to get food: I can go an entire year without eating or drinking.

**FrostyFur:** A year's nothing to **SwellShell**—he's at *least* a hundred years older than me. Do you even remember your birthday?

**SwellShell:** Nope! So I'll go ahead and celebrate today. Grass cake, anyone? 😊

### 2 p.m.

**SwellShell:** I feel like a mud bath. How's everyone else doing?

**TealToes:** I'm feeling blue.

**LionAround:** Can I snag you a fish? That always cheers me up.

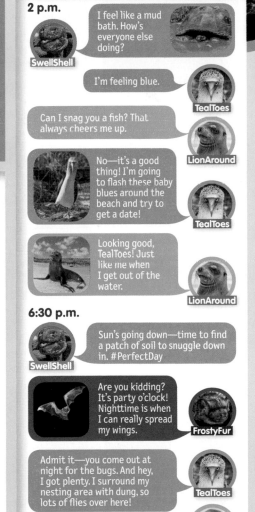
**TealToes:** No—it's a good thing! I'm going to flash these baby blues around the beach and try to get a date!

**LionAround:** Looking good, TealToes! Just like me when I get out of the water.

### 6:30 p.m.

**SwellShell:** Sun's going down—time to find a patch of soil to snuggle down in. #PerfectDay

**FrostyFur:** Are you kidding? It's party o'clock! Nighttime is when I can really spread my wings.

**TealToes:** Admit it—you come out at night for the bugs. And hey, I got plenty. I surround my nesting area with dung, so lots of flies over here!

**LionAround:** That's *fowl*. Get it? You're a bird—you're fowl. 😜

# WHAT IN THE WORLD?

## SPACED OUT

These images show close-up and faraway views of things that are associated with outer space. Unscramble the letters to identify each picture. Seeing stars?

ANSWERS ON PAGE 338

LAYAGX

_____

TUNRATOSA

_____

NOMO

_____

ECPSA ELTHUST

_____

NSU

_____

TMOEC

_____

RUANST

_____

RMSA REVRO

_____

IASEELTLT

_____

# FUNNY FILL-IN

Ask a friend to give you words to fill in the blanks in this story and write them on a separate sheet of paper. Then read the story out loud and fill in the words for a laugh.

I've never been more _____ (adjective). My baseball team, the _____ (color) _____ (noun, plural), was about to play the championship game. But Coach _____ (celebrity) announced that the official rules had changed! First, every player would _____ (verb) _____ (large number) times before going to bat. We also had to wear our gloves on our _____ (body part, plural) like _____ (article of clothing, plural) and run like a(n) _____ (animal). Before Coach could explain more, the umpire shouted, "_____ (verb) ball!" The umpire tossed me our new official bat, a(n) _____ (tool). When the _____ (type of job) threw the new official ball, a(n) _____ (fruit), it zoomed past me and _____ (past-tense verb) all over the catcher. After _____ (large number) tries, I finally hit the _____ (same fruit) all the way to _____ (faraway city). I started _____ (verb ending in -ing) as fast as I could until I slid into home base. This new game isn't so _____ (adjective) after all.

179

# AWESOME
# EXPLORATION

Wasfia Nazreen—Bangladeshi human rights activist and adventurer—paddles her canoe on the Columbia River Valley Wetlands, near Wilmer, British Columbia, Canada.

# EARTH EXPLORER
## Meet **Barrington Irving!**

**This National Geographic emerging explorer dares kids to fly high.**

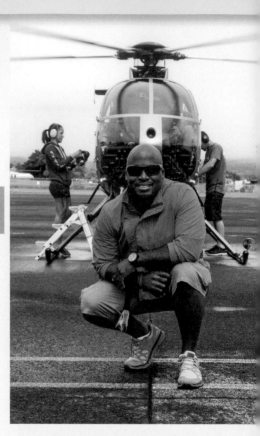

**B**arrington Irving's soaring career hit high altitude when he was just 23 years old. That's when he set out to pilot a single-engine airplane on a trip spanning the globe. During that 97-day journey he navigated through thunderstorms, monsoons, snowstorms, and sandstorms—and eventually landed in the history books as the youngest person and the first African American to fly solo around the world.

Barrington's 2007 record has since been broken, but he has yet to stop inspiring kids around the globe to spread their wings and go after their own high-flying ambitions. As the "captain" of the Flying Classroom (flyingclassroom.com), Barrington visits students and shares his own experiences while offering real-life lessons in science, technology, engineering, and math (also known as STEM+).

"I use STEM+ in everything I do," says Irving, who has worked with middle school kids to create things like a car that goes from 0 to 60 miles an hour (96.6 km/h) in less than three seconds. "Kids can build anything!"

Barrington also believes kids can be anything, even if their dreams seem out of reach.

"I was always fascinated with planes as a kid but never thought I was smart enough to fly one," he says. "Then I randomly met an airline pilot named Capt. Gary Robinson. Interest turned into passion and I fell in love with aviation because someone believed in me."

Today, Irving hopes to pay it forward when it comes to supporting kids and getting them to believe in themselves.

"You have to have confidence," he says. "If you don't believe, no one else will. Confidence will always keep you going."

One trip around the world is about 30,000 miles (48,280 km) long.

IRVING READING NOTES FROM STUDENTS AS HE CROSSES THE EQUATOR

"Always be willing to explore beyond what you don't know and can ever dream of. Never let anything limit you from soaring. See the world!"

During his 97-day trip around the world, Barrington made just 26 stops.

WORKING WITH THE INVASIVE CANE TOAD IN AUSTRALIA

## CALL TO ACTION!

Want to fly the friendly skies one day? You can build your knowledge base right in your own bedroom. "Start with YouTube videos [about flying and pilots]," suggests Barrington. Or, you can ask your parents to put you in touch with a pilot or someone who works in aviation. "I remember when I started I simply picked up the phone and would call offices to have a discussion with professionals," says Irving.

BARRINGTON AND CO-PILOT TOM

# Meet Your Shark Bestie

Some sharks grow over 30,000 teeth in their lifetime.

## YOU WON'T BELIEVE THESE PREDATOR PERSONALITIES.

While diving off the Bahama Islands, National Geographic photographer Brian Skerry noticed an oceanic whitetip shark swimming toward him. Soon the nine-foot (2.7-m)-long female was gently bumping her snout against Skerry's camera.

The shark's mouth was closed, so Skerry knew she wasn't trying to bite him. Instead, she just examined his photographic equipment like a curious kid. Skerry says this type of behavior shows that sharks have all sorts of personalities. And even individuals belonging to a species that's thought to be aggressive can have a major sweet side.

### PERSONALITY POWER

Hiking in the Bahamas through a mangrove forest—a group of shrubs or trees that grow in coastal waters—Skerry arrived at a wild nursery for lemon shark pups in about a foot (0.3 m) of water. He put on his snorkel gear and scrambled onto his stomach to snap pics of the fish, watching as three shark pups swished closer to investigate. "Certain sharks are quicker to explore new things in their environment," Skerry says. Meaning some sharks are also super social, while others within the same species prefer their me time.

Different sharks within the same species thrive in different situations. Social lemon sharks may do better when food is plentiful because they'll share the grub with each other. But when food is scarce, the loner lemon sharks might thrive, since they don't divide their meals.

### SUPERSIZE SHARK

On another diving trip, Skerry caught sight of a 14-foot (4.3-m)-long tiger shark in the Atlantic Ocean. Skerry admits to being nervous at first, but the shark just glided over him and actually allowed Skerry to touch her. The tiger shark, known as Emma, visited the dive site almost every day during Skerry's stay. "She was just a gentle giant," says Skerry.

Skerry hopes that by showing the different personalities of sharks, people will view them

SKERRY TOOK THIS PHOTO OF A LEMON SHARK PUP FROM THE WATERY FLOOR OF A MANGROVE FOREST.

More than 450 species of sharks exist, but at least 26 of them are endangered and at least 48 are vulnerable.

THIS PHOTO, TAKEN BY BRIAN SKERRY, SHOWS A DIVER INTERACTING WITH A TIGER SHARK OFF THE BAHAMA ISLANDS.

THE ULTIMATE BOOK OF SHARKS

Check out this book!

SKERRY READIES HIS CAMERA TO TAKE PHOTOS OF A SCHOOL OF CARIBBEAN REEF SHARKS.

less as scary animals and more as individuals that deserve our care and protection. Even if they do have a lot of teeth!

## GUARDIANS OF THE SEA

Want to help keep coral reefs in good condition? Call in the sharks! Certain sharks eat animals that prey on herbivorous (or plant-eating) fish. Since herbivorous fish eat harmful algae that grow on the reefs, a break in that chain would be bad news for coral. Thank goodness for hungry sharks.

A REMORA FISH CATCHES A RIDE ON A TIGER SHARK OFF THE BAHAMA ISLANDS.

# THE LOST SKULL

## Bones found in a submerged Mexican cave give clues about the first Americans.

DIVER SUSAN BIRD CLEANS THE SKULL WITH A BRUSH.

A man once dived more than 900 feet (274 m) underwater without an oxygen supply.

I n 2007, a team of scuba divers swimming off Mexico's Yucatán Peninsula came across an eerie, but exciting find. Deep within an underwater cave, in a chamber the size of two basketball courts, was the oldest complete human skeleton ever found in the Americas. These ancient remains held clues to ultimately reveal new things about the first people to live in North America.

### A JAW-DROPPING FIND

Experts suspected that the remains belonged to a teenage girl who lived in the last ice age some 12,000 years ago. They named her Naia, after a sea creature in Greek myths, and assessed that she likely died after falling into a large hole caused by dropping sea levels and erosion. Over time, sea levels rose again and water flooded the cave, burying Naia for the next 12 millennia.

### A LINK TO THE PAST

By examining the bones and other items found nearby like teeth, experts ran DNA tests to assess that Naia is a direct ancestor of present-day Native Americans. Naia's DNA also matches with people native to Siberia, a part of Russia. Scientists have long thought that ancient people from this region crossed to North America on land exposed between what is now Russia and Alaska during the last ice age. They were the first humans to inhabit the Americas, and Naia proves how far south they went.

Today, Naia's skull is in a lab. Researchers are still studying her skull to learn about early Americans, so she can continue to shed light on the past.

THE WATER IN WHICH NAIA WAS FOUND HELPED PRESERVE HER SKULL.

The Yucatán Peninsula has 2,500 Maya ruins.

NORTH AMERICA
ATLANTIC OCEAN
MEXICO
PACIFIC OCEAN
SOUTH AMERICA

UNITED STATES

MEXICO
Gulf of Mexico
Caribbean Sea

★ Mexico City

PACIFIC OCEAN

HOYO NEGRO

# Out of This World

## SCIENTISTS SPEND EIGHT MONTHS IN ISOLATION TO MIMIC LIFE ON MARS

**What's life like on Mars?** A crew of researchers have a pretty good idea about living on the red planet after spending eight straight months in a Mars-like habitat. In an initiative run by the University of Hawaii and sponsored by NASA, the six scientists lived inside a vinyl dome below the summit of Hawaii's Mauna Loa volcano, meant to mimic the rugged, rocky terrain on Mars.

### JUST LIKE THE REAL DEAL

Eating mostly freeze-dried and canned food, the crew conducted surveys and experiments while practicing protocols for an actual mission to Mars, including fixing equipment, mapping, and even growing fresh vegetables. Any communication with the outside world was on a 20-minute delay—the time it takes for signals to travel between Earth and Mars. And anytime they left the dome to do fieldwork outside, they'd put on their spacesuits, just like they'd need to do while on Mars.

### HEAD GAMES

The experiment also tested the crew's ability to be mostly cut off from the rest of the world. While the six of them bonded by playing games like Pictionary and watching movies together, it's hard to avoid conflict while living in isolation. Making matters a bit more, well, stressful? Sharing a space about the size of a two-bedroom home—including two composting toilets and one shower—a similar setup to what astronauts would have on Mars. Throughout the eight-month experiment, the team worked on practicing open and honest communication to resolve conflict so they could better focus on completing their tasks.

### MISSION ACCOMPLISHED

While the mock mission may seem out of this world, NASA says the experiment and others like it will help it better plan and prepare for an actual trip to Mars, which may be just a decade or two away.

NATIONAL GEOGRAPHIC KiDS

ALMANAC CHALLENGE 2020

# BE A 2020 VISIONARY!

**A** lot has happened in the world since the first *National Geographic Kids Almanac* was published 10 years ago. We've discovered evidence of water on Mars, mass-produced electric cars for consumers, and tracked the DNA sequence of the human genome. Smartphones took off and tons of apps were invented. Selfies, makerspaces, and 3D printers came into fashion.

In the past decade, National Geographic explorers have also accomplished great things to further our mission to understand and protect the planet. They've helped establish important new marine sanctuaries and national parks to preserve animal habitats and biodiversity all over the globe. These adventurers have explored the deepest realms of the ocean, and uncovered the oldest human fossils and new dinosaur species to shed light on the past—and the future.

NATIONAL GEOGRAPHIC

PHOTO ARK
JOEL SARTORE

National Geographic photographer Joel Sartore is photographing every animal species in captivity for his Photo Ark project to show the wonder of all animals and inspire people to protect them.

A new species of human ancestor, called *Homo naledi,* was discovered by National Geographic Explorer Lee Berger and his team in a South African cave.

# THIS YEAR'S CHALLENGE

To celebrate the Almanac's 10th anniversary, we invite you to be a 2020 Visionary. Think about the world 10 years from now, picture a positive change, invention, or discovery that you'd like to see happen, and share your vision with us. Focus on whatever you're interested in—animals, plants, people, places, science, medicine, technology, conservation. The sky's the limit! You don't have to be an expert on how to make your vision a reality. You just have to tell us what it is, how it would make the world better, and why it matters to you. Send us your visionary idea, and it could be featured in next year's Almanac!

Find inspiration and info on how to submit your entry at **natgeokids.com/almanac.**

## LAST YEAR'S CHALLENGE

Check out the winner of last year's Lions Forever poster contest. We received more than 500 entries with amazing artwork and inspiring messages of conservation. Thanks to all the kids from around the world who entered and shared their interest in saving lions. See more entries at **natgeokids.com/almanac.**

### RUNNERS-UP

NORA B., AGE 12, SEVERNA PARK, MARYLAND, U.S.A.

(LEFT) MARIAM S., AGE 11, PRAIRIE VILLAGE, KANSAS, U.S.A.
(MIDDLE) SHABAD S., AGE 11, BOWIE, MARYLAND, U.S.A.
(RIGHT) LILAH P., AGE 10, ST. LOUIS, MISSOURI, U.S.A.

# SEARCH-AND-RESCUE
# DOG

Have no fear, superdog is here!

SHAKA TAKES A BREAK FROM TRAINING AS MCGURK LOOKS ON.

## North Lake Tahoe, California, U.S.A.

Shaka the golden retriever digs in the snow. He's not pawing through the snow for fun, though—he's practicing to save lives. That's because Shaka is part of Squaw Dogs, a team of search-and-rescue dogs at the Squaw Valley Ski Resort. The animals assist their human handlers with finding lost skiers after avalanches.

Shaka's handler, ski patroller Ivan McGurk, says that though humans can use their eyes to look for injured skiers aboveground, they need help to find people under the snow. "Shaka's trained to search for humans using his nose," McGurk says. "I need his sense of smell to track down what I can't see."

When Shaka's not working, he's with his best friend, Kaya the Belgian Malinois, another Squaw Dog. And when they play something called "flying squirrel," look out! "Shaka runs at Kaya and leaps on her!" says Ben Stone, Kaya's handler.

He saves lives *and* he can fly? Someone get this dog a cape.

# HOW TO SURVIVE ...

## A LION ATTACK

**1 CATFIGHT**
Lions usually avoid confrontations with people. But if one lunges toward you, **swing a tree branch, throw rocks, even gouge its eyes.** Fighting back may make it slink away like the Cowardly Lion.

**2 DON'T TAKE IT "LION DOWN"**
**Never crouch, kneel, or play dead.** The lion might think you're ready to become a Kid McNugget.

**3 ACT LIKE A PRO WRESTLER**
Lions go after weaker prey, so show it that you rule. **Scream, snarl, and bare your teeth** (even if you have braces). Come on stronger than The Rock in a smackdown.

**4 STRENGTH IN NUMBERS**
Lions prefer to attack solitary prey, so make sure you safari with plenty of friends. Don't let the lion divide and conquer— **keep your pals close by at all times.**

**5 SEE YA LATER**
See an escape route? Don't wait for a permission slip, Einstein! **Slowly back away—but never turn tail and run.** You just might avoid a major *cat*-astrophe.

WARE!
CKSAND

## QUICKSAND

**1 NO MORE *SOUP*-ERSTITIONS**
**Quicksand isn't some bottom-less pit waiting to suck you in.** It's a soupy mixture of sand and water found near riverbanks, shorelines, and marshes. It's rarely more than a few feet deep, though it can be deeper.

**2 GO WITH THE FLOAT**
Not that you'd want to, but **quicksand is actually easier to float on than water.** So lean back, place your arms straight out from your sides, and let the sopping sand support your weight.

**3 YOU FLAIL, YOU FAIL**
Don't kick or struggle. That creates a vacuum, which only pulls you down. Ignore the gritty goop squishing into your underpants and remain calm.

**4 LEG LIFTS**
Conquer the quicksand with a slow stand. As you're lying back with your arms out, carefully inch one leg, then the other, to the surface.

**5 ROLL OVER!**
When both legs are afloat, pretend you're performing a dog trick. Keeping your face out of the muck, **gently roll over the quicksand** until you're on solid ground.

# awes8me
## EXTREME SPORTS

CLIFF JUMPERS!

**(2) WINGING IT**

At the World BASE Race, competitors soar from cliffs wearing wingsuits. Free-falling faster than a speeding train for about two minutes, the jumpers eventually pull a parachute to glide gently to the ground.

**(1) TAKE THE PLUNGE**

*Cannonball!* A brave diver leaps off the La Quebrada Cliffs in Acapulco, Mexico. The height of the jump? Some 150 feet (45.7 m)—four times taller than most platform diving boards.

**(4) GO WITH THE FLOW**

This sport is on fire. In ash boarding, you strap a wooden board onto your feet before shooting down the slope of an active volcano, reaching speeds up to 50 miles an hour (80.5 km/h).

**(3) CURVE APPEAL**

Cars and motorcycles drive sideways along a wall in this dizzying display in India. Thanks to centripetal force, vehicles stay stuck to the wall as they loop around the curved course.

## 5 WHEELS UP

Rock 'n' roll! A free rider sails over a steep rock wall in Moab, Utah, U.S.A. In free riding, cyclists use obstacles in nature—like rock formations and twisty trails—to do daring tricks and stunts.

## 6 BALANCING ACT

No fear here: A daredevil tiptoes along a wire as she crosses between two cliffs in the Italian Alps. A stumble at this height would be like falling from the top of the Empire State Building.

## 7 THROWN FOR A LOOP

Stunt cyclist Danny MacAskill seems to defy gravity by riding around a 16-foot (4.9-m)-tall loop. Here, he's shown in a time-lapsed photo making a full circle before riding away on his bike.

## 8 BIG AIR

A snowboarder is flying high during the slopestyle event at the 2014 Winter Olympics in Sochi, Russia. Slopestyle competitors race down a mountain dotted with obstacles like ramps, which allow them to catch major air.

**DUH!** Don't try these tricks on your own.

# PHOTO TIPS: Getting Started

**TAKING A PHOTO IS AS EASY AS PUSHING A BUTTON,** but taking a good photo requires patience and a general understanding of how photography works. Whether you're using a low-end smartphone or a high-end digital camera, check out National Geographic photographer Annie Griffith's top tips and tricks for taking better pictures. With these expert pointers, you'll discover how to get the shot you want.

## TIP 1

### Get Closer When You Photograph People

Remember, it's the face of a person that makes us love people pictures, not their shoes! So move in close and show that beautiful face!

## TIP 2

### Take Time to Think About Your Composition

**Composition** is the way you place objects or people inside the frame. This is where you can be most creative. Remember, what is left OUT of the frame is as important as what is left in, so look carefully to see if anything in the shot will distract from your subject. If so, find a way to recompose, or rearrange, the photo so the distraction is left out.

**composition:** the arrangement of the subject and its surroundings in a frame

## TIP 3
### Get Moving!

If you have taken lots of shots from one spot, try looking at the subject from another angle: above, behind, close up, far away. Professional photographers are moving all the time, always trying for a better shot.

## TIP 4
### Don't Photograph People in the Sun

Bright sun is usually the worst light for photographing people. The sun causes deep shadows and harsh light. Besides, everyone in the picture is usually squinting! It's much better to move your subjects to a shady spot where the light is softer.

## TIP 5
### Quality Not Quantity

It's far better to take fewer, more thoughtfully composed pictures, than it is to shoot like a maniac. It's not about how many pictures you take. It's about how cool those pictures are!

Check out the book!

GUIDE TO
PHOTO
GRAPHY

# QUIZ WHIZ

Discover just how much you know about exploration with this quiz!

Write your answers on a piece of paper. Then check them below.

**1** More than _____ species of sharks exist.
a. 45
b. 260
c. 450
d. 700

**2** **True or false?** It's easier to float on quicksand than water.

**3** Which location has a rocky terrain that's similar to Mars?
a. Chile
b. Hawaii
c. Mongolia
d. Tunisia

**4** Bright _____ is usually the worst light for photographing people.

**5** In _____ boarding, you strap a wooden board to your feet and shoot down an active volcano.
a. hot
b. ash
c. lava
d. snow

Not **STUMPED** yet? Check out the *NATIONAL GEOGRAPHIC KIDS QUIZ WHIZ* collection for more crazy **EXPLORATION** questions!

ANSWERS: 1. c; 2. True 3. b; 4. sun; 5. b

## HOMEWORK HELP

# How to Write a Perfect Essay

**Need to write an essay? Does the assignment feel as big as climbing Mount Everest? Fear not. You're up to the challenge! The following step-by-step tips will help you with this monumental task.**

**1** **BRAINSTORM.** Sometimes the subject matter of your essay is assigned to you, sometimes it's not. Either way, you have to decide what you want to say. Start by brainstorming some ideas, writing down any thoughts you have about the subject. Then read over everything you've come up with and consider which idea you think is the strongest. Ask yourself what you want to write about the most. Keep in mind the goal of your essay. Can you achieve the goal of the assignment with this topic? If so, you're good to go.

**2** **WRITE A TOPIC SENTENCE.** This is the main idea of your essay, a statement of your thoughts on the subject. Again, consider the goal of your essay. Think of the topic sentence as an introduction that tells your reader what the rest of your essay will be about.

**3** **OUTLINE YOUR IDEAS.** Once you have a good topic sentence, you then need to support that main idea with more detailed information, facts, thoughts, and examples. These supporting points answer one question about your topic sentence—"Why?" This is where research and perhaps more brainstorming come in. Then organize these points in the way you think makes the most sense, probably in order of importance. Now you have an outline for your essay.

**4** **ON YOUR MARK, GET SET, WRITE!** Follow your outline, using each of your supporting points as the topic sentence of its own paragraph. Use descriptive words to get your ideas across to the reader. Go into detail, using specific information to tell your story or make your point. Stay on track, making sure that everything you include is somehow related to the main idea of your essay. Use transitions to make your writing flow.

**5** **WRAP IT UP.** Finish your essay with a conclusion that summarizes your entire essay and restates your main idea.

**6** **PROOFREAD AND REVISE.** Check for errors in spelling, capitalization, punctuation, and grammar. Look for ways to make your writing clear, understandable, and interesting. Use descriptive verbs, adjectives, or adverbs when possible. It also helps to have someone else read your work to point out things you might have missed. Then make the necessary corrections and changes in a second draft. Repeat this revision process once more to make your final draft as good as you can.

199

Lightning flashes above Monument Valley Navajo Tribal Park on the border of Arizona and Utah, U.S.A.

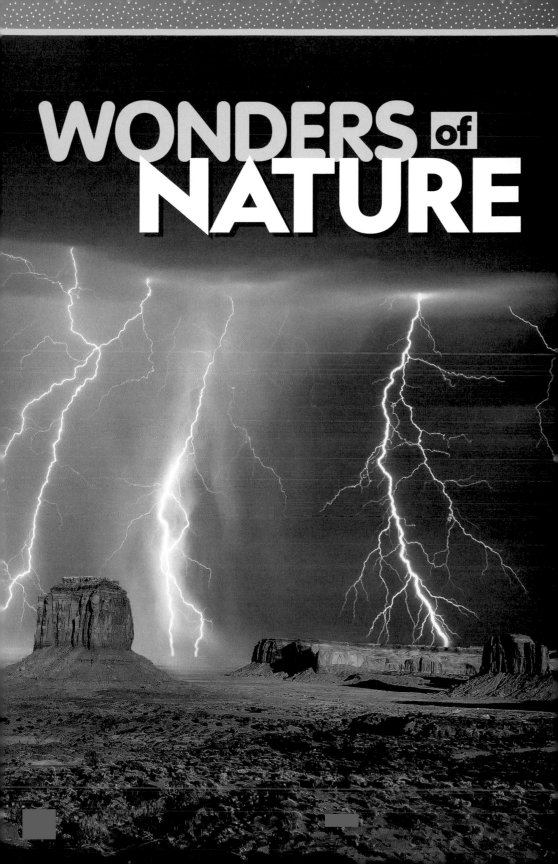

# WONDERS of
# NATURE

## EARTH EXPLORER
### Meet Enric Sala!

**This National Geographic explorer-in-residence is fighting to save the world's oceans, one fish at a time.**

Picture this: You're diving off the coast of Costa Rica when you look up to see 200 hammerhead sharks swimming above you. Later, you slowly cruise through a school of some 100 whitetip reef sharks, before setting your gaze on a pod of giant whale sharks—all in the same pocket of the Pacific Ocean.

This is what Enric Sala, a National Geographic explorer-in-residence, experienced on a recent dive trip off Cocos Island, a national park about 330 miles (530 km) from Costa Rica's mainland. As a marine ecologist, Enric travels the world studying the world's oceans and working to save marine life.

As amazing as some of those trips are, Enric has seen things that turned his career into his passion. He has seen sharks pierced with rusty steel hooks, whales washed up on shores with their bellies full of plastic, and coral reefs dying off at an alarming rate.

"Humans are destroying ocean life because of too much fishing, pollution, and climate change," says Enric. "But if we protect the ocean, marine life can come back."

Through his Pristine Seas project, Enric is hoping to save the oceans. He and his team are setting up Marine Protected Areas (MPAs) throughout the world. Like national parks on land, these are safe spaces in the ocean where human activities, like fishing, are strictly regulated.

So far, the Pristine Seas project has helped to establish 19 marine reserves across the globe, in spots like Russia and Chile. Still, less than 5 percent of the world's oceans are officially protected. But Enric is hopeful that number will continue to increase as people become more and more aware of the desperate need to save the oceans—and everything in them.

"The ocean is vital to our survival as it gives us food, more than half of the oxygen we breathe, and many more wonderful things," says Enric.

About 70 percent of Earth's surface is covered with water.

RAINBOW WRASSES IN THE MEDITERRANEAN SEA

" In only three years, we can see already more fish than before. In ten years, the abundance of fish inside a protected area is, on average, six times greater than outside. Everything comes back. "

GREEN SEA TURTLE, COCOS ISLAND, COSTA RICA

The Mariana Trench, the deepest part of the ocean, is deeper than Mount Everest is tall.

## CALL TO ACTION!

"Go in the ocean, swim, and snorkel. Or just go to any place where you can enjoy the natural world," says Enric. "Take a walk through a forest, explore a marsh, or run through a prairie. Spend time in nature and you'll fall in love with it."

TABUAERAN LAGOON, KIRIBATI

# Weather and Climate

Weather is the condition of the atmosphere—temperature, wind, humidity, and precipitation—at a given place at a given time. Climate, however, is the average weather for a particular place over a long period of time. Different places on Earth have different climates, but climate is not a random occurrence. It is a pattern that is controlled by factors such as latitude, elevation, prevailing winds, the temperature of ocean currents, and location on land relative to water. Climate is generally constant, but evidence indicates that human activity is causing a change in its patterns.

## WOW-WORTHY WEATHER

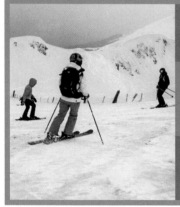

**CANADIAN COLD SNAP:** In December 2017, Toronto, Canada, cracked a 57-year-old weather record with temperatures dropping to minus 7.6°F (-22°C).

**SEEING ORANGE:** Dark orange snow sometimes falls on parts of Europe, the result of storms blowing dust from the Sahara into the atmosphere, where it mixes with the white stuff.

**RECORD RAIN:** A record-setting rainstorm soaked the Hawaiian island of Kauai in April 2018, with nearly 50 inches (127 cm) of rain falling in just one 24-hour period.

# GLOBAL CLIMATE ZONES

Climatologists, people who study climate, have created different systems for classifying climates. One that is often used is called the Köppen system, which classifies climate zones according to precipitation, temperature, and vegetation. It has five major categories—Tropical, Dry, Temperate, Cold, and Polar—with a sixth category for locations where high elevations override other factors.

ARCTIC OCEAN

ARCTIC CIRCLE

ATLANTIC OCEAN

TROPIC OF CANCER

PACIFIC OCEAN

EQUATOR

PACIFIC OCEAN

TROPIC OF CAPRICORN

INDIAN OCEAN

ANTARCTIC CIRCLE

**Climate**

■ Tropical  ■ Dry  ■ Humid temperate  ■ Humid cold  ■ Polar

# EXTREME CLIMATES

**Talk about a temperature swing!** The difference between the coldest place on Earth—east Antarctica—and the hottest—Death Valley, in Nevada and California, U.S.A.—is a whopping 270°F (150°C). Though they are both deserts, these two opposites are neck and neck in the race for world's most extreme climate.

## HOT
### DEATH VALLEY

| | |
|---|---|
| **CRAZY TEMPS** | Hottest temperature ever recorded: **134°F** (57°C) |
| **RAINFALL** | Death Valley is the driest place in North America. The average yearly rainfall is about **2 inches (5 cm)**. |
| **ELEVATION** | At **282 feet (86 m) below sea level**, Death Valley is the lowest point in North America. |
| **STEADY HEAT** | In 2001, Death Valley experienced **160 consecutive days** of temperatures **100°F (38°C)** or hotter. |

## COLD
### EAST ANTARCTIC PLATEAU

| | |
|---|---|
| **CRAZY TEMPS** | Coldest temperature ever recorded: **-135.8°F** (-93°C) |
| **RAINFALL** | East Antarctica gets less than **2 inches (5 cm)** of precipitation in a year. |
| **ELEVATION** | The record low temperature was recorded just below the plateau's **13,000-foot (3,962-m) ridge**. |
| **DARKNESS** | During parts of winter, there is **24 hours** of darkness. |

# WATER CYCLE

Precipitation falls

Water storage in ice and snow

Water vapor condenses in clouds

Water filters into the ground

Meltwater and surface runoff

Freshwater storage

Evaporation

Groundwater discharge

Water storage in ocean

## The amount of water on Earth is more or less constant—

only the form changes. As the sun warms Earth's surface, liquid water is changed into water vapor in a process called **evaporation.** Water on the surface of plants' leaves turns into water vapor in a process called **transpiration.** As water vapor rises into the air, it cools and changes form again. This time, it becomes clouds in a process called **condensation.** Water droplets fall from the clouds as **precipitation,** which then travels as groundwater or runoff back to the lakes, rivers, and oceans, where the cycle (shown above) starts all over again.

To a meteorologist— a person who studies the weather— a "light rain" is less than 1/48 inch (0.5 mm). A "heavy rain" is more than 1/6 inch (4 mm).

You drink the same water as the dinosaurs! Earth has been recycling water for more than four billion years.

# Types of Clouds

If you want a clue about the weather, look up at the clouds. They'll tell a lot about the condition of the air and what weather might be on the way. Clouds are made of both air and water. On fair days, warm air currents rise up and push against the water in clouds, keeping it from falling. But as the raindrops in a cloud get bigger, it's time to set them free. The bigger raindrops become too heavy for the air currents to hold up, and they fall to the ground.

**1 STRATUS** These clouds make the sky look like a bowl of thick gray porridge. They hang low in the sky, blanketing the day in dreary darkness. Stratus clouds form when cold, moist air close to the ground moves over a region.

**2 CIRRUS** These wispy tufts of clouds are thin and hang high up in the atmosphere where the air is extremely cold. Cirrus clouds are made of tiny ice crystals.

**3 CUMULONIMBUS** These are the monster clouds. Rising air currents force fluffy cumulus clouds to swell and shoot upward, as much as 70,000 feet (21,000 m). When these clouds bump against the top of the troposphere, or the tropopause, they flatten out on top like tabletops.

**4 CUMULUS** These white, fluffy clouds make people sing, "Oh, what a beautiful morning!" They form low in the atmosphere and look like marshmallows. They often mix with large patches of blue sky. Formed when hot air rises, cumulus clouds usually disappear when the air cools at night.

## How Much Does a Cloud Weigh?

A light, fluffy cumulus cloud typically weighs about 216,000 pounds (98,000 kg). That's about the weight of 18 elephants. A rain-soaked cumulonimbus cloud typically weighs 105.8 million pounds (48 million kg), or about the same as 9,000 elephants.

207

# HURRICANE
# HAPPENINGS

**A storm is coming!** But is it a tropical cyclone, a hurricane, or a typhoon? These weather events go by different names depending on where they form and how fast their winds get. Strong tropical cyclones are called hurricanes in the Atlantic and parts of the Pacific Ocean; in the western Pacific they are called typhoons. But any way you look at it, these storms pack a punch.

## 1,380 MILES (2,221 km)

diameter of the most massive tropical cyclone ever recorded, 1979's Typhoon Tip

## 82°F (27.8°C)

water surface temperature necessary for a tropical cyclone to form

## 16.6

average number of tropical storms each year in the Northeast and Central Pacific Basins

## 10

number of Hurricane Sandy–related pictures uploaded every second to Instagram on October 29, 2012

## 31

number of days Hurricane John lasted in 1994

# 12.1

average number of tropical storms in the Atlantic Basin each year

# 254 MPH

(408 km/h)

strongest gust of storm wind ever recorded

# 12-25 MILES

(20–40 km)

diameter of a hurricane eye

## HURRICANE NAMES FOR 2020

Hurricane names come from six official international lists. The names alternate between male and female. When a storm becomes a hurricane, a name from the list is used, in alphabetical order. Each list is reused every six years. A name "retires" if that hurricane caused a lot of damage or many deaths. Check out the names for 2020.

| | | |
|---|---|---|
| Arthur | Hanna | Omar |
| Bertha | Isaias | Paulette |
| Cristobal | Josephine | Rene |
| Dolly | Kyle | Sally |
| Edouard | Laura | Teddy |
| Fay | Marco | Vicky |
| Gonzalo | Nana | Wilfred |

## SCALE OF HURRICANE INTENSITY

| CATEGORY | ONE | TWO | THREE | FOUR | FIVE |
|---|---|---|---|---|---|
| DAMAGE | Minimal | Moderate | Extensive | Extreme | Catastrophic |
| WINDS | 74–95 mph (119–153 km/h) | 96–110 mph (154–177 km/h) | 111–129 mph (178–208 km/h) | 130–156 mph (209–251 km/h) | 157 mph or higher (252+ km/h) |

(DAMAGE refers to wind and water damage combined.)

# HURRICANE!

**W**ith warnings of a major hurricane heading toward Puerto Rico, the territory's governor declared a state of emergency and ordered an evacuation. Those who stayed stocked up on food and water, and boarded up their windows.

But no one could quite prepare for Hurricane Maria, which hit Puerto Rico on September 20, 2017. With winds whipping up to 155 miles an hour (250 km/h), this Category 4 hurricane brought catastrophic winds, heavy rainfall, and devastation throughout the island. Rivers rose to epic heights, buildings were destroyed, and power was wiped out across nearly the entire island. An estimated 2,975 people died as a result of the storm, with hundreds of others injured. All told, Maria was Puerto Rico's worst ever natural disaster.

For months, thousands of people remained without power, cell service, or internet as electrical grids and utility towers were slowly repaired or replaced. The storm racked up some $90 billion in damage, making it one of the most costly hurricanes ever.

After receiving support from around the world, Puerto Rico has begun to recover. Six months after the storm took out a road through Puerto Rico's popular El Yunque rain forest, parts of the park reopened. It's a promising sign that life is returning to usual on this island.

# EARTHQUAKE!

**I**n the wee hours of Monday, February 26, 2018, life was quiet in Papua New Guinea. But at 3:44 a.m., a powerful 7.5 earthquake split the ground open and devastated the nation in an instant.

Roads became impassable. Homes crumbled to the ground. Landslides caused contamination of safe drinking water. The quake destroyed crops and vegetable gardens, cutting off the primary food sources for a significant percentage of Papua New Guinea's 8.3 million citizens. Significant aftershocks, which lasted into March, caused additional damage.

With thousands of people impacted—and a death toll of more than 100—humanitarian groups such as World Food Programme stepped in to supply food, medical care, and other much needed aid. Countries such as Australia and New Zealand committed funding as well as the use of their military planes.

While the recovery after a natural disaster never happens right away, these types of efforts are helping Papua New Guinea piece itself back together.

# What is a *tornado?*

## THE ENHANCED FUJITA SCALE

The Enhanced Fujita (EF) Scale, named after tornado expert T. Theodore Fujita, classifies tornadoes based on wind speed and the intensity of damage that they cause.

**EF0**
65–85 mph winds
(105–137 km/h)
Slight damage

**EF1**
86–110 mph winds
(138–177 km/h)
Moderate damage

**EF2**
111–135 mph winds
(178–217 km/h)
Substantial damage

**EF3**
136–165 mph winds
(218–266 km/h)
Severe damage

**EF4**
166–200 mph winds
(267–322 km/h)
Massive damage

**EF5**
More than 200 mph winds
(322+ km/h)
Catastrophic damage

**TORNADOES, ALSO KNOWN AS TWISTERS,** are funnels of rapidly rotating air that are created during a thunderstorm. With wind speeds of up to 300 miles an hour (483 km/h), tornadoes have the power to pick up and destroy everything in their path.

**THIS ROTATING FUNNEL OF AIR,** formed in a cumulus or cumulonimbus cloud, becomes a tornado if it touches the ground.

**TORNADOES HAVE OCCURRED IN ALL 50 U.S. STATES AND ON EVERY CONTINENT EXCEPT ANTARCTICA.**

211

# Biomes

**A BIOME, OFTEN CALLED A MAJOR LIFE ZONE,** is one of the natural world's major communities where plants and animals adapt to their specific surroundings. Biomes are classified depending on the predominant vegetation, climate, and geography of a region. They can be divided into six major types: forest, freshwater, marine, desert, grassland, and tundra. Each biome consists of many ecosystems.

Biomes are extremely important. Balanced ecological relationships among biomes help to maintain the environment and life on Earth as we know it. For example, an increase in one species of plant, such as an invasive one, can cause a ripple effect throughout a whole biome.

## FOREST

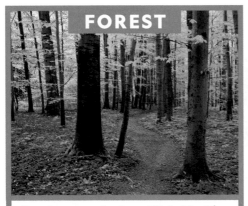

Forests occupy about one-third of Earth's land area. There are three major types of forests: tropical, temperate, and boreal (taiga). Forests are home to a diversity of plants, some of which may hold medicinal qualities for humans, as well as thousands of animal species, some still undiscovered. Forests can also absorb carbon dioxide, a greenhouse gas, and give off oxygen.

**The rabbit-size royal antelope lives in West Africa's dense forests.**

## FRESHWATER

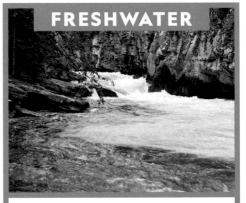

Most water on Earth is salty, but freshwater ecosystems—including lakes, ponds, wetlands, rivers, and streams—usually contain water with less than one percent salt concentration. The countless animal and plant species that live in freshwater biomes vary from continent to continent, but they include algae, frogs, turtles, fish, and the larvae of many insects.

**The place where fresh and salt water meet is called an estuary.**

## MARINE

The marine biome covers almost three-fourths of Earth's surface, making it the largest habitat on our planet. Oceans make up the majority of the saltwater marine biome. Coral reefs are considered to be the most biodiverse of any of the biome habitats. The marine biome is home to more than one million plant and animal species.

**Estimated to be up to 100,000 years old, sea grass growing in the Mediterranean Sea may be the oldest living thing on Earth.**

## DESERT

Covering about one-fifth of Earth's surface, deserts are places where precipitation is less than 10 inches (25 cm) per year. Although most deserts are hot, there are other kinds as well. The four major kinds of deserts are hot, semiarid, coastal, and cold. Far from being barren wastelands, deserts are biologically rich habitats.

**Some sand dunes in the Sahara are tall enough to bury a 50-story building.**

## GRASSLAND

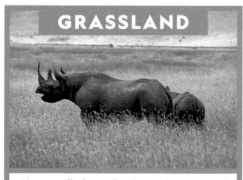

Biomes called grasslands are characterized by having grasses instead of large shrubs or trees. Grasslands generally have precipitation for only about half to three-fourths of the year. If it were more, they would become forests. Grasslands can be divided into two types: tropical (savannas) and temperate. Some of the world's largest land animals, such as elephants, live there.

**Grasslands in North America are called prairies; in South America, they're called pampas.**

## TUNDRA

The coldest of all biomes, a tundra is characterized by an extremely cold climate, simple vegetation, little precipitation, poor nutrients, and a short growing season. There are two types of tundra: arctic and alpine. A tundra is home to few kinds of vegetation. Surprisingly, though, there are quite a few animal species that can survive the tundra's extremes, such as wolves, caribou, and even mosquitoes.

**Formed 10,000 years ago, the arctic tundra is the world's youngest biome.**

# THE OC

## PACIFIC OCEAN

### STATS

Surface area
65,436,200 sq mi (169,479,000 sq km)

Portion of Earth's water area
47 percent

Greatest depth
Challenger Deep
(in the Mariana Trench)
-36,070 ft (-10,994 m)

Surface temperatures
Summer high: 90°F (32°C)
Winter low: 28°F (-2°C)

Tides
Highest: 30 ft (9 m) near Korean Peninsula
Lowest: 1 ft (0.3 m) near Midway Islands

Cool creatures: giant Pacific octopus,
bottlenose whale, clownfish, great
white shark

CLOWN ANEMONEFISH

## ATLANTIC OCEAN

### STATS

Surface area
35,338,500 sq mi (91,526,300 sq km)

Portion of Earth's water area
25 percent

Greatest depth
Puerto Rico Trench
-28,232 ft (-8,605 m)

Surface temperatures
Summer high: 90°F (32°C)
Winter low: 28°F (-2°C)

Tides
Highest: 52 ft (16 m)
Bay of Fundy, Canada
Lowest: 1.5 ft (0.5 m)
Gulf of Mexico and Mediterranean Sea

Cool creatures: blue whale, Atlantic spotted
dolphin, sea turtle

BOTTLENOSE DOLPHIN

214

# EANS

## INDIAN OCEAN

### STATS

Surface area
**28,839,800 sq mi (74,694,800 sq km)**

Portion of Earth's water area
**21 percent**

Greatest depth
**Java Trench**
**-23,376 ft (-7,125 m)**

Surface temperatures
**Summer high: 93°F (34°C)**
**Winter low: 28°F (-2°C)**

Tides
**Highest: 36 ft (11 m)**
**Lowest: 2 ft (0.6 m)**
**Both along Australia's west coast**

Cool creatures: **humpback whale, Portuguese man-of-war, dugong (sea cow)**

LEATHERBACK TURTLE

## ARCTIC OCEAN

### STATS

Surface area
**5,390,000 sq mi (13,960,100 sq km)**

Portion of Earth's water area
**4 percent**

Greatest depth
**Molloy Deep**
**-18,599 ft (-5,669 m)**

Surface temperatures
**Summer high: 41°F (5°C)**
**Winter low: 28°F (-2°C)**

Tides
**Less than 1 ft (0.3 m) variation throughout the ocean**

Cool creatures: **beluga whale, orca, harp seal, narwhal**

NARWHAL

To see the major oceans and bays in relation to landmasses, look at the map on pages 258 and 259.

# Coral Reefs

Just below the surface of the Caribbean Sea's crystal clear water, miles of vivid corals grow in fantastic shapes that shelter tropical fish of every color. Coral reefs account for a quarter of all life in the ocean and are often called the rain forests of the sea. Like big apartment complexes for sea creatures, coral reefs provide a tough limestone skeleton for fish, clams, and other organisms to live in—and plenty of food for them to eat, too.

And how does the coral get its color? It's all about the algae that cling to its limestone polyps. Algae and coral live together in a mutually helpful relationship. The coral provides a home to the algae and helps the algae convert sunlight into food that the corals consume. But as beautiful as coral reefs are, they are also highly sensitive. A jump of even 2°F (1.1°C) in water temperature makes the reef rid itself of the algae, leaving the coral with a sickly, bleached look. Pollution is another threat; it can poison the sensitive corals. Humans pose a threat, too: One clumsy kick from a swimmer can destroy decades of coral growth.

SEA STAR
ON A SPONGE

QUEEN
ANGELFISH

## BY THE NUMBERS

**25** percent of all marine creatures are supported by coral reefs.

**500** million is how many years ago the world's first coral reefs formed.

**4** is the number of countries that border the Mesoamerican Barrier Reef: Mexico, Honduras, Belize, and Guatemala.

THE
**GREAT**
BARRIER
**REEF**
IN
**AUSTRALIA**
IS THE
**BIGGEST**
**LIVING**
STRUCTURE
**ON EARTH.**

MANTA RAY

## Try This!
# CREATE A
# MOTION OCEAN

### Shake the jar and watch waves appear!

**YOU WILL NEED**
- clear jar with lid
- water
- blue food coloring
- glitter
- baby oil
- plastic floating toy

**WHAT TO DO**
1. Fill the jar halfway with water.
2. Add drops of food coloring until you like the color you see. Shake in a little glitter.
3. Pour in baby oil until the jar is three-quarters full.
4. Place a floating toy on top of the oil, then screw on the lid tightly.
5. Shake the jar gently to set your ocean in motion.

# QUIZ WHIZ

Quiz yourself to find out if you're a natural when it comes to nature knowledge!

Write your answers on a piece of paper. Then check them below.

**1** **True or false?** Wispy cirrus clouds usually appear where the air is warm.

**2** The Fujita scale measures the speed and intensity of which type of storm?
a. blizzard
b. tornado
c. hurricane
d. typhoon

**3** The world's first coral reefs formed some _____ years ago.
a. 5,000
b. 500,000
c. 500 million
d. 5 billion

**4** **True or false?** Hurricane John lasted for 31 days in 1994.

**5** What is the place called where freshwater and salt water meet?
a. estuary
b. tributary
c. tide pool
d. basin

Not **STUMPED** yet? Check out the *NATIONAL GEOGRAPHIC KIDS QUIZ WHIZ* collection for more crazy **NATURE** questions!

**ANSWERS:** 1. False, they appear where the air is cold; 2. b; 3. c; 4. True; 5. a

# Oral Reports Made Easy

**Does the thought of public speaking** start your stomach churning like a tornado? Would you rather get caught in an avalanche than give a speech?

Giving an oral report does not have to be a natural disaster. The basic format is very similar to that of a written essay. There are two main elements that make up a good oral report—the writing and the presentation. As you write your oral report, remember that your audience will be hearing the information as opposed to reading it. Follow the guidelines below, and there will be clear skies ahead.

## Writing Your Material

**Follow the steps in the "How to Write a Perfect Essay" section on p. 199, but prepare your report to be spoken rather than written.** Try to keep your sentences short and simple. Long, complex sentences are harder to follow. Limit yourself to just a few key points. You don't want to overwhelm your audience with too much information. To be most effective, hit your key points in the introduction, elaborate on them in the body, and then repeat them once again in your conclusion.

### AN ORAL REPORT HAS THREE BASIC PARTS:

- **Introduction**—This is your chance to engage your audience and really capture their interest in the subject you are presenting. Use a funny personal experience or a dramatic story, or start with an intriguing question.

- **Body**—This is the longest part of your report. Here you elaborate on the facts and ideas you want to convey. Give information that supports your main idea, and expand on it with specific examples or details. In other words, structure your oral report in the same way you would a written essay, so that your thoughts are presented in a clear and organized manner.

- **Conclusion**—This is the time to summarize the information and emphasize your most important points to the audience one last time.

## Preparing Your Delivery

**1** **Practice makes perfect.** Practice! Practice! Practice! Confidence, enthusiasm, and energy are key to delivering an effective oral report, and they can best be achieved through rehearsal. Ask family and friends to be your practice audience and give you feedback when you're done. Were they able to follow your ideas? Did you seem knowledgeable and confident? Did you speak too slowly or too fast, too softly or too loudly? The more times you practice giving your report, the more you'll master the material. Then you won't have to rely so heavily on your notes or papers, and you will be able to give your report in a relaxed and confident manner.

**2** **Present with everything you've got.** Be as creative as you can. Incorporate videos, sound clips, slide presentations, charts, diagrams, and photos. Visual aids help stimulate your audience's senses and keep them intrigued and engaged. They can also help to reinforce your key points. And remember that when you're giving an oral report, you're a performer. Take charge of the spotlight and be as animated and entertaining as you can. Have fun with it.

**3** **Keep your nerves under control.** Everyone gets a little nervous when speaking in front of a group. That's normal. But the more preparation you've done— meaning plenty of researching, organizing, and rehearsing—the more confident you'll be. Preparation is the key. And if you make a mistake or stumble over your words, just regroup and keep going. Nobody's perfect, and nobody expects you to be.

# HISTORY HAPPENS

An amphitheater opened by Emperor Titus in A.D. 80, the Colosseum is among Rome, Italy's most visited monuments today.

# EARTH EXPLORER
## Meet Guillermo de Anda!

The National Geographic emerging explorer dives deep to discover what lies beneath.

Guillermo de Anda's life changed the first time he laid eyes on a submerged human skull. Buried deep inside an underwater cave, this ancient remain intrigued Guillermo—and directed the course of his career.

"That discovery made me want to dedicate my work to underwater archaeology and the study of ancient humans and civilizations," says Guillermo, whose team recently discovered the world's largest underwater cave system in Mexico.

Guillermo's work focuses on the ancient Maya civilization, and his expeditions are centered around cavelike pools called cenotes, which were once used in ancient rituals. In the murky depths of these cenotes, he has found the remains of extinct elephants, saber-toothed cats, and giant sloths—nearly perfectly preserved for as many as 15,000 years.

In particular, Guillermo highlights the Holtun Cenote in Chichén Itzá, Mexico, which contained the well-preserved remains of human and animal bones as well as jade and ceramics. Because cenotes date back thousands and thousands of years, exploring them may reveal more about the mysterious Maya.

"I am working to get a better understanding of the development of life and civilization over the last 20,000 years," says Guillermo. "Underwater archaeology is amazing, and the potential for research is endless."

GUILLERMO AT A MAYA ARCHAEOLOGICAL SITE IN MEXICO

The world's largest underwater cave is 216 miles (347 km) long.

GUILLERMO IN A CENOTE CALLED "EL PIT"

> One of my biggest career highlights to date is the discovery of the first bears found in Mexico's Yucatán Peninsula. We didn't know they ever existed in this area, and they turned out to be over 12,000 years old.

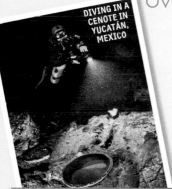

DIVING IN A CENOTE IN YUCATÁN, MEXICO

Guillermo's team discovered more than 120 artifacts in one cenote, including ceramics and burnt human bones—all dating back some 12,000 years.

## CALL TO ACTION!

Before you dive into underwater archaeology, Guillermo suggests you first learn all you can about archaeology in general. "Read books about the Ice Age, about the Maya civilization, and other parts of our past so that you know about a lot of different subjects," he says. As for a specific underwater career, you obviously have to be comfy taking the plunge. Guillermo says learning to scuba dive at an early age is key to avoiding fear when you're swimming through dark spaces. And to keep tabs on Guillermo and his team's progress in Mexico, check out granacuiferomaya.com.

# Buried Secrets

## Who built this ancient Egyptian monument?

A huge stone lion looms over the passing boats on Egypt's Nile River. It serves as a giant guardian to some of the country's famous pyramids, human-made tombs that seem to stretch all the way to the sun. The ancient sand-colored statue known as the Sphinx is as tall as the White House, with paws longer than a city bus.

How many hidden chambers are inside? Scientists are still digging up clues to answer that question, but they might have an answer for one of the monument's biggest mysteries: Who built it?

## SET IN STONE

In ancient Egypt, people worshipped sphinxes as mythical creatures with the power to ward off evil. Some think the Sphinx was built as a protector of the pyramids, which were once used as burial places for Egyptian kings. Nobody's sure when the Sphinx was built, but experts believe it was already ancient when Egyptian queen Cleopatra saw it around 47 B.C. Since then, many other historical figures have visited the monument. But which historical figure *built* the monument?

## FACE OFF

Historians' two top suspects are Pharaoh Khufu, who ruled Egypt from 2589 B.C. to 2566 B.C., and his son, Pharaoh Khafre, who reigned from 2558 B.C. to 2532 B.C. Most experts agree that one of these rulers oversaw the construction of the statue and had his own face carved atop the giant lion. But which one was it—Khufu or Khafre?

Some think the Sphinx is the work of Khufu. They say the statue's face matches a sculpture of the king discovered in 1903.

But most experts, including Egyptologist Mark Lehner, think Khufu's son, Khafre, built the Sphinx. As father and son, the pair shared a resemblance.

HISTORIANS THINK THE SPHINX MIGHT'VE LOOKED LIKE THIS BEFORE WIND AND WATER WORE AWAY ITS COLORS.

THE SPHINX SITS NEAR SIX PYRAMIDS, INCLUDING THE GREAT PYRAMID OF GIZA.

THE STATUE WASN'T FULLY UNCOVERED UNTIL 1936, ABOUT 70 YEARS AFTER THIS PIC WAS TAKEN.

Egypt's Nile River is the world's longest river, flowing over 4,400 miles (7,081 km) through eastern Africa.

ATLANTIC OCEAN
EUROPE
ASIA
EGYPT
AFRICA
INDIAN OCEAN

Early Egyptians named their land Kemet, or "black land," for its rich river mud.

In Egypt, camels are called "ships of the desert." Like ships, they carry goods and people.

Mediterranean Sea
ISRAEL
JORDAN
SPHINX ★ Cairo
LIBYA
SAUDI ARABIA
Nile River
EGYPT
Red Sea
SUDAN

But Lehner says the most convincing evidence lies in a temple that was built in front of the statue. Lehner believes that the temple and the Sphinx are part of the same master building plan overseen by one person. Ancient workers built the temple on top of part of another structure that's been proven to be the work of Khafre. Lehner believes that this means the Sphinx and its temple must have been constructed after Khafre's first structure was built—Khufu wouldn't have been around to build on top of Khafre's lower structure. "To me, that's strong evidence that the Sphinx couldn't have been Khufu's," Lehner says.

## DISAPPEARING ACT

Today the ancient Egyptians' work is crumbling. Centuries of wind and water have ground away at the Sphinx's limestone, and shifting sands have threatened to cover much of it. Archaeologists work tirelessly to repair the structure to keep it from completely disappearing.

By preserving the Sphinx, experts are also protecting clues that might still be hidden in the statue's stone. Someday, these could be the keys that unlock even more of the Sphinx's secrets.

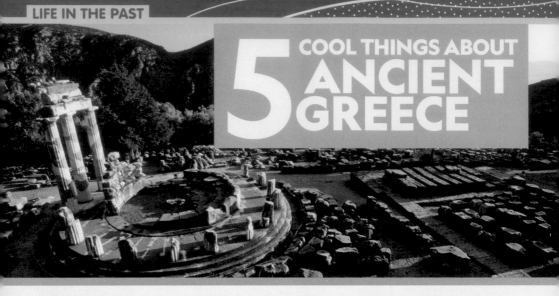

# 5 COOL THINGS ABOUT ANCIENT GREECE

**ALTHOUGH THEY LIVED MORE THAN 2,000 YEARS AGO,** the ancient Greeks were clearly ahead of their time. From science to sports, many Greek traditions are alive and well today. Here are some things that make this civilization stand out.

## 1 START-UP SCHOOL

In 387 B.C., the Greek philosopher Plato founded the Academy in Athens, which was the earliest example of a modern university. Students (including some women, against the traditions of the time) studied astronomy, biology, math, law, politics, and philosophy. Plato's hope was that the Academy would provide a place for all scholars to work toward better government in the Grecian cities. The Academy would become a center of learning for nearly 1,000 years.

## 2 OUTDOOR STAGE

The Greeks were among the first to perform plays. These performances sprang from festivals honoring their gods in which men would dress up, act out stories, and sing songs. They built large, outdoor theaters in most of their cities—some big enough to hold 15,000 people! The audience was so far away from the stage that the actors would wear elaborate costumes and sad- or happy-face masks so that people could see each character's expressions no matter where they were sitting.

## 3 CITY-STATES

Experts believe that ancient Greek civilization was likely begun nearly 4,000 years ago by the Mycenaeans of Crete, a Greek island. The ancient Greek Empire spread from Greece through Europe, and in 800 B.C. the Greeks began splitting their land into hundreds of city-states. Although most Greeks shared the same language and religion, each city-state maintained its own laws, customs, and rulers.

## 4 SUPERSTITIONS

The ancient Greeks were superstitious people. For instance, they originated the idea that breaking a mirror was bad luck. Believing mirrors showed the will of the gods, they thought a broken mirror meant the gods did not want you to see something unpleasant in your future. They also had unique ideas about food—some ancient Greeks would not eat beans because they believed they contained the souls of the dead.

## 5 ORIGINAL OLYMPICS

The ancient Greeks held many festivals in honor of their gods, including some serious sports competitions. The most famous took place in Olympia, Greece, starting in 776 B.C. Honoring the god Zeus, this two-day event—which inspired the modern-day Olympic Games—included contests in wrestling, boxing, long jump, javelin, discus, and chariot racing. Winners were given a wreath of leaves, free meals, and the best seats in the theater as prizes.

# ALEXANDER THE GREAT

A bold military leader, Alexander the Great had a need to lead—and he conquered enough land to create an empire that stretched across 3,000 miles (4,828 km). Get the scoop on the life of this legendary ruler.

Historians think Alexander likely had two different colored eyes—one hazel and one green.

**START**

**ca 356 B.C.**

Alexander is born to King Philip II and Queen Olympias, rulers of the ancient Greek kingdom of Macedon. Alexander's tutor is a famous philosopher named Aristotle, who teaches the young prince and his friends about medicine, religion, logic, and art. What, no gym class?

Um—my horse ate my homework?

**ca 336 B.C.**

Macedon's new king conquers his first city: Thessaly, a neighbor to the south. Alexander and his men sneak up behind Mount Ossa, a nearby mountain range separating the two locations, and surprise the Thessalian guards while they're sleeping. Guess it's true—you snooze, you lose.

**ca 338 B.C.**

Alexander helps his father command troops at the Battle of Chaeronea (Cair-oh-NEE-ah). He becomes ruler two years later at the age of 20, following King Philip's death.

Historians don't always know the exact dates of events from ancient times. That's why you'll see a "ca" next to the years listed below. It stands for "circa," meaning "around."

**ca 331 B.C.**

Alexander invades Egypt and takes over the kingdom. The ruler is crowned pharaoh and establishes the famous Egyptian city of Alexandria, naming it after (duh!) himself.

WELCOME TO ALEXANDR

MINE

MINE

MINE

**ca 323 B.C.**

Alexander gets sick and dies at the age of 32. In just 13 years, he has built a massive empire spreading from Africa to Asia, and introduced Greek culture to much of the world. Now that is pretty great.

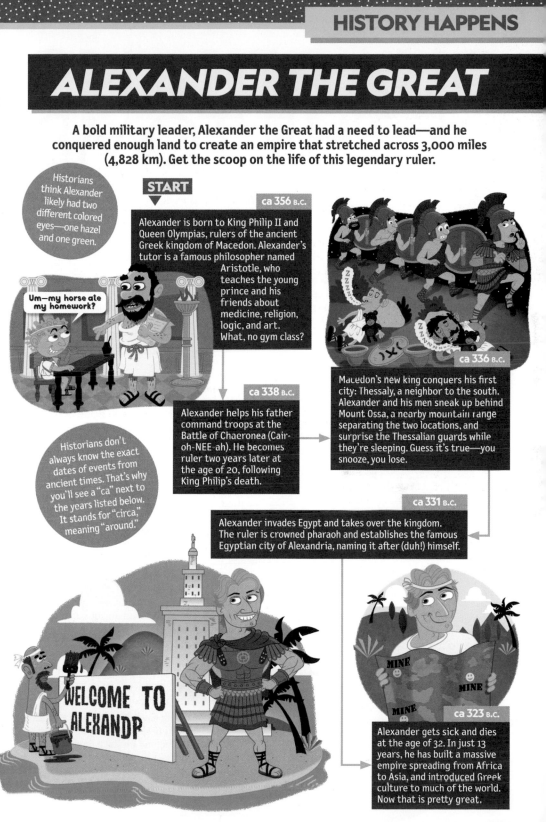

# GUARDIANS
# OF THE TOMB

**B**ack in 1974, some Chinese farmers were digging for water when they got a shock. Staring up from the soil was a face, eyes wide open, with features that looked almost human. But this was not a skeleton: It was one of thousands of life-size soldiers made of baked clay called terra-cotta—and they had been buried for 2,200 years.

## BURIED TREASURE

Row upon row of the soldiers—each face as different and as realistic as the next—were hidden in a pit the size of two football fields near Xi'an, which was China's capital city for nearly 2,000 years. Archaeologists eventually found four pits, some containing statues of horse-drawn chariots, cavalry (soldiers on horseback), and high-ranking officers.

## BODY GUARDS

Who could have built this huge underground army? Experts assume it was China's first emperor, Qin Shihuangdi (Chin She-hwong-dee). The brilliant but brutal ruler, who created the first unified China, was known for his big ideas and even bigger ego. It's believed that because Qin Shihuangdi had killed so many people during his reign, he may have wanted a large army to protect him from his victims' ghosts once he died. He probably had the clay soldiers created to guard his tomb, which was just one mile (1.6 km) away from where the pits were discovered.

## FINAL REWARDS

As it turned out, the emperor's living enemies took revenge—not the dead ones. In 206 B.C., a few years after Qin Shihuangdi's death, invading armies destroyed the pits, burying the warriors and cracking every figure. The pits caved in more as time went on, and the soldiers were lost to the ages.

Experts have since pieced a thousand soldiers back together. But some 6,000 figures are still buried. As work continues, who knows what secrets these soldiers have yet to tell?

STATUES OF ARCHERS, LIKE THE ONE ABOVE, WERE BURIED HOLDING REAL CROSSBOWS.

ANCIENT CRAFTSMEN MADE THOUSANDS OF LIFE-SIZE TERRA-COTTA WARRIORS, EACH WITH A UNIQUE FACE.

# UNDER
## RECONSTRUCTION

Experts have painstakingly rebuilt and restored a thousand terra-cotta warriors found in underground pits near the emperor's tomb. The complex is so vast that excavations may continue for generations.

A warrior's head poking out of the dirt still has traces of red paint. Originally all of the warriors were painted bright colors.

Workers brush dirt away from the collapsed roof that sheltered the terra-cotta warriors.

A toppled terra-cotta warrior lies in its 2,200-year-old underground tomb.

ASIA
CHINA
PACIFIC OCEAN

TERRA-COTTA WARRIORS

CHINA

HORSE-DRAWN CHARIOT

# Secrets of the

## SCIENTISTS USE CUTTING-EDGE TECHNOLOGY TO UNCOVER NEW EVIDENCE ABOUT HOW THE SHIP SANK.

Sunday, April 14, 1912: The R.M.S. *Titanic* steams across the North Atlantic Ocean. The 882-foot (269-m)-long passenger ship carries 2,208 people on its maiden voyage from Southampton, England, to New York City, in the United States of America.

Suddenly, a dark shape appears. An iceberg scrapes the ship, and within three hours, the *Titanic* sinks. Almost 1,500 people lose their lives.

Scientists have closely studied the *Titanic*'s wreck on the ocean floor since it was discovered in 1985. National Geographic Explorer-in-Residence James Cameron—director of the movies *Titanic* and *Avatar*—assembled a team of experts to examine the shipwreck anew. Using 3D modeling and state-of-the-art technology, the experts reveal new clues about how the *Titanic* sank.

## FLOODING

It might have been possible for the ship to sink more slowly, allowing more people to survive. Many of the ship's portholes were found open—most likely because passengers were airing out their rooms and never closed them. This caused the ship to take on water faster.

Something similar also may have happened in one of the grand lobbies, where a large door was found open. "The size of the door is twice the size of the original iceberg damage," Cameron says. "This would have sped up the sinking of the ship."

## BREAKING

As the *Titanic* took on water, the front of the ship, called the bow, sank below the surface, causing the back, or stern, to lift into the air. The great stress broke the ship in half. "When the *Titanic* broke in half and the bow pulled away, the bottom likely remained attached to the back of the ship until it, too, was pulled apart," Cameron says.

**EXPLORER JAMES CAMERON PILOTS AN UNDERWATER VEHICLE CALLED A SUBMERSIBLE.**

## SINKING

In its final resting place, the bow looks remarkably intact. But the stern looks like a bomb destroyed it. Why? The bow was filled with water when it sank, so the pressure was the same on the inside as the outside. The stern, however, sank with lots of air inside and imploded from the pressure.

## FINAL IMPACT

The sinking ship created a massive trail of water that followed it downward at 20 to 25 miles an hour (32 to 40 km/h). Experts think that this water trail pummeled the *Titanic* after it hit bottom. "Millions of gallons of water came pushing down on it," Cameron says. With all this new information, is our understanding of the *Titanic* tragedy complete? "I think we have a very good picture of what happened," Cameron says. "But there will always be mysteries."

# Titanic

TITANIC
·19·  ·12·
LONDON

**SUPERSIZE SHIP**
The *Titanic* was almost as long as three football fields. With its smokestacks, the ship was as tall as a 17-story building.

TITANIC

## WHAT IF ...
Scientists know a lot about how the *Titanic* sank, but other factors contributed as well.

**SAILING SCHEDULE**
The *Titanic* set sail more than three weeks behind schedule. If the ship had left on time, an iceberg probably wouldn't have been in its path.

**FROM CALM TO CHAOS**
The sea was unusually calm on April 14, 1912. Waves would have made the iceberg easier to spot.

**MISSED MESSAGES**
Two messages were telegraphed from other ships to warn the *Titanic* of icebergs, but they never reached the captain.

We asked oceanographer and National Geographic Explorer-in-Residence Robert Ballard, who led the team that discovered the *Titanic* in 1985, what it felt like to make the discovery of the century.

**"My first reaction** was one of excitement and celebration. But we were at the **very spot** on the **cold North Atlantic Ocean** where it all happened. So then we had **a quiet moment of remembrance."**

# THE GREATEST HEISTS OF ALL TIME!

How criminal masterminds pulled off daring thefts—but still got caught.

## TRAIN BANDITS

**Where:** Buckinghamshire, England
**Date:** August 8, 1963
**The Loot:** More than £2.6 million ($7 million) in Scottish banknotes from a Royal Mail Train.
**The Master Plan:** A team of 15 criminals rigs the train signal so the train stops unexpectedly. When it does, they jump into a car filled with mail sacks carrying the money. The thieves transfer the treasure to their vehicle and speed away to their hideout, a farmhouse 27 miles (43 km) away.
**The Outcome:** A tip leads investigators to the thieves' hideout, where they find stolen mail sacks and fingerprints on everything. Twelve thieves are taken to jail; three are never found.

## A DAZZLING CRIME

**Where:** Antwerp, Belgium
**Date:** February 16, 2003
**The Loot:** More than 75 million euros ($100 million) worth of jewels, gold, and money from a vault under the Antwerp World Diamond Centre.
**The Master Plan:** Thieves spend two and a half years planning the robbery. Using hair spray, tape, and Styrofoam boxes, the thieves block the heat, light, and motion sensors so they can't detect the men's body temperatures or movements. They figure out the combination to the vault's three-ton (2.7-t) steel door by installing a tiny hidden camera.
**The Outcome:** Police discover a bag in the woods with two of the robbers' DNA. Four of the thieves go to jail. The stolen gems are never recovered.

## THE ARTFUL CROOK

**Where:** Paris, France
**Date:** August 21, 1911
**The Loot:** The priceless "Mona Lisa"
**The Master Plan:** A man named Vincenzo Perugia poses as a workman at the Louvre art museum in Paris, grabs the famous painting, and walks past an unmanned guard station with it tucked under his smock.
**The Outcome:** After hiding the painting in a wooden trunk for two years, Perugia takes it to an art dealer in Florence, Italy—the same city where the "Mona Lisa" was painted by Leonardo da Vinci about 400 years earlier. The suspicious dealer calls the police, who arrest Perugia and return the "Mona Lisa" to the Louvre.

# CURSE OF THE HOPE DIAMOND

Is the Hope Diamond, one of the world's most valuable jewels, the bearer of bad luck? Legend has it that the stone was stolen from the eye of a sacred statue in India, and Hindu gods cursed the stone to punish the thieves. You decide if the curse is rock solid or just a gem of a tale!

## LOSING THEIR HEADS

The French royal family once owned the diamond, but not for too long. After King Louis XVI and his wife, Marie Antoinette, were imprisoned and beheaded during the French Revolution, the government confiscated the stone, which thieves later stole before it was bought by the wealthy Hope family.

## LOST HOPE

Lord Francis Hope eventually inherited the diamond, and then his wife left him and he had to sell the pricey stone to help pay off his huge debts. But the gem still bears the Hope family name.

## TEMPTING FATE

Millionaire Evalyn McLean bought the diamond in 1911. But luck was not on McLean's side, either. During her lifetime, two of her children died, her husband became mentally ill, and she fell into serious debt.

## DOOMED DELIVERY

In 1958 a mailman named James Todd delivered the diamond to its present home—the Smithsonian Institution in Washington, D.C., U.S.A. Within a year Todd's wife died and his house burned down. Was it the curse?

## REAL OR FAKE?

"The curse isn't true," says Richard Kurin, author of the book *Hope Diamond: The Legendary History of a Cursed Gem*. It may all just be an eerie coincidence, but one thing's for sure, "The Hope diamond is so valuable because it is a unique stone and because of its famous story," says Kurin.

## WHERE DO DIAMONDS COME FROM?

Natural diamonds form about 100 miles (160 km) underground and are the hardest known natural substance. Under extreme heat and pressure, carbon atoms are squeezed together into the hard, clear crystals. Volcanic eruptions carry the diamonds toward Earth's surface, where they are mined for use in industrial tools and sparkly jewelry.

# GOING TO WAR

Since the beginning of time, different countries, territories, and cultures have feuded with each other over land, power, and politics. Major military conflicts include the following wars:

## 1095-1291 THE CRUSADES
Starting late in the 11th century, these wars over religion were fought in the Middle East for nearly 200 years.

## 1337-1453 HUNDRED YEARS' WAR
France and England battled over rights to land for more than a century before the French eventually drove the English out in 1453.

## 1754-1763 FRENCH AND INDIAN WAR (part of Europe's Seven Years' War)
A nine-year war between the British and French for control of North America.

## 1775-1783 AMERICAN REVOLUTION
Thirteen British colonies in America united to reject the rule of the British government and to form the United States of America.

## 1861-1865 AMERICAN CIVIL WAR
Occurred when the northern states (the Union) went to war with the southern states, which had seceded, or withdrawn, to form the Confederate States of America. Slavery was one of the key issues in the Civil War.

## 1910-1920 MEXICAN REVOLUTION
The people of Mexico revolted against the rule of dictator President Porfirio Díaz, leading to his eventual defeat and to a democratic government.

## 1914-1918 WORLD WAR I
The assassination of Austria's Archduke Ferdinand by a Serbian nationalist sparked this wide-spreading war. The U.S. entered after Germany sank the British ship *Lusitania,* killing more than 120 Americans.

## 1918-1920 RUSSIAN CIVIL WAR
Following the 1917 Russian Revolution, this conflict pitted the Communist Red Army against the foreign-backed White Army. The Red Army won, leading to the establishment of the Union of Soviet Socialist Republics (U.S.S.R.) in 1922.

## 1936-1939 SPANISH CIVIL WAR
Aid from Italy and Germany helped the Nationalists gain victory over the Communist-supported Republicans. The war resulted in the loss of more than 300,000 lives and increased tension in Europe leading up to World War II.

## 1939-1945 WORLD WAR II
This massive conflict in Europe, Asia, and North Africa involved many countries that aligned with the two sides: the Allies and the Axis. After the bombing of Pearl Harbor in Hawaii in 1941, the U.S. entered the war on the side of the Allies. More than 50 million people died during the war.

## 1946–1949 CHINESE CIVIL WAR
Also known as the "War of Liberation," this war pitted the Communist and Nationalist Parties in China against each other. The Communists won.

## 1950–1953 KOREAN WAR
Kicked off when the Communist forces of North Korea, with backing from the Soviet Union, invaded their democratic neighbor to the south. A coalition of 16 countries from the United Nations stepped in to support South Korea. An armistice ended active fighting in 1953.

## 1950s–1975 VIETNAM WAR
Fought between the Communist North, supported by allies including China, and the government of South Vietnam, supported by the United States and other anticommunist nations.

## 1967 SIX-DAY WAR
A battle for land between Israel and the states of Egypt, Jordan, and Syria. The outcome resulted in Israel's gaining control of coveted territory, including the Gaza Strip and the West Bank.

## 1991–PRESENT SOMALI CIVIL WAR
Began when Somalia's last president, a dictator named Mohamed Siad Barre, was overthrown. The war has led to years of fighting and anarchy.

## 2001–2014 WAR IN AFGHANISTAN
After attacks in the U.S. by the terrorist group al Qaeda, a coalition that eventually included more than 40 countries invaded Afghanistan to find Osama bin Laden and other al Qaeda members and to dismantle the Taliban. Bin Laden was killed in a U.S. covert operation in 2011. The North Atlantic Treaty Organization (NATO) took control of the coalition's combat mission in 2003. That combat mission officially ended in 2014.

## 2003–2011 WAR IN IRAQ
A coalition led by the U.S., and including Britain, Australia, and Spain, invaded Iraq over suspicions that Iraq had weapons of mass destruction.

# Navajo Code Talkers

In 1942, the United States was embroiled in World War II over the South Pacific. The Japanese air attacks had crippled the U.S. Pacific Fleet at Pearl Harbor. To outwit Japanese forces, the U.S. needed a secret way to relay sensitive information, like battle plans and enemy positions—without anyone on the outside catching wind of it.

Enter Philip Johnston, a World War I veteran with a plan. Having grown up on a Navajo reservation, he spoke the Navajo language and pitched it to the U.S. Marines as an uncrackable spoken code. After all, the language was unwritten and known to fewer than 30 non-Navajo people. The Marines agreed to recruit other soldiers to test it out. A crew of 29 Navajo speakers were trained as Code Talkers to communicate in a way that would throw off the Japanese.

But the Code Talkers didn't just speak straight Navajo. When they were talking about important military terms, they'd use Navajo words that loosely translated to the term, like "besh-lo," or iron fish, for submarine and "atsá," or eagle, for transport plane. To the enemy's ears, the communication sounded like a bunch of random syllables strung together, but the Code Talkers understood every word.

The Code Talkers were able to deliver thousands of messages to the battlefields and assist in many major turning points during the war, including the U.S. victory at the Battle of Iwo Jima. By the end of World War II, there were more than 400 Code Talkers working to keep opposing forces in the dark.

# THE CONSTITUTION & THE BILL OF RIGHTS

The United States Constitution was written in 1787 by a group of political leaders from the 13 states that made up the U.S. at the time. Thirty-nine men, including Benjamin Franklin and James Madison, signed the document to create a national government. While some feared the creation of a strong federal government, all 13 states eventually ratified, or approved, the Constitution, making it the law of the land. The Constitution has three major parts: the preamble, the articles, and the amendments.

**Here's a summary of what topics are covered in each part of the Constitution. Check out the Constitution online or at your local library for the full text.**

**THE PREAMBLE** outlines the basic purposes of the government: *We the People of the United States, in order to form a more perfect Union, establish justice, insure domestic tranquility, provide for the common defense, promote the general welfare, and secure the blessings of liberty to ourselves and our posterity, do ordain and establish this Constitution for the United States of America.*

**SEVEN ARTICLES** outline the powers of Congress, the president, and the court system:

**Article I** outlines the legislative branch—the Senate and the House of Representatives—and its powers and responsibilities.

**Article II** outlines the executive branch—the presidency—and its powers and responsibilities.

**Article III** outlines the judicial branch—the court system—and its powers and responsibilities.

**Article IV** describes the individual states' rights and powers.

**Article V** outlines the amendment process.

**Article VI** establishes the Constitution as the law of the land.

**Article VII** gives the requirements for the Constitution to be approved.

**THE AMENDMENTS,** or additions to the Constitution, were put in later as needed. In 1791, the first 10 amendments, known as the **Bill of Rights,** were added. Since then, another 17 amendments have been added. This is the Bill of Rights:

**1st Amendment:** guarantees freedom of religion, speech, and the press, and the right to assemble and petition. The U.S. may not have a national religion.

**2nd Amendment:** discusses the militia and the right of people to bear arms

**3rd Amendment:** prohibits the military or troops from using private homes without consent

**4th Amendment:** protects people and their homes from search, arrest, or seizure without probable cause or a warrant

**5th Amendment:** grants people the right to have a trial and prevents punishment before prosecution; protects private property from being taken without compensation

**6th Amendment:** guarantees the right to a speedy and public trial

**7th Amendment:** guarantees a trial by jury in certain cases

**8th Amendment:** forbids "cruel and unusual punishments"

**9th Amendment:** states that the Constitution is not all-encompassing and does not deny people other, unspecified rights

**10th Amendment:** grants the powers not covered by the Constitution to the states and the people

Read the full text version of the United States Constitution at constitutioncenter.org/constitution/full-text

White House

# BRANCHES OF GOVERNMENT

The **UNITED STATES GOVERNMENT** is divided into three branches: executive, legislative, and judicial. The system of checks and balances is a way to control power and to make sure one branch can't take the reins of government. For example, most of the president's actions require the approval of Congress. Likewise, the laws passed in Congress must be signed by the president before they can take effect.

## Executive Branch

**The Constitution lists the central powers of the president:** to serve as commander in chief of the armed forces; make treaties with other nations; grant pardons; inform Congress on the state of the union; and appoint ambassadors, officials, and judges. The executive branch includes the president and the 15 governmental departments.

## Legislative Branch

This branch is made up of Congress—the Senate and the House of Representatives. The Constitution grants Congress the power to make laws. Congress is made up of elected representatives from each state. Each state has two representatives in the Senate, while the number of representatives in the House is determined by the size of the state's population. Washington, D.C., and the territories elect nonvoting representatives to the House of Representatives. The Founding Fathers set up this system as a compromise between big states—which wanted representation based on population—and small states—which wanted all states to have equal representation rights.

The U.S. Capitol in Washington, D.C.

## Judicial Branch

The judicial branch is composed of the federal court system—the U.S. Supreme Court, the courts of appeals, and the district courts. The Supreme Court is the most powerful court. Its motto is "Equal Justice Under Law." This influential court is responsible for interpreting the Constitution and applying it to the cases that it hears. The decisions of the Supreme Court are absolute—they are the final word on any legal question.

The U.S. Supreme Court Building in Washington, D.C.

There are nine justices on the Supreme Court. They are appointed by the president of the United States and confirmed by the Senate.

237

# The American Indian Experience

**American Indians are indigenous** to North and South America—they are the people who were here before Columbus and other European explorers came to these lands. They lived in nations, tribes, and bands across both continents. For decades following the arrival of Europeans in 1492, American Indians clashed with the newcomers who had ruptured the Indians' ways of living.

## Tribal Land

During the 19th century, both United States legislation and military action restricted the movement of American Indians, forcing them to live on reservations and attempting to dismantle tribal structures. For centuries, Indians were displaced or killed, or became assimilated into the general U.S. population. In 1924 the Indian Citizenship Act granted citizenship to all American Indians. Unfortunately, this was not enough to end the social discrimination and mistreatment that many Indians have faced. Today, American Indians living in the U.S. still face many challenges.

## Healing the Past

Many members of the 560-plus recognized tribes in the United States live primarily on reservations. Some tribes have more than one reservation, while others have none. Together these reservations make up less than 3 percent of the nation's land area. The tribal governments on reservations have the right to form their own governments and to enforce laws, similar to individual states. Many feel that this sovereignty is still not enough to right the wrongs of the past: They hope for a change in the U.S. government's relationship with American Indians.

Arizona, California, and Oklahoma have the largest American Indian populations by state.

American Indians invented kayaks, snowshoes, and lacrosse.

Top: A Cherokee and Catawba man dances at a powwow.
Middle: A Monacan girl dances in a traditional jingle dress.
Bottom: Little Shell men in traditional costume

**The president of the United States** is the chief of the executive branch, the commander in chief of the U.S. armed forces, and head of the federal government. Elected every four years, the president is the highest policy-maker in the nation. The 22nd Amendment (1951) says that no person may be elected to the office of president more than twice. There have been 45 presidencies and 44 presidents.

## JAMES MONROE
*5th President of the United States ★ 1817–1825*
BORN April 28, 1758, in Westmoreland County, VA
POLITICAL PARTY Democratic-Republican
NO. OF TERMS two
VICE PRESIDENT Daniel D. Tompkins
DIED July 4, 1831, in New York, NY

## GEORGE WASHINGTON
*1st President of the United States ★ 1789–1797*
BORN Feb. 22, 1732, in Pope's Creek, Westmoreland County, VA
POLITICAL PARTY Federalist
NO. OF TERMS two
VICE PRESIDENT John Adams
DIED Dec. 14, 1799, at Mount Vernon, VA

**MONROVIA, the capital of the African country Liberia, is named after JAMES MONROE.**

Monrovia

## JOHN ADAMS
*2nd President of the United States ★ 1797–1801*
BORN Oct. 30, 1735, in Braintree (now Quincy), MA
POLITICAL PARTY Federalist
NO. OF TERMS one
VICE PRESIDENT Thomas Jefferson
DIED July 4, 1826, in Quincy, MA

## JOHN QUINCY ADAMS
*6th President of the United States ★ 1825–1829*
BORN July 11, 1767, in Braintree (now Quincy), MA
POLITICAL PARTY Democratic-Republican
NO. OF TERMS one
VICE PRESIDENT John Caldwell Calhoun
DIED Feb. 23, 1848, at the U.S. Capitol, Washington, D.C.

## THOMAS JEFFERSON
*3rd President of the United States ★ 1801–1809*
BORN April 13, 1743, at Shadwell, Goochland (now Albemarle) County, VA
POLITICAL PARTY Democratic-Republican
NO. OF TERMS two
VICE PRESIDENTS 1st term: Aaron Burr
2nd term: George Clinton
DIED July 4, 1826, at Monticello, Charlottesville, VA

## ANDREW JACKSON
*7th President of the United States ★ 1829–1837*
BORN March 15, 1767, in the Waxhaw region, NC and SC
POLITICAL PARTY Democrat
NO. OF TERMS two
VICE PRESIDENTS 1st term: John Caldwell Calhoun
2nd term: Martin Van Buren
DIED June 8, 1845, in Nashville, TN

## JAMES MADISON
*4th President of the United States ★ 1809–1817*
BORN March 16, 1751, at Belle Grove, Port Conway, VA
POLITICAL PARTY Democratic-Republican
NO. OF TERMS two
VICE PRESIDENTS 1st term: George Clinton
2nd term: Elbridge Gerry
DIED June 28, 1836, at Montpelier, Orange County, VA

## MARTIN VAN BUREN
*8th President of the United States ★ 1837–1841*
BORN Dec. 5, 1782, in Kinderhook, NY
POLITICAL PARTY Democrat
NO. OF TERMS one
VICE PRESIDENT Richard M. Johnson
DIED July 24, 1862, in Kinderhook, NY

### WILLIAM HENRY HARRISON

*9th President of the United States ★ 1841*

BORN Feb. 9, 1773, in Charles City County, VA

POLITICAL PARTY Whig

NO. OF TERMS one (cut short by death)

VICE PRESIDENT John Tyler

DIED April 4, 1841, in the White House, Washington, D.C.

### JOHN TYLER

*10th President of the United States ★ 1841–1845*

BORN March 29, 1790, in Charles City County, VA

POLITICAL PARTY Whig

NO. OF TERMS one (partial)

VICE PRESIDENT none

DIED Jan. 18, 1862, in Richmond, VA

### JAMES K. POLK

*11th President of the United States ★ 1845–1849*

BORN Nov. 2, 1795, near Pineville, Mecklenburg County, NC

POLITICAL PARTY Democrat

NO. OF TERMS one

VICE PRESIDENT George Mifflin Dallas

DIED June 15, 1849, in Nashville, TN

### ZACHARY TAYLOR

*12th President of the United States ★ 1849–1850*

BORN Nov. 24, 1784, in Orange County, VA

POLITICAL PARTY Whig

NO. OF TERMS one (cut short by death)

VICE PRESIDENT Millard Fillmore

DIED July 9, 1850, in the White House, Washington, D.C.

### MILLARD FILLMORE

*13th President of the United States ★ 1850–1853*

BORN Jan. 7, 1800, in Cayuga County, NY

POLITICAL PARTY Whig

NO. OF TERMS one (partial)

VICE PRESIDENT none

DIED March 8, 1874, in Buffalo, NY

### FRANKLIN PIERCE

*14th President of the United States ★ 1853–1857*

BORN Nov. 23, 1804, in Hillsborough (now Hillsboro), NH

POLITICAL PARTY Democrat

NO. OF TERMS one

VICE PRESIDENT William Rufus De Vane King

DIED Oct. 8, 1869, in Concord, NH

### JAMES BUCHANAN

*15th President of the United States ★ 1857–1861*

BORN April 23, 1791, in Cove Gap, PA

POLITICAL PARTY Democrat

NO. OF TERMS one

VICE PRESIDENT John Cabell Breckinridge

DIED June 1, 1868, in Lancaster, PA

### ABRAHAM LINCOLN

*16th President of the United States ★ 1861–1865*

BORN Feb. 12, 1809, near Hodgenville, KY

POLITICAL PARTY Republican (formerly Whig)

NO. OF TERMS two (assassinated)

VICE PRESIDENTS 1st term: Hannibal Hamlin
2nd term: Andrew Johnson

DIED April 15, 1865, in Washington, D.C.

### ANDREW JOHNSON

*17th President of the United States ★ 1865–1869*

BORN Dec. 29, 1808, in Raleigh, NC

POLITICAL PARTY Democrat

NO. OF TERMS one (partial)

VICE PRESIDENT none

DIED July 31, 1875, in Carter's Station, TN

## Before becoming a politician, ANDREW JOHNSON was a TAILOR.

## ULYSSES S. GRANT

*18th President of the United States ★ 1869–1877*

BORN April 27, 1822, in Point Pleasant, OH
POLITICAL PARTY Republican
NO. OF TERMS two
VICE PRESIDENTS 1st term: Schuyler Colfax
2nd term: Henry Wilson
DIED July 23, 1885, in Mount McGregor, NY

## GROVER CLEVELAND

*22nd and 24th President of the United States 1885–1889 ★ 1893–1897*

BORN March 18, 1837, in Caldwell, NJ
POLITICAL PARTY Democrat
NO. OF TERMS two (nonconsecutive)
VICE PRESIDENTS 1st administration:
Thomas Andrews Hendricks
2nd administration:
Adlai Ewing Stevenson
DIED June 24, 1908, in Princeton, NJ

## RUTHERFORD B. HAYES

*19th President of the United States ★ 1877–1881*

BORN Oct. 4, 1822, in Delaware, OH
POLITICAL PARTY Republican
NO. OF TERMS one
VICE PRESIDENT William Almon Wheeler
DIED Jan. 17, 1893, in Fremont, OH

## BENJAMIN HARRISON

*23rd President of the United States ★ 1889–1893*

BORN Aug. 20, 1833, in North Bend, OH
POLITICAL PARTY Republican
NO. OF TERMS one
VICE PRESIDENT Levi Parsons Morton
DIED March 13, 1901, in Indianapolis, IN

President Rutherford B. Hayes's wife, Lucy, loved pets. The couple owned the **FIRST SIAMESE CAT IN THE COUNTRY.**

## WILLIAM MCKINLEY

*25th President of the United States ★ 1897–1901*

BORN Jan. 29, 1843, in Niles, OH
POLITICAL PARTY Republican
NO. OF TERMS two (assassinated)
VICE PRESIDENTS 1st term:
Garret Augustus Hobart
2nd term:
Theodore Roosevelt
DIED Sept. 14, 1901, in Buffalo, NY

## JAMES A. GARFIELD

*20th President of the United States ★ 1881*

BORN Nov. 19, 1831, near Orange, OH
POLITICAL PARTY Republican
NO. OF TERMS one (assassinated)
VICE PRESIDENT Chester A. Arthur
DIED Sept. 19, 1881, in Elberon, NJ

## THEODORE ROOSEVELT

*26th President of the United States ★ 1901–1909*

BORN Oct. 27, 1858, in New York, NY
POLITICAL PARTY Republican
NO. OF TERMS one, plus balance of McKinley's term
VICE PRESIDENTS 1st term: none
2nd term: Charles Warren Fairbanks
DIED Jan. 6, 1919, in Oyster Bay, NY

## CHESTER A. ARTHUR

*21st President of the United States ★ 1881–1885*

BORN Oct. 5, 1829, in Fairfield, VT
POLITICAL PARTY Republican
NO. OF TERMS one (partial)
VICE PRESIDENT none
DIED Nov. 18, 1886, in New York, NY

## WILLIAM HOWARD TAFT

*27th President of the United States ★ 1909–1913*

BORN Sept. 15, 1857, in Cincinnati, OH
POLITICAL PARTY Republican
NO. OF TERMS one
VICE PRESIDENT James Schoolcraft Sherman
DIED March 8, 1930, in Washington, D.C.

## WOODROW WILSON

*28th President of the United States ★ 1913–1921*

BORN Dec. 29, 1856, in Staunton, VA

POLITICAL PARTY Democrat

NO. OF TERMS two

VICE PRESIDENT Thomas Riley Marshall

DIED Feb. 3, 1924, in Washington, D.C.

## WARREN G. HARDING

*29th President of the United States ★ 1921–1923*

BORN Nov. 2, 1865, in Caledonia
(now Blooming Grove), OH

POLITICAL PARTY Republican

NO. OF TERMS one (died while in office)

VICE PRESIDENT Calvin Coolidge

DIED Aug. 2, 1923, in San Francisco, CA

## CALVIN COOLIDGE

*30th President of the United States ★ 1923–1929*

BORN July 4, 1872, in Plymouth, VT

POLITICAL PARTY Republican

NO. OF TERMS one, plus balance of
Harding's term

VICE PRESIDENTS 1st term: none
2nd term:
Charles Gates Dawes

DIED Jan. 5, 1933, in Northampton, MA

## HERBERT HOOVER

*31st President of the United States ★ 1929–1933*

BORN Aug. 10, 1874,
in West Branch, IA

POLITICAL PARTY Republican

NO. OF TERMS one

VICE PRESIDENT Charles Curtis

DIED Oct. 20, 1964, in New York, NY

## FRANKLIN D. ROOSEVELT

*32nd President of the United States ★ 1933–1945*

BORN Jan. 30, 1882, in Hyde Park, NY

POLITICAL PARTY Democrat

NO. OF TERMS four (died while in office)

VICE PRESIDENTS 1st & 2nd terms: John
Nance Garner; 3rd term:
Henry Agard Wallace;
4th term: Harry S. Truman

DIED April 12, 1945,
in Warm Springs, GA

## HARRY S. TRUMAN

*33rd President of the United States ★ 1945–1953*

BORN May 8, 1884, in Lamar, MO

POLITICAL PARTY Democrat

NO. OF TERMS one, plus balance of
Franklin D. Roosevelt's term

VICE PRESIDENTS 1st term: none
2nd term:
Alben William Barkley

DIED Dec. 26, 1972, in Independence, MO

## DWIGHT D. EISENHOWER

*34th President of the United States ★ 1953–1961*

BORN Oct. 14, 1890, in Denison, TX

POLITICAL PARTY Republican

NO. OF TERMS two

VICE PRESIDENT Richard Nixon

DIED March 28, 1969,
in Washington, D.C.

## JOHN F. KENNEDY

*35th President of the United States ★ 1961–1963*

BORN May 29, 1917, in Brookline, MA

POLITICAL PARTY Democrat

NO. OF TERMS one (assassinated)

VICE PRESIDENT Lyndon B. Johnson

DIED Nov. 22, 1963, in Dallas, TX

## LYNDON B. JOHNSON

*36th President of the United States ★ 1963–1969*

BORN Aug. 27, 1908, near Stonewall, TX

POLITICAL PARTY Democrat

NO. OF TERMS one, plus balance of
Kennedy's term

VICE PRESIDENTS 1st term: none
2nd term: Hubert
Horatio Humphrey

DIED Jan. 22, 1973, near San Antonio, TX

Lyndon B. Johnson's beagles were named HIM and HER.

### RICHARD NIXON
*37th President of the United States ★ 1969–1974*
BORN Jan. 9, 1913, in Yorba Linda, CA
POLITICAL PARTY Republican
NO. OF TERMS two (resigned)
VICE PRESIDENTS 1st term & 2nd term (partial): Spiro Theodore Agnew; 2nd term (balance): Gerald R. Ford
DIED April 22, 1994, in New York, NY

### GERALD R. FORD
*38th President of the United States ★ 1974–1977*
BORN July 14, 1913, in Omaha, NE
POLITICAL PARTY Republican
NO. OF TERMS one (partial)
VICE PRESIDENT Nelson Aldrich Rockefeller
DIED Dec. 26, 2006, in Rancho Mirage, CA

### JIMMY CARTER
*39th President of the United States ★ 1977–1981*
BORN Oct. 1, 1924, in Plains, GA
POLITICAL PARTY Democrat
NO. OF TERMS one
VICE PRESIDENT Walter Frederick (Fritz) Mondale

### RONALD REAGAN
*40th President of the United States ★ 1981–1989*
BORN Feb. 6, 1911, in Tampico, IL
POLITICAL PARTY Republican
NO. OF TERMS two
VICE PRESIDENT George H. W. Bush
DIED June 5, 2004, in Los Angeles, CA

### GEORGE H. W. BUSH
*41st President of the United States ★ 1989–1993*
BORN June 12, 1924, in Milton, MA
POLITICAL PARTY Republican
NO. OF TERMS one
VICE PRESIDENT James Danforth (Dan) Quayle III
DIED November 30, 2018, in Houston, TX

### BILL CLINTON
*42nd President of the United States ★ 1993–2001*
BORN Aug. 19, 1946, in Hope, AR
POLITICAL PARTY Democrat
NO. OF TERMS two
VICE PRESIDENT Albert Arnold Gore, Jr.

### GEORGE W. BUSH
*43rd President of the United States ★ 2001–2009*
BORN July 6, 1946, in New Haven, CT
POLITICAL PARTY Republican
NO. OF TERMS two
VICE PRESIDENT Richard Bruce Cheney

### BARACK OBAMA
*44th President of the United States ★ 2009–2017*
BORN Aug. 4, 1961, in Honolulu, HI
POLITICAL PARTY Democrat
NO. OF TERMS two
VICE PRESIDENT Joseph R. Biden, Jr.

**To avoid germs, Donald J. Trump prefers HIGH FIVES to HANDSHAKES.**

### DONALD TRUMP
*45th President of the United States ★ 2017–present*
BORN June 14, 1946, in Queens, NY
POLITICAL PARTY Republican
VICE PRESIDENT Mike Pence

# PRANKSTERS IN CHIEF

## Real-life practical jokes played by U.S. presidents

The job of president of the United States is a stressful one. But even the most serious commanders in chief had fun while working in the White House. Check out seven of the best pranks ever pulled by U.S. presidents.

### BARRY FUNNY

Barack Obama is best known as the 44th president of the United States—not as "Barry," a childhood nickname. But the former president dusted off his old title in 2009 to prank call then Virginia governor Tim Kaine. Kaine was being interviewed on a radio show when Obama dialed in to pose as a regular local citizen, Barry in D.C. The in-disguise president quickly revealed his true identity, then thanked the good-natured Kaine for his service to the state of Virginia.

### LOST LETTERS

In 2001, incoming president George W. Bush's staff faced an unexpected problem: They couldn't type Bush's full name! That's because pranksters working for the previous president, Bill Clinton, had pried the W's from dozens of keyboards across the White House complex.

### COPYCAT IN CHIEF

Before President Abraham Lincoln was known as the "Great Emancipator" for freeing the slaves during the Civil War of 1861 to 1865, he earned a reputation as a great imitator. In 1840, Lincoln mimicked the mannerisms of political rival Jesse Thomas so well that he had the audience cracking up. His impersonation was talked about for years afterward.

## HIDE AND SNEAK

The job of president comes with many perks—including the ability to summon Secret Service agents at the push of a button. President Calvin Coolidge reportedly liked this power a little too much when he was in office from 1923 to 1929. He would supposedly call in his security detail to the Oval Office, then hide under his desk as his employees searched the office for the man they were sworn to protect.

## BIG SHOT

When reporter Tony Vaccaro was told he might need an immunization shot to travel with President Harry S. Truman to South America in 1947, he wasn't happy—especially when Vaccaro saw the giant needle. That's when a man burst into the room and said, "This won't hurt a bit, Tony." It was President Truman, who had learned of Vaccaro's fear of needles and decided to make the reporter sweat.

## WATER LANDING

President Lyndon B. Johnson, who served from 1963 to 1969, loved to collect vehicles. One of his favorites was a blue convertible that he kept at his Texas ranch. But disaster always seemed to strike as he and his guests sped down a hill toward a lake. "The brakes don't work—we're going in!" he'd yell as the car hit the water. But just as his passengers tried to escape, President Johnson would laugh. The convertible was actually an Amphicar, a vehicle that looked like a car ... but could float like a boat!

## UP AND AWAY

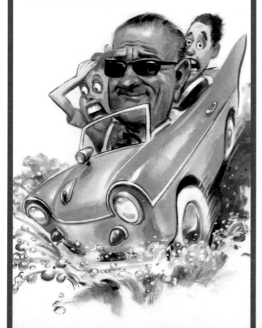

President Franklin D. Roosevelt, who was in office from 1933 to 1945, once told a Secret Service agent to climb on the roof of a farm building to fetch something. But Roosevelt didn't stick around for the agent to climb down. The president had the ladder removed and drove away, leaving the agent (temporarily) stranded.

# CIVIL RIGHTS

A lthough the Constitution protects the civil rights of American citizens, it has not always been able to protect all Americans from persecution or discrimination. During the first half of the 20th century, many Americans, particularly African Americans, were subjected to widespread discrimination and racism. By the mid-1950s, many people were eager to end the bonds of racism and bring freedom to all men and women.

The civil rights movement of the 1950s and 1960s sought to end racial discrimination against African Americans, especially in the southern states. The movement wanted to restore the fundamentals of economic and social equality to those who had been oppressed.

## Woolworth Counter Sit-in

On February 1, 1960, four African-American college students strolled into a Woolworth's "five-and-dime" store in Greensboro, North Carolina. They planned to have lunch there, but were refused service as soon as they sat down at the counter. In a time of heightened racial tension, the Woolworth's manager had a strict whites-only policy. But the students wouldn't take no for an answer. The men—later dubbed the "Greensboro Four"—stayed seated, peacefully and quietly, at the lunch counter until closing. The next day, they returned with 15 additional college students. The following day, even more. By February 5, some 300 students gathered at Woolworth's, forming one of the most famous sit-ins of the civil rights movement. The protest—which sparked similar sit-ins throughout the country—worked: Just six months later, restaurants across the south began to integrate.

## Key Events in the Civil Rights Movement

| | |
|---|---|
| 1954 | The Supreme Court case *Brown* v. *Board of Education* declares school segregation illegal. |
| 1955 | Rosa Parks refuses to give up her bus seat to a white passenger and spurs a bus boycott. |
| 1957 | The Little Rock Nine help to integrate schools. |
| 1960 | Four black college students begin sit-ins at a restaurant in Greensboro, North Carolina. |
| 1961 | Freedom Rides to southern states begin as a way to protest segregation in transportation. |
| 1963 | Martin Luther King, Jr., leads the famous March on Washington. |
| 1964 | The Civil Rights Act, signed by President Lyndon B. Johnson, prohibits discrimination based on race, color, religion, sex, and national origin. |
| 1967 | Thurgood Marshall becomes the first African American to be named to the Supreme Court. |
| 1968 | President Lyndon B. Johnson signs the Civil Rights Act of 1968, which prohibits discrimination in the sale, rental, and financing of housing. |

# STONE OF HOPE:
## THE LEGACY OF MARTIN LUTHER KING, JR.

On April 4, 1968, Dr. Martin Luther King, Jr., was shot by James Earl Ray while standing on a hotel balcony in Memphis, Tennessee. The news of his death sent shock waves throughout the world: Dr. King, a Baptist minister and founder of the Southern Christian Leadership Conference (SCLC), was the most prominent civil rights leader of his time. His nonviolent protests and marches against segregation, as well as his powerful speeches—including his famous "I Have a Dream" speech—motivated people to fight for justice for all.

More than 50 years after his death, Dr. King's dream lives on through a memorial on the National Mall in Washington, D.C. Built in 2011, the memorial features a 30-foot (9-m) statue of Dr. King carved into a granite boulder named the "Stone of Hope."

Today, Dr. King continues to inspire people around the world with his words and his vision for a peaceful world without racism. He will forever be remembered as one of the most prominent leaders of the civil rights movement.

"The time is always right to do what is right."

Martin Luther King, Jr. Memorial in Washington, D.C.

The Smithsonian's National Museum of African American History and Culture in Washington, D.C., is filled with powerful artifacts, including stools from the Woolworth's lunch counter in Greensboro, North Carolina, and a dress Rosa Parks was making the day she was famously arrested for refusing to give up her bus seat for a white person.

The average person spends six hours at the Museum of African American History—compared to two hours at other museums.

# WOMEN

## FIGHTING FOR EQUALITY

Women in New York City cast their votes for the first time in November 1920.

**Today, women make up about half of the country's workforce. But a little over a century ago, less than 20 percent worked outside the home. In fact, they didn't even have the right to vote!**

That began to change in the mid-1800s when women, led by pioneers like Elizabeth Cady Stanton and Susan B. Anthony, started speaking up about inequality. They organized public demonstrations, gave speeches, published documents, and wrote newspaper articles to express their ideas. In 1848, about 300 people attended the Seneca Falls Convention in New York State to address the need for equal rights. By the late 1800s, the National American Woman Suffrage Association had made great strides toward giving women the freedom to vote. One by one, states began allowing women to vote. By 1920, the U.S. Constitution was amended, giving women across the country the ability to cast a vote during any election.

But the fight for equality did not end there. In the 1960s and 1970s, the women's rights movement experienced a rebirth, as feminists protested against injustices in areas such as the workplace and in education.

While these efforts enabled women to make great strides in our society, the efforts to even the playing field among men and women continue today.

New Zealand gave women the right to vote in 1893, becoming the world's first country to do so.

In 2018, Saudi Arabia allowed women to drive for the first time.

Women's March in Boston, Massachusetts, on January 21, 2017

# Key Events in Women's History

**1848:** **Elizabeth Cady Stanton** and **Lucretia Mott** organize the Seneca Falls Convention in New York. Attendees rally for equitable laws, equal educational and job opportunities, and the right to vote.

**1920: The 19th Amendment,** guaranteeing women the right to vote, is ratified.

**1964: Title VII of the Civil Rights Act of 1964,** which prohibits employment discrimination on the basis of sex, is successfully amended.

**1971: Gloria Steinem** heads up the National Women's Political Caucus, which encourages women to be active in government. She also launches *Ms.*, a magazine about women's issues.

**1972:** Congress approves **the Equal Rights Amendment** (ERA), proposing that women and men have equal rights under the law. It is ratified by 35 of the necessary 38 states, and is still not part of the U.S. Constitution.

**1981:** President Ronald Reagan appoints **Sandra Day O'Connor** as the first female Supreme Court justice.

**2009:** President Obama signs **the Lilly Ledbetter Fair Pay Act** to protect against pay discrimination among men and women.

**2013:** The **ban against women in military combat** positions is removed, overturning a 1994 Pentagon decision restricting women from combat roles.

**2016:** Democratic presidential nominee **Hillary Rodham Clinton** becomes the first woman to lead the ticket of a major U.S. party.

**2017:** A crowd of some four million people turned out for the first-ever **Women's March**, a protest advocating women's rights. Events were held in locations throughout the country.

## Ruth Bader Ginsburg Rises to the Top

Soft-spoken and small in stature, Ruth Bader Ginsburg's relentless ambition has allowed her to shine as a justice of the United States Supreme Court. Throughout her career, she has broken boundaries by working tirelessly to fight for equal pay for women and was instrumental in changing laws throughout America to favor gender equality. She has also played a role in a ruling that allowed women into the Virginia Military Institute for the first time in the school's 158-year history. Bader Ginsburg will be forever remembered for her contributions to make the world an equal place for everyone.

## Maria Mitchell Shoots for the Stars

On a clear evening in October 1847, Maria Mitchell, a 29-year-old librarian from Nantucket, Massachusetts, sat atop the roof of the bank where her father worked as a cashier. A budding astronomer, Mitchell often watched the night skies through the lens of a telescope. That night, a small blurry object caught her eye. It was a comet— previously uncharted by scientists. Now known as Miss Mitchell's Comet, the discovery rocketed Mitchell into the forefront of the astronomy world. She received a gold medal from the king of Denmark, became the first professional female astronomer in the United States, and traveled throughout the country and Europe. Mitchell later went on to have a successful career as a professor of astronomy at Vassar College in New York, where she continued to make discoveries among the stars—and inspired hundreds of students to do the same.

# QUIZ WHIZ

## Go back in time to seek the answers to this history quiz!

Write your answers on a piece of paper. Then check them below.

**1** **True or false?** Ancient Egyptians believed that sphinxes could ward off evil.

**2** Including its smokestacks, the R.M.S. *Titanic* was as tall as a _____-story building.
a. 5
b. 30
c. 100
d. 17

**3** Bandits in England once stole how much from a Royal Mail Train?
a. $1.7 million
b. $7 million
c. $17 million
d. $170 million

**4** **True or false?** Volcanic eruptions help carry diamonds formed underground to Earth's surface.

**5** Some ancient Greeks did not eat beans because they believed they contained _____.
a. methane gas
b. the souls of the dead
c. magical powers
d. poison

Not **STUMPED** yet? Check out the *NATIONAL GEOGRAPHIC KIDS QUIZ WHIZ* collection for more crazy **HISTORY** questions!

**ANSWERS:** 1. True ; 2. d ; 3. b ; 4. True 5. b

## HOMEWORK HELP

# Brilliant Biographies

Malala Yousafzai

**A biography is the story of a person's life.** It can be a brief summary or a long book. Biographers—those who write biographies—use many different sources to learn about their subjects. You can write your own biography of a famous person you find inspiring.

## How to Get Started

Choose a subject you find interesting. If you think Cleopatra is cool, you have a good chance of getting your reader interested, too. If you're bored by ancient Egypt, your reader will be snoring after your first paragraph.

Your subject can be almost anyone: an author, an inventor, a celebrity, a politician, or a member of your family. To find someone to write about, ask yourself these simple questions:

1. Who do I want to know more about?
2. What did this person do that was special?
3. How did this person change the world?

## Do Your Research

- Find out as much about your subject as possible. Read books, news articles, and encyclopedia entries. Watch video clips and movies, and search the internet. Conduct interviews, if possible.
- Take notes, writing down important facts and interesting stories about your subject.

## Write the Biography

- Come up with a title. Include the person's name.
- Write an introduction. Consider asking a probing question about your subject.
- Include information about the person's childhood. When was this person born? Where did he or she grow up? Who did he or she admire?
- Highlight the person's talents, accomplishments, and personal attributes.
- Describe the specific events that helped to shape this person's life. Did this person ever have a problem and overcome it?
- Write a conclusion. Include your thoughts about why it is important to learn about this person.
- Once you have finished your first draft, revise and then proofread your work.

Here's a SAMPLE BIOGRAPHY of Malala Yousafzai, a human rights advocate and the youngest ever recipient of the Nobel Peace Prize. Of course, there is so much more for you to discover and write about on your own!

## Malala Yousafzai

Malala Yousafzai was born in Pakistan on July 12, 1997. Malala's father, Ziauddin, a teacher, made it his priority for his daughter to receive a proper education. Malala loved school. She learned to speak three different languages and even wrote a blog about her experiences as a student.

Around the time Malala turned 10, the Taliban—a group of strict Muslims who believe women are to stay at home—took over the region where she lived. The Taliban did not approve of Malala's outspoken love of learning. One day, on her way home from school, Malala was shot in the head by a Taliban gunman. Very badly injured, she was sent to a hospital in England.

Not only did Malala survive the shooting—she thrived. She used her experience as a platform to fight for girls' education worldwide. She began speaking out about educational opportunities for all. Her efforts gained worldwide attention and eventually, she was awarded the Nobel Peace Prize in 2014 at the age of 17. She is the youngest person to earn the prestigious prize.

Each year on July 12, World Malala Day honors her heroic efforts to bring attention to human rights issues.

The all-natural rock rainbows of the Zhangye Danxia National Geological Park in north-central China took millions of years to form.

# GEOGRAPHY ROCKS

# EARTH EXPLORER
## Meet **Alex Tait!**

**How National Geographic's Geographer put his passion on the map.**

When an iceberg the size of Delaware recently sheared off the Antarctic Peninsula, Alex Tait was watching—and waiting. As the Geographer at National Geographic, Alex keeps the maps up to date. So as the giant iceberg, one of the world's largest, broke away and essentially changed the shape of the continent, Alex took note.

Updating National Geographic's maps of Antarctica to reflect the fractured ice shelf is just one of many jobs Alex tackles in his position. He also monitors other shifts in the world, like boundary changes; creates custom maps; updates existing maps; and makes sure that there's consistency among all of the many maps published in National Geographic's books and magazines, and on its website.

"Maps tell us stories and give us an easier way to understand and care about our world," says Alex.

Alex fell in love with geography as a kid while poring over paper maps as he planned hiking trips with his dad. While technology has changed the way many of us view maps today, Alex believes that the beauty of geography remains the same, whether maps are on a screen or folded out in front of you.

And as technology continues to advance, so will our access to see places from around the globe, says Alex. Want to see the top of Mount Everest? You may one day soon be able to get live images of the famous summit and other far-flung places around the planet.

"Geographic data is getting so comprehensive and maps are getting more and more realistic," says Alex. "And with virtual reality (VR) and augmented reality (AR), you will be able to use a map to go anywhere you want—from the tops of mountains to the bottom of the ocean. Maps literally change the way we view the world."

A person who makes and studies maps is called a cartographer.

A MAP OF MOUNT WASHINGTON IN NEW HAMPSHIRE, U.S.A., THAT ALEX WORKED ON

"Maps are tools to show changes happening on our planet. We recently made a map showing the impact of human activity on the planet, like fishing, shipping, and climate change."

The earliest maps were drawn on clay tablets some 3,500 years ago.

## CALL TO ACTION!

Want to get into geography? It all starts with learning to understand and read maps—and even making some of your own. Whether you use a paper and pencil to draw out the boundaries of your backyard or create a map on your computer, Alex says that making and studying maps will help you get a stronger grip on geography. "I still make my own maps sometimes," says Alex. "Understanding maps is like learning a language. The more you do it and the more you practice, the better you'll be at interpreting it all." (Get started on your own maps by visiting mapmaker.nationalgeographic.org today!)

# THE POLITICAL WORLD

Earth's land area is made up of seven continents, but people have divided much of the land into smaller political units called countries. Australia is a continent made up of a single country, and Antarctica is used for scientific research. But the other five continents include almost 200 independent countries. The political map shown here depicts boundaries—imaginary lines created by treaties—that separate countries. Some boundaries, such as the one between the United States and Canada, are very stable and have been recognized for many years.

ARCTIC

Queen Elizabeth Is.

Chukchi Sea

Beaufort Sea

RUSSIA

Baffin Bay

Greenland (Denmark)

Greenland Sea

Alaska (U.S.)

Bering Sea

60°

Gulf of Alaska

Great Bear Lake

Great Slave Lake

ARCTIC CIRCLE

ICELAND

Hudson Bay

CANADA

Labrador Sea

UNITED KINGDOM

Lake Winnipeg

Great Lakes

IRELAND (ÉIRE)

FRANCE

Great Salt Lake

UNITED STATES

**See Europe map for more detail.**

PORT. SPAIN

30°

MOROCCO

TROPIC OF CANCER

Gulf of Mexico

MEXICO

BAHAMAS

DOMINCAN REP.

Puerto Rico (U.S.)

Western Sahara (Morocco)

Hawai'i (U.S.)

CUBA

HAITI

ST. KITTS & NEVIS

ANTIGUA & BARBUDA

Guadeloupe (France)

DOMINICA

CABO VERDE

MAURITANIA

MALI

BELIZE

JAMAICA

Caribbean Sea

ST. LUCIA

Martinique (France)

BARBADOS

SENEGAL

BURKINA FASO

GUATEMALA

HONDURAS

EL SALVADOR

NICARAGUA

GRENADA

ST. VINCENT & THE GRENADINES

TRINIDAD AND TOBAGO

GAMBIA

GUINEA-BISSAU

GHANA

COSTA RICA

PANAMA

VENEZUELA

GUYANA

GUINEA

SIERRA LEONE

PACIFIC

COLOMBIA

French Guiana (France)

LIBERIA

150°

120°

90°

SURINAME

30°

CÔTE D'IVOIRE (IVORY COAST)

KIRIBATI

EQUATOR

0°

OCEAN

Galápagos Islands (Ecuador)

ECUADOR

EQ. GUINEA

Marquesas Islands (France)

PERU

BRAZIL

SAO TOME AND PRINCIPE

SAMOA

American Samoa (U.S.)

French Polynesia (France)

BOLIVIA

ATLANTIC

TONGA

PARAGUAY

TROPIC OF CAPRICORN

OCEAN

30°

0

miles

2000

URUGUAY

0

kilometers

3000

CHILE

ARGENTINA

*Winkel Tripel Projection*

Chatham Is. (N.Z.)

Falkland Islands (U.K.)

Tierra del Fuego

Strait of Magellan

Drake Passage

Meridian of Greenwich (London)

ANTARCTIC

60°

Weddell Sea

Ross Sea

A N T

Other boundaries, such as the one between Sudan and South Sudan in northeast Africa, are relatively new and still disputed. Countries come in all shapes and sizes. Russia and Canada are giants; others, such as El Salvador and Qatar, are small. Some countries are long and skinny—look at Chile in South America! Still other countries—such as Indonesia and Japan in Asia—are made up of groups of islands. The political map is a clue to the diversity that makes Earth so fascinating.

OCEAN

Barents Sea
Svalbard (Norway)
Novaya Zemlya
Kara Sea
North Land
New Siberian Islands
Laptev Sea
East Siberian Sea

NORWAY
SWEDEN
FINLAND
DEN.
GERMANY
EST.
LATV.
LITH.
BELARUS
POLAND

R U S S I A

Bering Sea
Sea of Okhotsk
Lake Baikal

60°

ITALY
ALBANIA
GREECE
Mediterranean Sea
TUNISIA
CYPRUS
LEBANON
ISRAEL
JORDAN
SYRIA
IRAQ
TURKEY
GEORGIA
ARM.
AZERB.
Caspian Sea

UKRAINE
MOLD.
ROMANIA
BULGARIA

KAZAKHSTAN

MONGOLIA

NORTH KOREA
SOUTH KOREA
JAPAN

TAIWAN
The People's Republic of China claims Taiwan as its 23rd province. Taiwan's government (Republic of China) maintains that there are two political entities.

30°

UZBEK.
TURKMEN.
KYRGYZSTAN
TAJIKISTAN
AFGHAN.

C H I N A

ALGERIA
LIBYA
EGYPT
IRAN
BAHRAIN
QATAR
SAUDI ARABIA
U.A.E.
Red Sea
OMAN

NEPAL
BHUTAN
BANGLADESH
INDIA
MYANMAR (BURMA)
LAOS
VIETNAM
THAILAND

South China Sea

Philippine Sea

Taiwan

Northern Mariana Islands (U.S.)
Guam (U.S.)

PACIFIC

MARSHALL ISLANDS

NIGER
CHAD
SUDAN
ERITREA
YEMEN
DJIBOUTI
Arabian Sea

Bay of Bengal

CAMBODIA
PHILIPPINES

PALAU

OCEAN

BENIN
NIGERIA
TOGO
C.A.R.
SOUTH SUDAN
ETHIOPIA
SOMALIA
SRI LANKA
MALDIVES

BRUNEI
MALAYSIA
SINGAPORE

FEDERATED STATES OF MICRONESIA

KIRIBATI
EQUATOR
NAURU
0°

GABON
Cabinda (Angola)
CONGO
DEM. REP. OF THE CONGO
RWANDA
BURUNDI
UGANDA
KENYA
TANZANIA
SEYCHELLES
COMOROS

60°
90°

INDIAN

150°

I N D O N E S I A
New Guinea
PAPUA NEW GUINEA
SOLOMON ISLANDS

TUVALU

ANGOLA
ZAMBIA
ZIMBABWE
NAMIBIA
BOTSWANA
MALAWI
MOZAMBIQUE
MADAGASCAR
MAURITIUS
Réunion (France)
ESWATINI (SWAZILAND)
SOUTH AFRICA
LESOTHO

OCEAN

TIMOR-LESTE (EAST TIMOR)

Coral Sea
VANUATU
FIJI

New Caledonia (France)

30°

Kerguelen Islands (France)

A U S T R A L I A

Great Australian Bight

Tasman Sea
North Island

Tasmania
NEW ZEALAND
South Island

CIRCLE

60°

Ross Sea

A R C T I C A

# THE PHYSICAL WORLD

Earth is dominated by large landmasses called continents—seven in all—and by an interconnected global ocean that is divided into four parts by the continents. More than 70 percent of Earth's surface is covered by oceans, and the rest is made up of land areas.

Different landforms give variety to the surface of the continents. The Rocky Mountains divide North America, the Andes mark the western edge of South America, and the Himalaya tower above South Asia. The Plateau of Tibet forms the rugged core of Asia, while

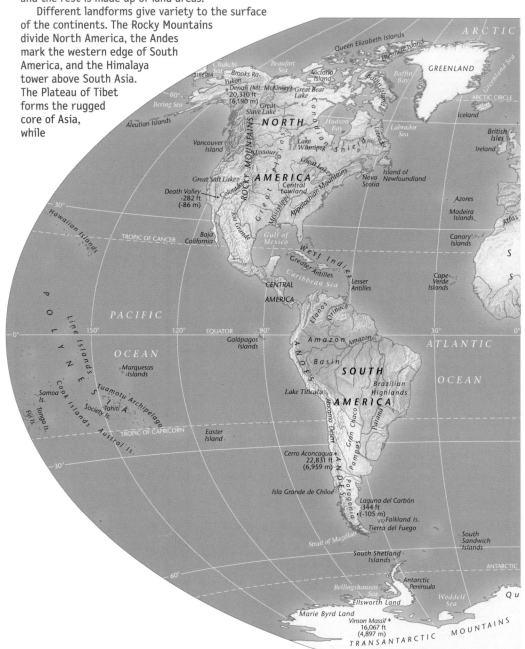

the Northern European Plain extends from the North Sea to the Ural Mountains. Much of Africa is a plateau, and dry plains cover large areas of Australia. Mountains rise more than 16,000 feet (4,877 m) above Antarctica's massive ice sheets. Mountains and trenches make the ocean floors as varied as any continent. A mountain chain called the Mid-Atlantic Ridge runs the length of the Atlantic Ocean. In the western Pacific, trenches drop deep into the ocean floor.

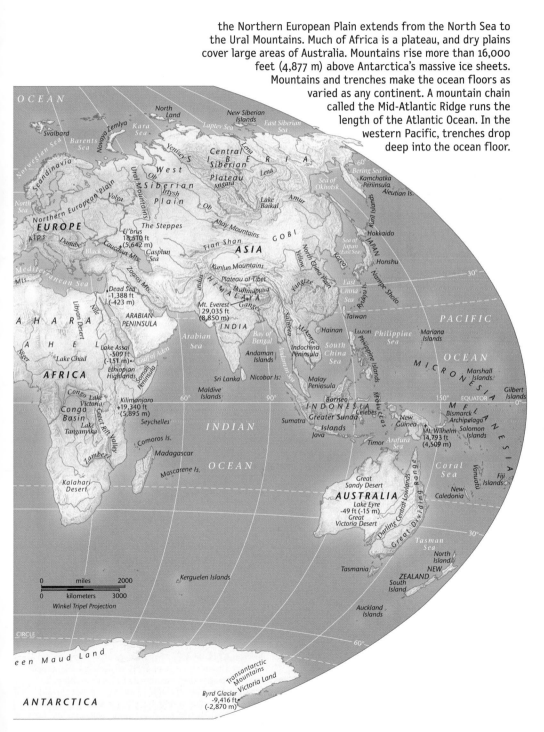

# KINDS OF MAPS

Maps are special tools that geographers use to tell a story about Earth. Maps can be used to show just about anything related to places. Some maps show physical features, such as mountains or vegetation. Maps can also show climates or natural hazards and other things we cannot easily see. Other maps illustrate different features on Earth—political boundaries, urban centers, and economic systems.

## AN IMPERFECT TOOL

Maps are not perfect. A globe is a scale model of Earth with accurate relative sizes and locations. Because maps are flat, they involve distortions of size, shape, and direction. Also, cartographers—people who create maps—make choices about what information to include. Because of this, it is important to study many different types of maps to learn the complete story of Earth. Three commonly found kinds of maps are shown on this page.

**PHYSICAL MAPS.** Earth's natural features—landforms, water bodies, and vegetation—are shown on physical maps. The map above uses color and shading to illustrate mountains, lakes, rivers, and deserts of central South America. Country names and borders are added for reference, but they are not natural features.

**POLITICAL MAPS.** These maps represent characteristics of the landscape created by humans, such as boundaries, cities, and place-names. Natural features are added only for reference. On the map above, capital cities are represented with a star inside a circle, while other cities are shown with black dots.

**THEMATIC MAPS.** Patterns related to a particular topic or theme, such as population distribution, appear on these maps. The map above displays the region's climate zones, which range from tropical wet (bright green) to tropical wet and dry (light green) to semiarid (dark yellow) to arid or desert (light yellow).

# **MAKING** MAPS

Long ago, cartographers worked with pen and ink, carefully handcrafting maps based on explorers' observations and diaries. Today, mapmaking is a high-tech business. Cartographers use Earth data stored in "layers" in a Geographic Information System (GIS) and special computer programs to create maps that can be easily updated as new information becomes available.

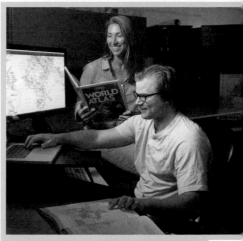

National Geographic staff cartographers Mike McNey and Rosemary Wardley review a map of Africa for the *National Geographic Kids World Atlas*.

Satellites in orbit around Earth act as eyes in the sky, recording data about the planet's land and ocean areas. The data is converted to numbers that are transmitted back to computers that are specially programmed to interpret the data. They record it in a form that cartographers can use to create maps.

# MAP **PROJECTIONS**

To create a map, cartographers transfer an image of the round Earth to a flat surface, a process called projection. All projections involve distortion. For example, an interrupted projection (bottom map) shows accurate shapes and relative sizes of land areas, but oceans have gaps. Other types of projections are cylindrical, conic, or azimuthal—each with certain advantages, but all with some distortion.

# GEOGRAPHIC FEATURES

From roaring rivers to parched deserts, from underwater canyons to jagged mountains, Earth is covered with beautiful and diverse environments. Here are examples of the most common types of geographic features found around the world.

## WATERFALL

Waterfalls form when a river reaches an abrupt change in elevation. At left, the Iguazú waterfall system—on the border of Brazil and Argentina—is made up of 275 falls.

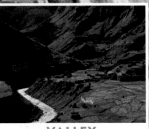

## VALLEY

Valleys, cut by running water or moving ice, may be broad and flat or narrow and steep, such as the Indus River Valley in Ladakh, India (above).

## RIVER

As a river moves through flatlands, it twists and turns. Above, the Rio Los Amigos winds through a rain forest in Peru.

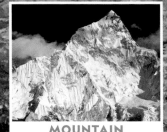

## MOUNTAIN

Mountains are Earth's tallest landforms, and Mount Everest (above) rises highest of all, at 29,035 feet (8,850 m) above sea level.

## GLACIER

Glaciers—"rivers" of ice— such as Alaska's Hubbard Glacier (above) move slowly from mountains to the sea. Global warming is shrinking them.

## CANYON

Steep-sided valleys called canyons are created mainly by running water. Buckskin Gulch in Utah (above) is the deepest "slot" canyon in the American Southwest.

## DESERT

Deserts are land features created by climate, specifically by a lack of water. Here, a camel caravan crosses the Sahara in North Africa.

**Bet You Didn't Know!**

# 7 awesome facts about Earth

**1** There are **volcanoes inside glaciers** in **Iceland.**

**2** **Antarctica** is the only **continent** with **no rain forests.**

**3** There are more **geysers** in **U.S.A.'s Yellowstone National Park** than anywhere else on **Earth.**

**4** More than **100 million years ago, India** was an island.

**5** The **oldest water** on **Earth—** some 1 to 2.5 billion years old— **was found 1.5 miles** (2.4 km) down a mine in **Canada.**

**6** The **ocean below** the **North Pole** is more than **13,000** feet (3,960 m) deep.

**7** **Two lakes** continue to exist in the **Sahara,** fed by water from underground.

Old Faithful geyser, in Yellowstone National Park, Wyoming, U.S.A.

# AFRICA

In 1979 and 2012, snow fell in parts of the Sahara in North Africa.

A zebra's night vision is thought to be as good as an owl's.

Zebra

The massive continent of Africa, where humankind began millions of years ago, is second only to Asia in size. Stretching nearly as far from west to east as it does from north to south, Africa is home to both the longest river in the world (the Nile) and the largest hot desert on Earth (the Sahara).

The Great Sphinx at Giza in Egypt

## SPEEDY SPECIES

Some of the world's fastest animals live in Africa, such as cheetahs, pronghorn antelopes, wildebeests, and lions. Each of these species can reach speeds topping 50 miles an hour (80 km/h).

## ADVANCED ANCESTORS

Our earliest ancestors lived in Africa—and experts say these humans were rather evolved. Artifacts recently discovered in Kenya from some 320,000 years ago show that the *Homo sapiens*—our early ancestor—made tools with sharp blades from volcanic rock and created their own bright red dye from clay, which they may have used as body paint. Scientists think this early civilization also traded for goods with other groups in distant lands, a surprisingly sophisticated system for people who lived so long ago.

## Protecting the Environment

| Country | Percent |
|---|---|
| Namibia | 43.2%* |
| Seychelles | 42.0% |
| Zambia | 37.8% |
| Botswana | 37.2% |
| Tanzania | 32.2% |
| Congo | 30.4% |

*Figures represent percent of total land area set aside as protected area

## MAJOR MINES

Bling it on! Africa is home to many gold and diamond mines, including the deepest mine in the world. The Mponeng mine in South Africa is deeper than 13,000 feet (3,960 m) and features tunnels that are many miles long. It takes over an hour to get to the bottom, where temps top 140°F (60°C). As for diamonds? Botswana's Jwaneng mine produces up to 15 million carats of bling every year—making it the world's most valuable diamond mine.

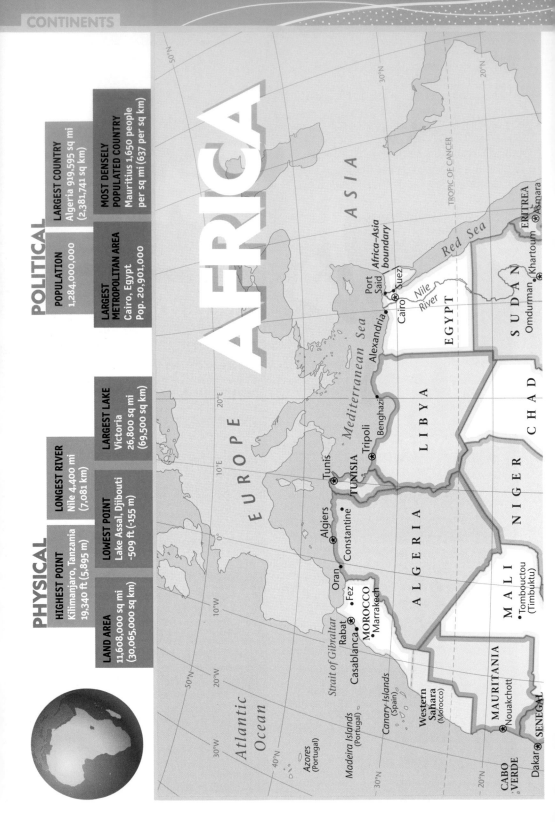

## PHYSICAL

**LAND AREA**
11,608,000 sq mi
(30,065,000 sq km)

**HIGHEST POINT**
Kilimanjaro, Tanzania
19,340 ft (5,895 m)

**LOWEST POINT**
Lake Assal, Djibouti
-509 ft (-155 m)

**LONGEST RIVER**
Nile 4,400 mi
(7,081 km)

**LARGEST LAKE**
Victoria
26,800 sq mi
(69,500 sq km)

## POLITICAL

**POPULATION**
1,284,000,000

**LARGEST
METROPOLITAN AREA**
Cairo, Egypt
Pop. 20,901,000

**LARGEST COUNTRY** Algeria 919,595 sq mi
(2,381,741 sq km)

**MOST DENSELY
POPULATED COUNTRY**
Mauritius 1,650 people
per sq mi (637 per sq km)

AFRICA

ASIA

EUROPE

Atlantic
Ocean

Mediterranean Sea

Red Sea

Azores
(Portugal)

Madeira Islands
(Portugal)

Canary Islands
(Spain)

Strait of Gibraltar

Rabat ⊛
Casablanca •
Fez •
Marrakech •
MOROCCO

Oran •
Algiers •
Constantine •
Tunis •
⊛ TUNISIA

Tripoli •
Benghazi •
LIBYA

Alexandria •
Port
Said •
Cairo ⊛
Suez •
Nile
River
EGYPT
Africa-Asia
boundary

Asmara ⊛
ERITREA
Omdurman • Khartoum ⊛
SUDAN

Western
Sahara
(Morocco)

ALGERIA

MALI
Tombouctou
(Timbuktu) •

NIGER

CHAD

MAURITANIA
Nouakchott •

SENEGAL
Dakar ⊛

CABO
VERDE

TROPIC OF CANCER

**Map Key**
- ⊛ National capital
- • Other city
- ▲ Highest point
- ▼ Lowest point

Azimuthal Equal-Area Projection

800 Miles
800 Kilometers

SEYCHELLES

Victoria ⊛

MAURITIUS ⊛
Port Louis ○
Réunion (France)

MADAGASCAR
Antananarivo ⊛

COMOROS
Moroni •

Indian
Ocean

Mozambique Channel

SOMALIA
Mogadishu ⊛

Gulf of Aden
SOMALILAND

DJIBOUTI Djibouti ⊛
Lake Assal
(-155 m) -509 ft. ▼

ETHIOPIA
Addis Ababa ⊛

SOUTH SUDAN
Juba ⊛

UGANDA
Kampala ⊛

KENYA
Nairobi ⊛
Mombasa •

Kilimanjaro ▲
19,340 ft.
(5,895 m)

TANZANIA
Dodoma ⊛
Dar es Salaam •

Lake Victoria

RWANDA
Kigali ⊛

BURUNDI
Bujumbura ⊛

DEMOCRATIC REPUBLIC OF THE CONGO
Kisangani •
Kananga •
Mbuji-Mayi •
Kinshasa ⊛

MALAWI
Lilongwe ⊛

ZAMBIA
Lusaka ⊛
Kitwe •
Kolwezi •
Lubumbashi •

ZIMBABWE
Harare ⊛

MOZAMBIQUE
Maputo ⊛

ESWATINI (SWAZILAND)
Lobamba ⊛
Mbabane ⊛

LESOTHO
Maseru ⊛

Durban •

Pretoria (Tshwane) ⊛
Johannesburg •
Bloemfontein ⊛

BOTSWANA
Gaborone ⊛

SOUTH AFRICA
Port Elizabeth •
Cape Town ⊛

NAMIBIA
Windhoek ⊛

ANGOLA
Luanda ⊛

CONGO
Brazzaville ⊛
Pointe-Noire •

Cabinda (Angola)

GABON
Libreville ⊛

CENTRAL AFRICAN REPUBLIC
Bangui ⊛

CAMEROON
Yaoundé ⊛
Douala •

EQUATORIAL GUINEA
Malabo ⊛

SAO TOME & PRINCIPE
São Tomé ⊛

NIGERIA
Abuja ⊛
Kano •
Ogbomosho •
Lagos •

BENIN
Porto-Novo ⊛
Cotonou •

TOGO
Lomé ⊛

GHANA
Accra ⊛

CÔTE D'IVOIRE (IVORY COAST)
Yamoussoukro ⊛
Abidjan •

BURKINA FASO
Ouagadougou ⊛

NIGER
Niamey ⊛

N'Djamena ⊛

MALI
Bamako ⊛

GUINEA
Conakry ⊛

SIERRA LEONE
Freetown ⊛

LIBERIA
Monrovia ⊛

GUINEA-BISSAU
Bissau ⊛

GAMBIA
Banjul ⊛

DARFUR

Atlantic
Ocean

St. Helena (U.K.)

Ascension (U.K.)

EQUATOR

TROPIC OF CAPRICORN

# ANTARCTICA

Gentoo penguin

There are mountains buried under ice in Antarctica.

An adult gentoo penguin makes as many as 450 dives a day looking for food.

This frozen continent may be a cool place to visit, but unless you're a penguin, you probably wouldn't want to hang out in Antarctica for long. The fact that it's the coldest, windiest, and driest continent helps explain why humans never colonized this ice-covered land surrounding the South Pole.

Weddell seal

## A DAY TO CELEBRATE

DECEMBER

**1**

Signed in 1959, the Antarctic Treaty, which governs Antarctica, says that the continent should be used only for peaceful purposes. The treaty, which has now been signed by 53 countries, also established Antarctica as a scientific reserve and a place for scientific exploration. Any activities that may disrupt the natural environment are prohibited. Each year on December 1, World Antarctica Day marks the signing of the treaty and celebrates this unique and fascinating place on Earth.

## GOING THE DISTANCE

Each year, a few hundred runners from around the world compete in the Antarctica Marathon and Half-Marathon, a hilly and twisty race along the continent's icy peninsula.

## FREAKY FALLS

Five-story-tall Blood Falls in Antarctica oozes red water from an ancient lake trapped under Taylor Glacier. First discovered in 1911, the falls' creepy color baffled experts, who originally thought it came from red algae. But recent studies show that the lake deep beneath the glacier is super-salty and full of iron, which turns the water red. Another fascinating fact about the falls? Scientists say it takes approximately 1.5 million years for the ancient lake water to travel through tiny cracks and channels in Taylor Glacier before it sees the light of day.

## Earth's Largest Deserts

Largest hot desert:
Sahara, Africa
3,475,000 square miles
(9,000,000 sq km)

Largest cold desert:
Antarctica
5,100,000 square miles
(13,209,000 sq km)

Not to scale

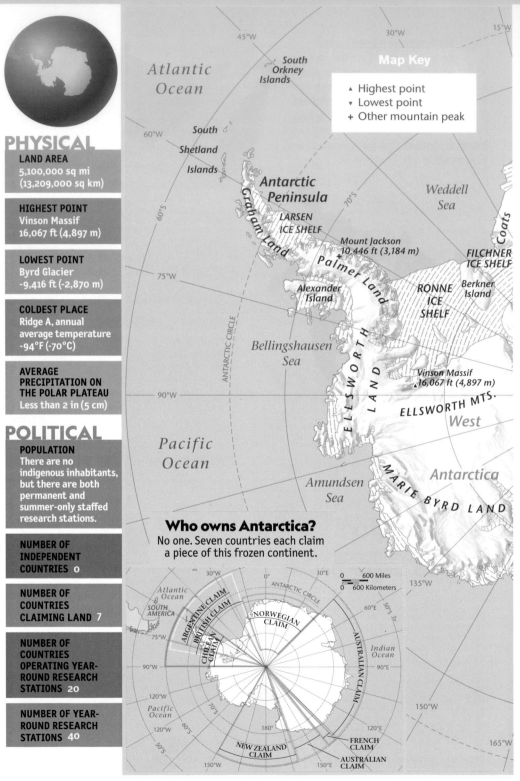

## PHYSICAL

**LAND AREA**
5,100,000 sq mi
(13,209,000 sq km)

**HIGHEST POINT**
Vinson Massif
16,067 ft (4,897 m)

**LOWEST POINT**
Byrd Glacier
-9,416 ft (-2,870 m)

**COLDEST PLACE**
Ridge A, annual
average temperature
-94°F (-70°C)

**AVERAGE
PRECIPITATION ON
THE POLAR PLATEAU**
Less than 2 in (5 cm)

## POLITICAL

**POPULATION**
There are no
indigenous inhabitants,
but there are both
permanent and
summer-only staffed
research stations.

**NUMBER OF
INDEPENDENT
COUNTRIES** 0

**NUMBER OF
COUNTRIES
CLAIMING LAND** 7

**NUMBER OF
COUNTRIES
OPERATING YEAR-
ROUND RESEARCH
STATIONS** 20

**NUMBER OF YEAR-
ROUND RESEARCH
STATIONS** 40

### Map Key

▲ Highest point
▼ Lowest point
+ Other mountain peak

*Atlantic
Ocean*

South
Orkney
Islands

South
Shetland
Islands

*Antarctic
Peninsula*

LARSEN
ICE SHELF

Mount Jackson
10,446 ft (3,184 m)

Alexander
Island

*Bellingshausen
Sea*

*Weddell
Sea*

Coats

FILCHNER
ICE SHELF

RONNE
ICE
SHELF

Berkner
Island

Vinson Massif
16,067 ft (4,897 m)

ELLSWORTH MTS.

*West*

*Pacific
Ocean*

Amundsen
Sea

MARIE BYRD LAND

*Antarctica*

ANTARCTIC CIRCLE

ELLSWORTH LAND

Graham Land

Palmer Land

### Who owns Antarctica?

No one. Seven countries each claim
a piece of this frozen continent.

*Atlantic
Ocean*

SOUTH
AMERICA

ARGENTINE CLAIM

BRITISH CLAIM

CHILEAN
CLAIM

NORWEGIAN
CLAIM

AUSTRALIAN CLAIM

*Indian
Ocean*

*Pacific
Ocean*

NEW ZEALAND
CLAIM

FRENCH
CLAIM

AUSTRALIAN
CLAIM

ANTARCTIC CIRCLE

0   600 Miles
0   600 Kilometers

# ANTARCTICA

FIMBUL
ICE SHELF

0°

RIISER-LARSEN
ICE SHELF

Q U E E N   M A U D   L A N D

Land

ENDERBY
LAND

60°E

Indian
Ocean

Valkyrie
Dome

MacKenzie Bay

75°E

Lambert
Glacier

AMERY ICE SHELF

AMERICAN

HIGHLAND

Ridge A +

WEST
ICE SHELF

POLAR PLATEAU

East

90°E

South Pole

Antarctica

SHACKLETON
ICE SHELF

T R A N S A N T A R C T I C   M O U N T A I N S

80°S

ROSS
ICE
SHELF

Byrd Glacier
-9,416 ft (-2,870 m)

105°E

Roosevelt
Island

Taylor
Glacier

W I L K E S   L A N D

Ross Island

Mount Erebus
12,448 ft
(3,794 m)

V I C T O R I A   L A N D

70°S

Ross
Sea

120°E

Talos
Dome

60°S

180°

Indian
Ocean

0          600 Miles
0          600 Kilometers

Azimuthal Equidistant Projection

150°E

135°E

# ASIA

Children with a water buffalo
in Sa Pa, Vietnam

A water buffalo's wide hooves keep it from sinking in mud.

About 73 percent of Japan is covered with mountains.

272

Made up of 46 countries, Asia is the world's largest continent. Just how big is it? From western Turkey to the eastern tip of Russia, Asia spans nearly half the globe! Home to more than four billion citizens—that's three out of five people on the planet—Asia's population is bigger than that of all the other continents combined.

Kuala Lumpur, Malaysia

## ON THE MOVE

About a third of the population of Mongolia moves seasonally. They live in portable huts called *ger* while traveling up to 70 miles (112 km) on foot to find food sources for their livestock.

## ON THE BORDER

Asia is the only continent that shares borders with two other continents: Africa and Europe. Here a marker identifies the border between Europe and Asia in western Russia.

## GOING BATTY

From the hefty golden-crowned flying fox to the itty-bitty bumblebee bat, Asia is home to at least 435 of the world's more than 1,300 species of bats. Indonesia has the world's largest number of species, with more than 175 different types of bats. And in Malaysia? Bats outnumber all other mammals in the country, including humans! The winged mammals help keep the ecosystem healthy, especially in Southeast Asia's forests where the bats play a key role in spreading the seeds of trees and other plants.

## Tallest Peaks by Continent

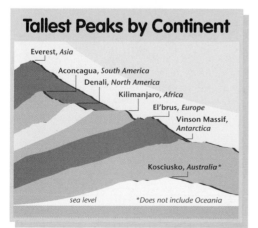

Everest, *Asia*

Aconcagua, *South America*

Denali, *North America*

Kilimanjaro, *Africa*

El'brus, *Europe*

Vinson Massif, *Antarctica*

Kosciusko, *Australia\**

sea level          *\*Does not include Oceania*

# PHYSICAL

**LAND AREA**
17,208,000 sq mi
(44,570,000 sq km)

**HIGHEST POINT**
Mount Everest,
China–Nepal
29,035 ft (8,850 m)

**LOWEST POINT**
Dead Sea,
Israel–Jordan
-1,388 ft (-423 m)

**LONGEST RIVER**
Yangtze, China
3,880 mi (6,244 km)

**LARGEST LAKE
ENTIRELY IN ASIA**
Lake Baikal, Russia
12,200 sq mi
(31,500 sq km)

# POLITICAL

**POPULATION**
4,536,000,000

**LARGEST
METROPOLITAN AREA**
Tokyo, Japan
Pop. 37,393,000

**LARGEST COUNTRY
ENTIRELY IN ASIA**
China
3,705,406 sq mi
(9,596,960 sq km)

**MOST DENSELY
POPULATED COUNTRY**
Singapore
22,745 people
per sq mi
(8,788 per sq km)

# ASIA

★ North Pole

*Arctic Ocean*

**Map Key**

- ⊛ National capital
- ◎ Other capital
- • Other city
- ▲ Highest point
- ▼ Lowest point

Magadan

*Sea of Okhotsk*

A commonly accepted division between Asia and Europe—marked here by a maroon, dashed line—is formed by the Ural Mountains, Ural River, Caspian Sea, Caucasus Mountains, and the Black Sea with its outlets, the Bosporus and Dardanelles.

R U S S I A

Tomsk
Novosibirsk
Lake Baikal
Irkutsk
Ulan-Ude
Khabarovsk
Sapporo
Qiqihar
Harbin
Vladivostok
Sendai

Ulaanbaatar ⊛
M O N G O L I A

Changchun
Fushun
Jilin
Shenyang
NORTH KOREA
Anshan
Pyongyang
JAPAN
⊛ Tokyo
Kyoto
Nagoya

Ürümqi
Beijing
Shijiazhuang
Dalian
Seoul ⊛
SOUTH KOREA
Osaka
Hiroshima
Fukuoka

Taiyuan
Zhengzhou
Xuzhou
Qingdao

*East China Sea*

Lanzhou
Luoyang
Nanjing

C H I N A
Xi'an
*Yangtze River*
Shanghai

TROPIC OF CANCER

Mount Everest
29,035 ft
(8,850 m)
BHUTAN
Chengdu
Chongqing
Nanchang
Fuzhou

Lhasa
Guiyang
Changsha
Taipei
*Taiwan*
Kaohsiung

▲ Thimphu
⊛ Kathmandu
Kunming
Shantou
Guangzhou

The People's Republic of China claims Taiwan as its 23rd province. Taiwan's government (Republic of China) maintains that there are two political entities.

BANGLADESH
Dhaka
Chittagong
Kolkata
MYANMAR (BURMA)
Nanning
Macau
Hong Kong

Hanoi
LAOS
Haiphong

*South China Sea*

Quezon City

Nay Pyi Taw
Vientiane
Da Nang
Manila

THAILAND
VIETNAM
PHILIPPINES

*Pacific Ocean*

Bangkok ⊛
CAMBODIA
Phnom Penh
Ho Chi Minh City (Saigon)
Cagayan de Oro

Bandar Seri Begawan

EQUATOR

Oceania
Asia
Jayapura

Banda Aceh
BRUNEI
Manado

M A L A Y S I A
Medan
Kuala Lumpur ⊛
Balikpapan

I N D O N E S I A

⊛ SINGAPORE
Jambi
Palembang
Bandung
Semarang
Dili
TIMOR-LESTE (EAST TIMOR)
AUSTRALIA

Jakarta ⊛
Surabaya

# AUSTRALIA,
## NEW ZEALAND, AND OCEANIA

More than one-third of New Zealand's population lives in the city of Auckland.

Australia's capitol building was designed in the shape of a boomerang.

Auckland Harbour in Auckland, New Zealand

G'day, mate! This vast region, covering almost 3.3 million square miles (8.5 million sq km), includes Australia—the world's smallest and flattest continent—and New Zealand, as well as a fleet of mostly tiny islands scattered across the Pacific Ocean. Also known as "down under," most of the countries in this region are in the Southern Hemisphere, and below the Equator.

Aboriginal children of Australia in ceremonial dress

## ROCK STARS

Most of Australia is a rural desert, also known as the outback. Here you can also find a giant rock formation called Uluru, or Ayers Rock, which appears to change color during the day.

## FOR THE DOGS

Dingos are wild dogs found almost exclusively in Australia. But these canines aren't actually native to down under— they likely arrived 1,000–5,000 years ago by boat from Asia. Today, these social dogs travel in packs throughout the forests, plains, mountains, and deserts of northern, northwestern, and central Australia. As the largest land predator in Australia, they prey on small to medium animals, such as lizards, rodents, and rabbits.

## Sizing Up the Great Barrier Reef

Just how big is the Great Barrier Reef Marine Park? It's approximately as large as:

Great Barrier Reef Marine Park

Germany

Vietnam

Australia

or the Republic of Congo

*Based on an area of 133,000 square miles (344,400 sq km)

## GROW ON

About 80 percent of the plants in New Zealand are not found anywhere else in the world. And some of them doubled as dinosaur snacks! Plants like the kauri—a coniferous tree—have ancestors that date back to the Jurassic period. And New Zealand's magnificent lowland forests have been nicknamed "dinosaur forests" because of the prehistoric plants that grow there.

# PHYSICAL

**LAND AREA**
3,278,000 sq mi
(8,490,000 sq km)

**HIGHEST POINT***
Mount Wilhelm,
Papua New Guinea
14,793 ft (4,509 m)
*includes Oceania

**LOWEST POINT**
Lake Eyre, Australia
-49 ft (-15 m)

**LONGEST RIVER**
Murray-Darling,
Australia
2,282 mi (3,672 km)

**LARGEST LAKE**
Lake Eyre, Australia
3,741 sq mi
(9,690 sq km)

# POLITICAL

**POPULATION**
41,000,000

**LARGEST
METROPOLITAN AREA**
Melbourne, Australia
Pop. 4,968,000

**LARGEST COUNTRY**
Australia
2,988,901 sq mi
(7,741,220 sq km)

**MOST DENSELY
POPULATED COUNTRY**
Nauru
1,250 people per sq mi
(476 per sq km)

**Map Key**

⊛ National capital
• Other city
▲ Highest point
▼ Lowest point

30°N

135°E          150°E

A S I A

15°N

**Northern Mariana
Islands**
(U.S.)

• Capital Hill

M i c r o n e s i a

Guam
(U.S.)

*Yap
Islands*

*Truk Islands*

**PALAU**
⊛
Melekeok

C a r o l i n e   I s l a n d s

⊛ Palikir

**FEDERATED STATES
OF MICRONESIA**

0°

M e l a n e s i a

Oceania–Asia
boundary

**PAPUA NEW GUINEA**
▲ Mount Wilhelm
14,793 ft
(4,509 m)

Honiara ⊛

Port Moresby •

Solomon Islands

15°S

**Coral Sea
Islands
Territory**
(Australia)

C o r a l   S e a

A U S T R A L I A

• Brisbane

-49 ft ▼ *Lake
Eyre*
(-15 m)

• Perth

*Darling
River*

Sydney •

*Lord Howe
Island*
(Australia)

Adelaide •

*Murray
River*

Canberra, ⊛
A.C.T.

Melbourne •

*Tasman
Sea*

*Indian
Ocean*

45°S

*Tasmania*

Hobart •

0          800 Miles
0          800 Kilometers

*Mercator Projection*

120°E          135°E          150°E

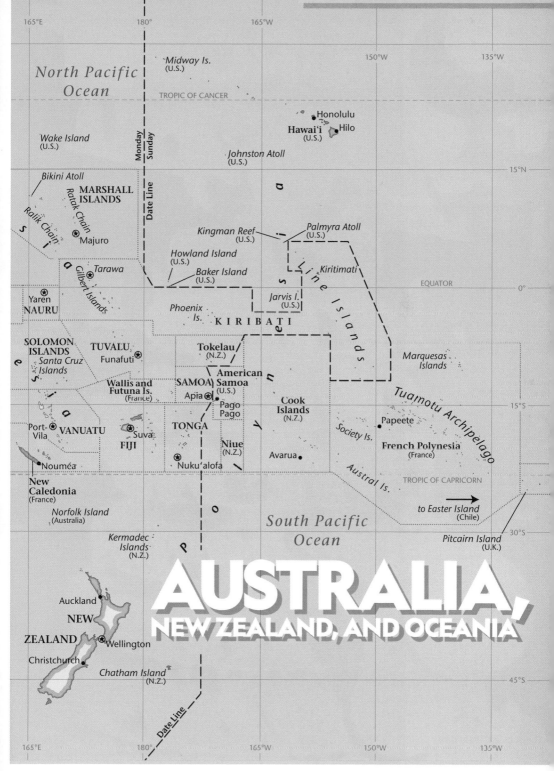

165°E  180°  165°W  150°W  135°W

**North Pacific Ocean**

Midway Is. (U.S.)

TROPIC OF CANCER

Wake Island (U.S.)

Monday | Sunday

Honolulu

Hawai'i (U.S.)  Hilo

Johnston Atoll (U.S.)

15°N

Bikini Atoll

**MARSHALL ISLANDS**

Ralik Chain

Ratak Chain

Date Line

Majuro

Kingman Reef (U.S.)

Palmyra Atoll (U.S.)

Howland Island (U.S.)

Line Islands

Kiritimati

EQUATOR  0°

Tarawa

Baker Island (U.S.)

Gilbert Islands

Yaren

**NAURU**

Jarvis I. (U.S.)

Phoenix Is.

**K I R I B A T I**

**SOLOMON ISLANDS**

Santa Cruz Islands

**TUVALU**

Funafuti

Tokelau (N.Z.)

Marquesas Islands

Wallis and Futuna Is. (France)

**SAMOA**

American Samoa (U.S.)

Apia

Pago Pago

Cook Islands (N.Z.)

15°S

Port-Vila

**VANUATU**

Suva

**TONGA**

**FIJI**

Niue (N.Z.)

Avarua

Society Is.

Papeete

Tuamotu Archipelago

**French Polynesia** (France)

Nouméa

Nuku'alofa

**New Caledonia** (France)

Norfolk Island (Australia)

Austral Is.

TROPIC OF CAPRICORN

to Easter Island (Chile)

Kermadec Islands (N.Z.)

**South Pacific Ocean**

30°S

Pitcairn Island (U.K.)

# AUSTRALIA, NEW ZEALAND, AND OCEANIA

Auckland

**NEW ZEALAND**

Wellington

Christchurch

Chatham Island (N.Z.)

45°S

Date Line

165°E  180°  165°W  150°W  135°W

# EUROPE

A pastry chef in Paris is known for his foie gras macarons—or goose liver cookies.

It's considered rude to write in red ink in Portugal.

Macarons in a pastry shop

A cluster of islands and peninsulas jutting west from Asia, Europe is bordered by the Atlantic and Arctic Oceans and more than a dozen seas. Here you'll find a variety of scenery, from mountains to countryside to coastlines. Europe is also known for its rich culture and fascinating history, which make it one of the most visited continents on Earth.

Traditional dance performed in Greece

## SPOT IT

Dalmatians get their name from Dalmatia, a region of Croatia along the Adriatic Sea. The spotted canines have served as border guard dogs during conflicts in the region.

## BERRY GOOD

Most of the world's raspberries are grown in Europe. Russia, Serbia, and Poland rank among the world's leading producers. The fertile soil and temperate climate in those countries create ideal growing conditions. Raspberries are native to Europe, and there are records of them being cultivated in Greece and Turkey more than 2,000 years ago. Now that's some sweet history!

## SEEING THE LIGHT

The midnight sun is a natural phenomenon that occurs every summer near the Arctic Circle when the sun can still be seen at midnight. Several places in northern Europe—including parts of Iceland, Norway, Finland, Sweden, Denmark, and Russia—experience the phenomena. Svalbard, Norway, experiences the longest period of the midnight sun in that country, with the sun staying visible in the night sky between April 20 and August 22.

## Europe's Longest Rivers

| | |
|---|---|
| Volga | 2,290 miles (3,685 km) |
| Danube | 1,770 miles (2,848 km) |
| Dnieper | 1,420 miles (2,285 km) |
| Rhine | 765 miles (1,230 km) |
| Elbe | 724 miles (1,165 km) |

# PHYSICAL

**LAND AREA**
3,841,000 sq mi
(9,947,000 sq km)

**HIGHEST POINT**
El'brus, Russia
18,510 ft (5,642 m)

**LOWEST POINT**
Caspian Sea
-92 ft (-28 m)

**LONGEST RIVER**
Volga, Russia
2,290 mi
(3,685 km)

**LARGEST LAKE
ENTIRELY IN EUROPE**
Ladoga, Russia
6,900 sq mi
(17,872 sq km)

# POLITICAL

**POPULATION**
746,000,000

**LARGEST
METROPOLITAN AREA**
Moscow, Russia
Pop. 12,538,000

**LARGEST COUNTRY
ENTIRELY IN EUROPE**
Ukraine
233,030 sq mi
(603,550 sq km)

**MOST DENSELY
POPULATED COUNTRY**
Monaco
50,000 people per sq
mi (20,000 per sq km)

**Map Key**

⊛ National capital
• Other city
▫ Small country
▲ Highest point
▼ Lowest point

Jan Mayen
(Norway)

ICELAND
⊛ Reykjavík

ARCTIC CIRCLE

Norwegian
Sea

Faroe Islands
(Denmark)

Shetland
Islands

Orkney Islands

Oslo

SCOTLAND
Glasgow
Edinburgh
N. IRELAND
Belfast
IRELAND
(ÉIRE)
Dublin
UNITED KINGDOM
Liverpool • Manchester
WALES
Birmingham
Cardiff • ENGLAND
London ⊛
The
Hague

North
Sea

Göteborg

DENMARK
Copenhagen ⊛
Kiel

Hamburg
NETH.
Amsterdam ⊛
Berlin ⊛

Brussels ⊛
BELGIUM

GERMANY
Frankfurt

Prague ⊛

Atlantic
Ocean

⊛ Paris

LUX.

• Nantes

Bay of
Biscay

FRANCE
Zürich
Bern ⊛
SWITZ.
Munich
LIECH.

AUSTRIA
Ljubljana ⊛
SLOV.

• Bordeaux
Lyon •

Milan •
Turin •
Venice

Genoa

Oporto
Lisbon
PORTUGAL
Madrid ⊛
SPAIN
Valencia
Seville
Murcia
Málaga
Gibraltar (U.K.)

Bilbao
Valladolid

ANDORRA
Zaragoza

Barcelona

Balearic Is.
(Spain)

Toulouse

MONACO
Marseille

Corsica
(France)

Nice

SAN
MARINO
ITALY

VATICAN
CITY ⊛
Rome

Sardinia
(Italy)

Naples

Messina
Palermo
Catania
Sicily

Valletta ⊛
MALTA

M e d i t e r r a n e a n

AFRICA

0                    400 Miles
0      400 Kilometers
*Azimuthal Equidistant Projection*

# EUROPE

10°E 20°E 30°E 40°E 50°E

*Barents Sea*

60°E

70°E

Murmansk

Asia
Europe

ASIA

60°N

Archangel

RUSSIA

N O R W A Y

S W E D E N

F I N L A N D

*Lake Ladoga*

Helsinki

St. Petersburg

Stockholm • Tallinn
ESTONIA

*Baltic Sea*

Riga
LATVIA

LITHUANIA

Yaroslavl'

Volga River
Kazan'

Ufa

Tver'

Moscow

Nizhniy
Novgorod

Samara
Orenburg

Ryazan'

50°N

Kaliningrad
(Russia)

Vitsyebsk
Vilnius
Kaunas

Smolensk

Penza

Gdańsk

Minsk

Bryansk

Saratov

POLAND
Warsaw

BELARUS

Homyel'

Kursk

KAZAKHSTAN

Bydgoszcz
Łódź

Kiev

Volgograd

Wrocław
Kraków

UKRAINE

Kharkiv

CZECHIA
(CZECH REP.)

L'viv

Poltava
Donets'k

Astrakhan'

Vinnytsya

Rostov

-92 ft ▽
(-28 m)

Vienna
SLOVAKIA
Bratislava

Dnipropetrovs'k

MOLDOVA
Chișinău

El'brus
(5,642 m) 18,510 ft ▲

Groznyy

Caspian Sea

Budapest

Baku

HUNGARY
Zagreb

ROMANIA

Odesa
Simferopol'
CRIMEA

Sochi

GEORGIA

40°N

CROATIA

Belgrade
Bucharest

Sevastopol'

AZERBAIJAN

BOSNIA &
HERZEGOVINA

Sarajevo
SERBIA

*Black Sea*

MONTENEGRO
KOSOVO
Pristina

Varna

Podgorica
Skopje

BULGARIA
Sofia

Bosporus

Tirana
MACED.

ALBANIA

Thessaloniki

Istanbul

T U R K E Y

*Dardanelles*

GREECE

Athens

*Sea*

Crete

NORTHERN CYPRUS
Nicosia

CYPRUS

20°E 30°E 40°E

A commonly accepted division
between Asia and Europe—
marked here by a maroon,
dashed line—is formed by the
Ural Mountains, Ural River, Caspian
Sea, Caucasus Mountains, and
the Black Sea with its outlets, the
Bosporus and Dardanelles.

**283**

# NORTH AMERICA

There are more than 100,000 coffee farms in Mexico.

Polar bears have no natural predators.

Polar bear with cub,
Manitoba, Canada

From the Great Plains of the United States and Canada to the rain forests of Panama, North America stretches 5,500 miles (8,850 km) from north to south. The third largest continent, North America can be divided into five regions: the mountainous west (including parts of Mexico and Central America's western coast), the Great Plains, the Canadian Shield, the varied eastern region (including Central America's lowlands and coastal plains), and the Caribbean.

Onlookers celebrate the opening of the Panama Canal expansion in 2016.

## VIKINGS LIVED HERE

Some 1,000 years ago, a troop of Norse explorers traveled by boat from Norway to the banks of Newfoundland, Canada. There, they found plenty of salmon, wild grapes, and timber—and set up camp. Today, the only known Viking settlement in North America can be found at L'Anse aux Meadows in the northernmost tip of Newfoundland. Archaeological evidence shows that these adventurous seafarers may have spent time in northeastern New Brunswick as well.

## HIGH ENERGY

The United States is one of the top producers of geothermal energy— energy from the natural heat of the ground. Among the states, California leads the geothermal charge, with some 5 percent of the state's total power generated from underground heat. In New York City, St. Patrick's Cathedral (above) recently installed a geothermal plant for heating and cooling that stretches as deep as 2,200 feet (670 m) below the building.

## TAKING FLIGHT

Millions of monarchs migrate up to 3,000 miles (4,828 km) to Mexico every year from the United States and Canada. They're the only butterflies to make such a massive journey.

## World's Longest Coastlines

| Country | Coastline |
|---|---|
| Canada | 151,023 miles (243,048 km) |
| Indonesia | 33,998 miles (54,716 km) |
| Russia | 23,397 miles (37,653 km) |
| Philippines | 22,549 miles (36,289 km) |
| Japan | 18,486 miles (29,751 km) |

## PHYSICAL

| LAND AREA | HIGHEST POINT | LARGEST LAKE |
|---|---|---|
| 9,449,000 sq mi (24,474,000 sq km) | Denali, Alaska 20,320 ft (6,194 m) | Lake Superior, U.S.–Canada 31,700 sq mi (82,100 sq km) |

| LONGEST RIVER | LOWEST POINT |
|---|---|
| Mississippi–Missouri, United States 3,780 mi (6,083 km) | Death Valley, California -282 ft (-86 m) |

## POLITICAL

| POPULATION | LARGEST METROPOLITAN AREA |
|---|---|
| 587,000,000 | Mexico City, Mexico Pop. 21,782,000 |

| LARGEST COUNTRY | MOST DENSELY POPULATED COUNTRY |
|---|---|
| Canada 3,855,103 sq mi (9,984,670 sq km) | Barbados / 1,807 people per sq mi (698 per sq km) |

Map Key

⊛ National capital
• Other city
▲ Highest point
▼ Lowest point

EUROPE

Greenland (Denmark)

ARCTIC CIRCLE

Arctic Ocean

ASIA

Alaska (U.S.)

(Mount McKinley) Denali ▲ (6,190 m) 20,310 ft

Anchorage

C A N A D A

Edmonton
Calgary
Winnipeg
Thunder Bay
Montréal

Vancouver
Victoria
Seattle

80°N

60°N

180°

160°W

40°N

0°

20°W

40°W

N 40°N

20°N

800 Miles
800 Kilometers

Azimuthal Equidistant Projection

286

NORTH
AMERICA

AREA ENLARGED

SOUTH AMERICA

North America–
South America boundary

Central America PANAMA
COSTA RICA
NICARAGUA
HONDURAS
EL SALVADOR
GUATEMALA
BELIZE

Panama
City
San José
Managua
Tegucigalpa
Belmopan
Guatemala City
San Salvador

Caribbean Sea

Atlantic
Ocean

Bermuda Is.
(U.K.)

West Indies

BAHAMAS
Nassau
CUBA
Havana

Boston
New York
Philadelphia
Washington, D.C.
Ottawa
Toronto
Detroit
Cleveland
Charlotte
Jacksonville
Indianapolis
Nashville
Atlanta
Tampa
Miami
Memphis
New
Orleans
Birmingham
Chicago
Minneapolis
St. Paul
St. Louis
Omaha
Houston

Lake
Superior

Mississippi River

Missouri River

UNITED STATES

Denver
Las Vegas
Phoenix
El Paso
Ciudad
Juárez
Chihuahua
Oklahoma
City
Fort
Worth
Dallas
San Antonio
Austin
Tulsa

Portland
San Francisco
San Jose
Fresno
Sacramento
Death Valley –282 ft
(–86 m)
Los Angeles
San Diego
Tijuana

Pacific
Ocean

TROPIC OF CANCER

Monterrey
MEXICO
Guadalajara
Mexico City
Acapulco
San Luis Potosí
Veracruz

Gulf of
Mexico

20°N
60°W
20°W
0°
EQUATOR
100°W
120°W
140°W
80°W
70°W
60°W
20°N

Caribbean Sea

Cayman
Islands
(U.K.)
JAMAICA Kingston
CUBA

HAITI
Port-au-
Prince
DOMINICAN
REPUBLIC
Santo
Domingo

Virgin Islands
(U.S.)
San Juan
Puerto Rico
(U.S.)

ST. KITTS
& NEVIS
Basseterre
ANTIGUA & BARBUDA
St. John's
DOMINICA
Roseau
ST. LUCIA
Castries
ST. VINCENT &
THE GRENADINES
Kingstown
BARBADOS
Bridgetown
GRENADA
St. George's
TRINIDAD & TOBAGO
Port of
Spain

Aruba
(Neth.)
Bonaire
(Neth.)
Curaçao
(Neth.)

400 Miles
400 Kilometers
0
Azimuthal Equidistant Projection

15°N
10°N

287

# SOUTH AMERICA

Brazil has participated in the FIFA World Cup 21 times—more than any other team.

Ancient tombs in Peru contain kernels of popcorn, some of which still pop.

A boy plays soccer in Manaus, Brazil.

outh America is bordered by three major bodies of water—the Caribbean Sea, Atlantic Ocean, and Pacific Ocean. The world's fourth largest continent extends over a range of climates from tropical in the north to subarctic in the south. South America produces a rich diversity of natural resources, including nuts, fruits, sugar, grains, coffee, and chocolate.

Santiago Cathedral in Santiago, Chile

## BIG BIRD

The Andean condor, which lives exclusively in the mountains and valleys of the Andes, is the largest raptor in the world and the largest flying bird in South America.

## OCEANS ALL AROUND

South America is surrounded by both the Pacific and Atlantic Oceans. Experts think that the two oceans used to be one massive body of water until North and South America joined together at the Isthmus of Panama some three million years ago. That move, scientists think, divided the original ocean into two. Today, Colombia and Chile are the only two countries in South America with a coastline on each ocean.

## South America's Deepest Canyon

Peru's Cotahuasi Canyon is more than 11,500 feet (3,500 m) deep!

Almost twice as deep as the Grand Canyon — 6,000 feet (1,830 m) —

Burj Khalifa 2,717 feet (828 m)

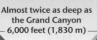

## ICE LAND

Patagonia in southern Chile is home to one of the largest ice fields in the world. The Southern Patagonia Icefield, which stretches across the Andes Mountains and occupies parts of Argentina and Chile, feeds some 50 major glaciers that flow into the Pacific Ocean or freshwater lakes. The ice field takes up an area almost as large as the Bahamas and is so big, it can be seen from space on a clear day.

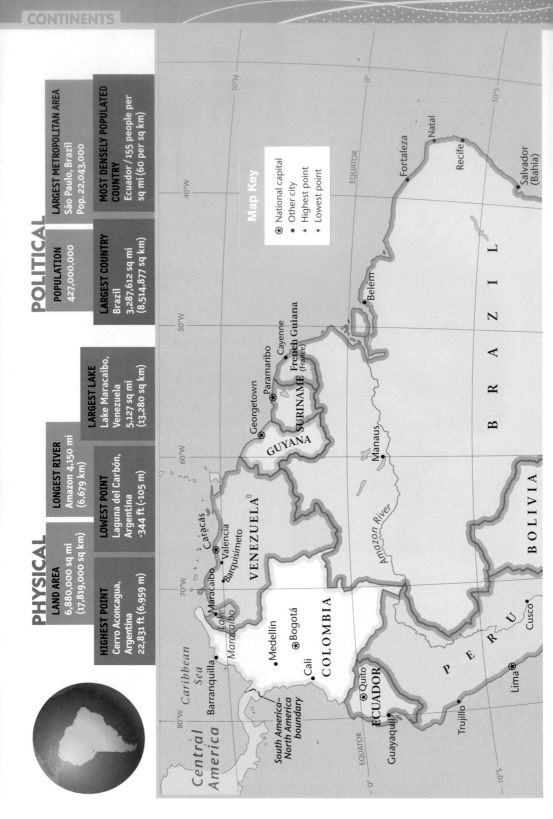

## PHYSICAL

**LAND AREA**
6,880,000 sq mi
(17,819,000 sq km)

**HIGHEST POINT**
Cerro Aconcagua,
Argentina
22,831 ft (6,959 m)

**LOWEST POINT**
Laguna del Carbón,
Argentina
-344 ft (-105 m)

**LONGEST RIVER**
Amazon 4,150 mi
(6,679 km)

**LARGEST LAKE**
Lake Maracaibo,
Venezuela
5,127 sq mi
(13,280 sq km)

## POLITICAL

**POPULATION**
427,000,000

**LARGEST COUNTRY**
Brazil
3,287,612 sq mi
(8,514,877 sq km)

**LARGEST METROPOLITAN AREA**
São Paulo, Brazil
Pop. 22,043,000

**MOST DENSELY POPULATED COUNTRY**
Ecuador / 155 people per
sq mi (60 per sq km)

**Map Key**
⊛ National capital
• Other city
▲ Highest point
▼ Lowest point

Central America

South America–
North America
boundary

Caribbean Sea

Barranquilla
Maracaibo
Lake Maracaibo
Medellín
⊛ Bogotá
Cali
COLOMBIA
Caracas
Valencia
⊛ Barquisimeto
VENEZUELA
⊛ Quito
ECUADOR
Guayaquil
Trujillo
Lima ⊛
Cusco
P E R U
BOLIVIA
Georgetown ⊛
GUYANA
Paramaribo
SURINAME
Cayenne
French Guiana
(France)
Manaus
Amazon River
B R A Z I L
Belém
Fortaleza
Natal
Recife
Salvador
(Bahia)

EQUATOR
80°W
70°W
60°W
50°W
40°W
10°N
0°
10°S
EQUATOR
0°

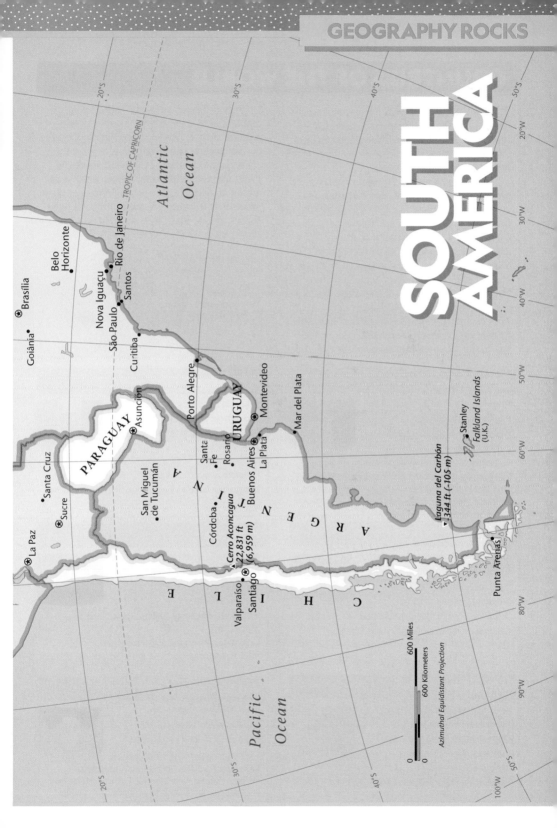

SOUTH AMERICA

Atlantic Ocean

Pacific Ocean

TROPIC OF CAPRICORN

Brasília

Belo Horizonte

Goiânia

Rio de Janeiro

Nova Iguaçu

São Paulo

Santos

Curitiba

Porto Alegre

Asunción

PARAGUAY

URUGUAY

Santa Cruz

Sucre

La Paz

San Miguel de Tucumán

Santa Fe

Rosario

Córdoba

Cerro Aconcagua
22,831 ft
(6,959 m)

Valparaíso

Santiago

A R G E N T I N A

C H I L E

Buenos Aires

La Plata

Montevideo

Mar del Plata

Laguna del Carbón
-344 ft (-105 m)

Stanley

Falkland Islands
(U.K.)

Punta Arenas

600 Miles

600 Kilometers

Azimuthal Equidistant Projection

0
0

20°S
30°S
40°S
50°S

20°W
30°W
40°W
50°W
60°W
70°W
80°W
90°W
100°W

20°S
30°S
40°S
50°S

# COUNTRIES OF THE WORLD

**The following pages** present a general overview of all 195 independent countries recognized by the National Geographic Society, including the newest nation, South Sudan, which gained independence in 2011.

The flags of each independent country symbolize diverse cultures and histories. The statistical data cover highlights of geography and demography and provide a brief overview of each country. They present general characteristics and are not intended to be comprehensive. For example, not every language spoken in a specific country can be listed. Thus, languages shown are the most representative of that area. This is also true of the religions mentioned.

A country is defined as a political body with its own independent government, geographical space, and, in most cases, laws, military, and taxes.

Disputed areas such as Northern Cyprus and Taiwan, and dependencies of independent nations, such as Bermuda and Puerto Rico, are not included in this listing.

Note the color key at the bottom of the pages and the locator map below, which assign a color to each country based on the continent on which it is located. Some capital city populations include that city's metro area. All information is accurate as of press time.

Color Key by Continent

## Afghanistan

**Area:** 251,773 sq mi (652,090 sq km)
**Population:** 36,500,000
**Capital:** Kabul, pop. 4,012,000
**Currency:** afghani
**Religions:** Sunni Muslim, Shiite Muslim
**Languages:** Afghan Persian (Dari), Pashto, Turkic languages (primarily Uzbek and Turkmen), Baluchi, 30 minor languages (including Pashai)

## Albania

**Area:** 11,100 sq mi (28,748 sq km)
**Population:** 2,900,000
**Capital:** Tirana, pop. 476,000
**Currency:** lek
**Religions:** Muslim, Albanian Orthodox, Roman Catholic
**Languages:** Albanian, Greek, Vlach, Romani, Slavic dialects

## Algeria

**Area:** 919,595 sq mi (2,381,741 sq km)
**Population:** 42,700,000
**Capital:** Algiers, pop. 2,694,000
**Currency:** Algerian dinar
**Religion:** Sunni Muslim
**Languages:** Arabic, French, Berber dialects

## Andorra

**Area:** 181 sq mi (469 sq km)
**Population:** 80,000
**Capital:** Andorra la Vella, pop. 23,000
**Currency:** euro
**Religion:** Roman Catholic
**Languages:** Catalan, French, Castilian, Portuguese

## Angola

**Area:** 481,354 sq mi (1,246,700 sq km)
**Population:** 30,400,000
**Capital:** Luanda, pop. 7,774,000
**Currency:** kwanza
**Religions:** indigenous beliefs, Roman Catholic, Protestant
**Languages:** Portuguese, Bantu, other African languages

## Antigua and Barbuda

**Area:** 171 sq mi (442 sq km)
**Population:** 100,000
**Capital:** St. John's, pop. 21,000
**Currency:** East Caribbean dollar
**Religions:** Anglican, Seventh-day Adventist, Pentecostal, Moravian, Roman Catholic, Methodist, Baptist, Church of God, other Christian
**Languages:** English, local dialects

## Argentina

**Area:** 1,073,518 sq mi (2,780,400 sq km)
**Population:** 44,500,000
**Capital:** Buenos Aires, pop. 14,967,000
**Currency:** Argentine peso
**Religion:** Roman Catholic
**Languages:** Spanish, English, Italian, German, French

## Armenia

**Area:** 11,484 sq mi (29,743 sq km)
**Population:** 3,000,000
**Capital:** Yerevan, pop. 1,080,000
**Currency:** dram
**Religions:** Armenian Apostolic, other Christian
**Language:** Armenian

## 3 cool things about ARMENIA

1. As the first country in the world to adopt Christianity as a state religion, Armenia earns its nickname, "Land of Churches," for its many places of worship. Some still-standing churches date back thousands of years.

2. A 5,500-year-old leather shoe—considered the oldest—was found in an Armenian cave. It looked like a moccasin and was stuffed with grasses.

3. The town of Yerevan is also known as the "Pink City" because many of its buildings and homes are made from a blush-colored volcanic rock.

## Australia

**Area:** 2,988,901 sq mi (7,741,220 sq km)
**Population:** 24,100,000
**Capital:** Canberra, A.C.T., pop. 448,000
**Currency:** Australian dollar
**Religions:** Roman Catholic, Anglican
**Language:** English

## Austria

**Area:** 32,378 sq mi (83,858 sq km)
**Population:** 8,800,000
**Capital:** Vienna, pop. 1,901,000
**Currency:** euro
**Religions:** Roman Catholic, Protestant, Muslim
**Language:** German

## Azerbaijan

**Area:** 33,436 sq mi (86,600 sq km)
**Population:** 9,900,000
**Capital:** Baku, pop. 2,286,000
**Currency:** Azerbaijani manat
**Religion:** Muslim
**Language:** Azerbaijani (Azeri)

## Bahamas

**Area:** 5,382 sq mi (13,939 sq km)
**Population:** 400,000
**Capital:** Nassau, pop. 280,000
**Currency:** Bahamian dollar
**Religions:** Baptist, Anglican, Roman Catholic, Pentecostal, Church of God
**Languages:** English, Creole

## Bahrain

**Area:** 277 sq mi (717 sq km)
**Population:** 1,500,000
**Capital:** Manama, pop. 565,000
**Currency:** Bahraini dinar
**Religions:** Shiite Muslim, Sunni Muslim, Christian
**Languages:** Arabic, English, Farsi, Urdu

## Bangladesh

**Area:** 55,598 sq mi (143,998 sq km)
**Population:** 166,400,000
**Capital:** Dhaka, pop. 19,578,000
**Currency:** taka
**Religions:** Muslim, Hindu
**Languages:** Bangla (Bengali), English

## Barbados

**Area:** 166 sq mi (430 sq km)
**Population:** 300,000
**Capital:** Bridgetown, pop. 89,000
**Currency:** Barbadian dollar
**Religions:** Anglican, Pentecostal, Methodist, other Protestant, Roman Catholic
**Language:** English

## Bhutan

**Area:** 17,954 sq mi (46,500 sq km)
**Population:** 800,000
**Capital:** Thimphu, pop. 203,000
**Currencies:** ngultrum; Indian rupee
**Religions:** Lamaistic Buddhist, Indian- and Nepalese-influenced Hindu
**Languages:** Dzongkha, Tibetan dialects, Nepalese dialects

## Belarus

**Area:** 80,153 sq mi (207,595 sq km)
**Population:** 9,500,000
**Capital:** Minsk, pop. 2,005,000
**Currency:** Belarusian ruble
**Religions:** Eastern Orthodox, other (includes Roman Catholic, Protestant, Jewish, Muslim)
**Languages:** Belarusian, Russian

## Bolivia

**Area:** 424,164 sq mi (1,098,581 sq km)
**Population:** 11,300,000
**Capitals:** La Paz, pop. 1,814,000; Sucre, pop. 278,000
**Currency:** boliviano
**Religions:** Roman Catholic, Protestant (includes Evangelical Methodist)
**Languages:** Spanish, Quechua, Aymara

## Belgium

**Area:** 11,787 sq mi (30,528 sq km)
**Population:** 11,400,000
**Capital:** Brussels, pop. 2,050,000
**Currency:** euro
**Religions:** Roman Catholic, other (includes Protestant)
**Languages:** Dutch, French

## Bosnia and Herzegovina

**Area:** 19,741 sq mi (51,129 sq km)
**Population:** 3,500,000
**Capital:** Sarajevo, pop. 343,000
**Currency:** konvertibilna marka (convertible mark)
**Religions:** Muslim, Orthodox, Roman Catholic
**Languages:** Bosnian, Croatian, Serbian

## Belize

**Area:** 8,867 sq mi (22,965 sq km)
**Population:** 400,000
**Capital:** Belmopan, pop. 23,000
**Currency:** Belizean dollar
**Religions:** Roman Catholic, Protestant (includes Pentecostal, Seventh-day Adventist, Mennonite, Methodist)
**Languages:** Spanish, Creole, Mayan dialects, English, Garifuna (Carib), German

## Botswana

**Area:** 224,607 sq mi (581,730 sq km)
**Population:** 2,200,000
**Capital:** Gaborone, pop. 269,000
**Currency:** pula
**Religions:** Christian, Badimo
**Languages:** Setswana, Kalanga

## Benin

**Area:** 43,484 sq mi (112,622 sq km)
**Population:** 11,500,000
**Capitals:** Porto-Novo, pop. 285,000; Cotonou, pop. 685,000
**Currency:** Communauté Financière Africaine franc
**Religions:** Christian, Muslim, Vodoun
**Languages:** French, Fon, Yoruba, tribal languages

## Brazil

**Area:** 3,287,612 sq mi (8,514,877 sq km)
**Population:** 209,400,000
**Capital:** Brasília, pop. 4,470,000
**Currency:** real
**Religions:** Roman Catholic, Protestant
**Language:** Portuguese

## Brunei

**Area:** 2,226 sq mi (5,765 sq km)
**Population:** 400,000
**Capital:** Bandar Seri Begawan, pop. 41,000
**Currency:** Bruneian dollar
**Religions:** Muslim, Buddhist, Christian, other (includes indigenous beliefs)
**Languages:** Malay, English, Chinese

## Burkina Faso

**Area:** 105,869 sq mi (274,200 sq km)
**Population:** 20,300,000
**Capital:** Ouagadougou, pop. 2,531,000
**Currency:** Communauté Financière Africaine franc
**Religions:** Muslim, indigenous beliefs, Christian
**Languages:** French, native African languages

## Bulgaria

**Area:** 42,855 sq mi (110,994 sq km)
**Population:** 7,000,000
**Capital:** Sofia, pop. 1,272,000
**Currency:** lev
**Religions:** Bulgarian Orthodox, Muslim
**Languages:** Bulgarian, Turkish, Roma

## Burundi

**Area:** 10,747 sq mi (27,834 sq km)
**Population:** 11,800,000
**Capital:** Bujumbura, pop. 899,000
**Currency:** Burundi franc
**Religions:** Roman Catholic, indigenous beliefs, Muslim, Protestant
**Languages:** Kirundi, French, Swahili

SNAPSHOT
# Bulgaria

Traditional clothing is worn during the Festival of the National Costume in Zheravna, Bulgaria.

● Asia  ● Europe  ● North America  ● South America

## Cabo Verde

**Area:** 1,558 sq mi (4,036 sq km)
**Population:** 600,000
**Capital:** Praia, pop. 168,000
**Currency:** Cape Verdean escudo
**Religions:** Roman Catholic (infused with indigenous beliefs), Protestant (mostly Church of the Nazarene)
**Languages:** Portuguese, Crioulo

## Cameroon

**Area:** 183,569 sq mi (475,442 sq km)
**Population:** 25,600,000
**Capital:** Yaoundé, pop. 3,656,000
**Currency:** Communauté Financière Africaine franc
**Religions:** indigenous beliefs, Christian, Muslim
**Languages:** 24 major African language groups, English, French

## Cambodia

**Area:** 69,898 sq mi (181,035 sq km)
**Population:** 16,000,000
**Capital:** Phnom Penh, pop. 1,952,000
**Currency:** riel
**Religion:** Theravada Buddhist
**Language:** Khmer

## Canada

**Area:** 3,855,103 sq mi (9,984,670 sq km)
**Population:** 37,200,000
**Capital:** Ottawa, pop. 1,363,000
**Currency:** Canadian dollar
**Religions:** Roman Catholic, Protestant (includes United Church, Anglican), other Christian
**Languages:** English, French

# SNAPSHOT Colombia

A long-tailed sylph hummingbird feeds on a tropical flower in Colombia.

**COLOR KEY** ● Africa ● Australia, New Zealand, and Oceania

## Central African Republic

**Area:** 240,535 sq mi (622,984 sq km)
**Population:** 4,700,000
**Capital:** Bangui, pop. 851,000
**Currency:** Communauté Financière Africaine franc
**Religions:** indigenous beliefs, Protestant, Roman Catholic, Muslim
**Languages:** French, Sangho, tribal languages

## Chad

**Area:** 495,755 sq mi (1,284,000 sq km)
**Population:** 15,400,000
**Capital:** N'Djamena, pop. 1,323,000
**Currency:** Communauté Financière Africaine franc
**Religions:** Muslim, Catholic, Protestant, animist
**Languages:** French, Arabic, Sara, more than 120 languages and dialects

## Chile

**Area:** 291,930 sq mi (756,096 sq km)
**Population:** 18,600,000
**Capital:** Santiago, pop. 6,680,000
**Currency:** Chilean peso
**Religions:** Roman Catholic, Evangelical
**Language:** Spanish

## China

**Area:** 3,705,406 sq mi (9,596,960 sq km)
**Population:** 1,393,800,000
**Capital:** Beijing, pop. 19,618,000
**Currency:** renminbi (yuan)
**Religions:** Taoist, Buddhist, Christian
**Languages:** Standard Chinese or Mandarin, Yue, Wu, Minbei, Minnan, Xiang, Gan, Hakka dialects

## Colombia

**Area:** 440,831 sq mi (1,141,748 sq km)
**Population:** 49,800,000
**Capital:** Bogotá, pop. 10,574,000
**Currency:** Colombian peso
**Religion:** Roman Catholic
**Language:** Spanish

## Comoros

**Area:** 863 sq mi (2,235 sq km)
**Population:** 800,000
**Capital:** Moroni, pop. 62,000
**Currency:** Comoran franc
**Religion:** Sunni Muslim
**Languages:** Arabic, French, Shikomoro

## Congo

**Area:** 132,047 sq mi (342,000 sq km)
**Population:** 5,400,000
**Capital:** Brazzaville, pop. 2,230,000
**Currency:** Communauté Financière Africaine franc
**Religions:** Christian, animist
**Languages:** French, Lingala, Monokutuba, local languages

## Costa Rica

**Area:** 19,730 sq mi (51,100 sq km)
**Population:** 5,000,000
**Capital:** San José, pop. 1,358,000
**Currency:** Costa Rican colón
**Religions:** Roman Catholic, Evangelical
**Languages:** Spanish, English

## Côte d'Ivoire (Ivory Coast)

**Area:** 124,503 sq mi (322,462 sq km)
**Population:** 24,900,000
**Capitals:** Abidjan, pop. 4,921,000; Yamoussoukro, pop. 231,000
**Currency:** Communauté Financière Africaine franc
**Religions:** Muslim, indigenous beliefs, Christian
**Languages:** French, Dioula, other native dialects

## Croatia

**Area:** 21,831 sq mi (56,542 sq km)
**Population:** 4,100,000
**Capital:** Zagreb, pop. 686,000
**Currency:** kuna
**Religions:** Roman Catholic, Orthodox
**Language:** Croatian

## Cuba

**Area:** 42,803 sq mi (110,860 sq km)
**Population:** 11,100,000
**Capital:** Havana, pop. 2,136,000
**Currency:** Cuban peso
**Religions:** Roman Catholic, Protestant, Jehovah's Witnesses, Jewish, Santería
**Language:** Spanish

## 3 cool things about CUBA

1. The world's smallest bird, the bee hummingbird, inhabits Cuba's Isla de la Juventud. The tiny birds, which grow to be about the size of the insect they're named for, build nests the size of quarters and lay pea-size eggs.

2. The national sport of Cuba is baseball, which was brought to the country in the 1860s. Today, the country has one of the top national teams in the world and many major league players come from Cuba.

3. Cuba is nicknamed *El Cocodrilo* (Spanish for crocodile), after the shape of the island. It's also home to some 3,000 Cuban crocodiles, a critically endangered species that can grow to be almost as long as a full-size car.

## Cyprus

**Area:** 3,572 sq mi (9,251 sq km)
**Population:** 1,200,000
**Capital:** Nicosia, pop. 269,000
**Currencies:** euro; new Turkish lira in Northern Cyprus
**Religions:** Greek Orthodox, Muslim, Maronite, Armenian Apostolic
**Languages:** Greek, Turkish, English

## Czechia (Czech Republic)

**Area:** 30,450 sq mi (78,866 sq km)
**Population:** 10,600,000
**Capital:** Prague, pop. 1,292,000
**Currency:** koruny
**Religion:** Roman Catholic
**Language:** Czech

## Democratic Republic of the Congo

**Area:** 905,365 sq mi (2,344,885 sq km)
**Population:** 84,300,000
**Capital:** Kinshasa, pop. 13,171,000
**Currency:** Congolese franc
**Religions:** Roman Catholic, Protestant, Kimbanguist, Muslim, syncretic sects, indigenous beliefs
**Languages:** French, Lingala, Kingwana, Kikongo, Tshiluba

## Denmark

**Area:** 16,640 sq mi (43,098 sq km)
**Population:** 5,800,000
**Capital:** Copenhagen, pop. 1,321,000
**Currency:** Danish krone
**Religions:** Evangelical Lutheran, other Protestant, Roman Catholic
**Languages:** Danish, Faroese, Greenlandic, German, English as second language

## Djibouti

**Area:** 8,958 sq mi (23,200 sq km)
**Population:** 1,000,000
**Capital:** Djibouti, pop. 562,000
**Currency:** Djiboutian franc
**Religions:** Muslim, Christian
**Languages:** French, Arabic, Somali, Afar

## Dominica

**Area:** 290 sq mi (751 sq km)
**Population:** 70,000
**Capital:** Roseau, pop. 15,000
**Currency:** East Caribbean dollar
**Religions:** Roman Catholic, Seventh-day Adventist, Pentecostal, Baptist, Methodist, other Christian
**Languages:** English, French patois

## Dominican Republic

**Area:** 18,704 sq mi (48,442 sq km)
**Population:** 10,800,000
**Capital:** Santo Domingo, pop. 3,172,000
**Currency:** Dominican peso
**Religion:** Roman Catholic
**Language:** Spanish

## Ecuador

**Area:** 109,483 sq mi (283,560 sq km)
**Population:** 17,000,000
**Capital:** Quito, pop. 1,822,000
**Currency:** U.S. dollar
**Religion:** Roman Catholic
**Languages:** Spanish, Quechua, other Amerindian languages

## Egypt

**Area:** 386,874 sq mi (1,002,000 sq km)
**Population:** 97,000,000
**Capital:** Cairo, pop. 20,901,000
**Currency:** Egyptian pound
**Religions:** Muslim (mostly Sunni), Coptic Christian
**Languages:** Arabic, English, French

## El Salvador

**Area:** 8,124 sq mi (21,041 sq km)
**Population:** 6,500,000
**Capital:** San Salvador, pop. 1,107,000
**Currency:** U.S. dollar
**Religions:** Roman Catholic, Protestant
**Languages:** Spanish, Nahua

## Equatorial Guinea

**Area:** 10,831 sq mi (28,051 sq km)
**Population:** 1,300,000
**Capital:** Malabo, pop. 297,000
**Currency:** Communauté Financière Africaine franc
**Religions:** Christian (predominantly Roman Catholic), pagan practices
**Languages:** Spanish, French, Fang, Bubi

## Eritrea

**Area:** 45,406 sq mi (117,600 sq km)
**Population:** 6,000,000
**Capital:** Asmara, pop. 896,000
**Currency:** nakfa
**Religions:** Muslim, Coptic Christian, Roman Catholic
**Languages:** Afar, Arabic, Tigre, Kunama, Tigrinya, other Cushitic languages

## Estonia

**Area:** 17,462 sq mi (45,227 sq km)
**Population:** 1,300,000
**Capital:** Tallinn, pop. 437,000
**Currency:** euro
**Religions:** Evangelical Lutheran, Orthodox
**Languages:** Estonian, Russian

## Eswatini

**Area:** 6,704 sq mi (17,363 sq km)
**Population:** 1,400,000
**Capitals:** Mbabane, pop. 68,000; Lobamba, pop. 11,000
**Currency:** lilangeni
**Religions:** Zionist, Roman Catholic, Muslim
**Languages:** English, siSwati

## Ethiopia

**Area:** 426,373 sq mi (1,104,300 sq km)
**Population:** 107,500,000
**Capital:** Addis Ababa, pop. 4,400,000
**Currency:** birr
**Religions:** Christian, Muslim, traditional
**Languages:** Amharic, Oromigna, Tigrinya, Guaragigna

## Fiji

**Area:** 7,095 sq mi (18,376 sq km)
**Population:** 900,000
**Capital:** Suva, pop. 178,000
**Currency:** Fijian dollar
**Religions:** Christian (Methodist, Roman Catholic, Assembly of God), Hindu (Sanatan), Muslim (Sunni)
**Languages:** English, Fijian, Hindustani

## Finland

**Area:** 130,558 sq mi (338,145 sq km)
**Population:** 5,500,000
**Capital:** Helsinki, pop. 1,279,000
**Currency:** euro
**Religion:** Lutheran Church of Finland
**Languages:** Finnish, Swedish

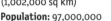

## France

**Area:** 210,026 sq mi (543,965 sq km)
**Population:** 65,100,000
**Capital:** Paris, pop. 10,901,000
**Currency:** euro
**Religions:** Roman Catholic, Muslim
**Language:** French

## Gambia

**Area:** 4,361 sq mi (11,295 sq km)
**Population:** 2,200,000
**Capital:** Banjul, pop. 437,000
**Currency:** dalasi
**Religions:** Muslim, Christian
**Languages:** English, Mandinka, Wolof, Fula, other indigenous vernaculars

## Gabon

**Area:** 103,347 sq mi (267,667 sq km)
**Population:** 2,100,000
**Capital:** Libreville, pop. 813,000
**Currency:** Communauté Financière Africaine franc
**Religions:** Christian, animist
**Languages:** French, Fang, Myene, Nzebi, Bapounou/Eschira, Bandjabi

## Georgia

**Area:** 26,911 sq mi (69,700 sq km)
**Population:** 3,900,000
**Capital:** Tbilisi, pop. 1,077,000
**Currency:** lari
**Religions:** Orthodox Christian, Muslim, Armenian-Gregorian
**Languages:** Georgian, Russian, Armenian, Azeri, Abkhaz

SNAPSHOT
# Georgia

Tbilisi, Georgia

**COLOR KEY** ● Africa ● Australia, New Zealand, and Oceania

## Germany

**Area:** 137,847 sq mi
(357,022 sq km)
**Population:** 82,800,000
**Capital:** Berlin, pop. 3,552,000
**Currency:** euro
**Religions:** Protestant, Roman Catholic, Muslim
**Language:** German

## Ghana

**Area:** 92,100 sq mi (238,537 sq km)
**Population:** 29,500,000
**Capital:** Accra, pop. 2,439,000
**Currency:** Ghana cedi
**Religions:** Christian (Pentecostal/Charismatic, Protestant, Roman Catholic, other), Muslim, traditional beliefs
**Languages:** Asante, Ewe, Fante, Boron (Brong), Dagomba, Dangme, Dagarte (Dagaba), Akyem, Ga, English

## Greece

**Area:** 50,949 sq mi (131,957 sq km)
**Population:** 10,600,000
**Capital:** Athens, pop. 3,156,000
**Currency:** euro
**Religion:** Greek Orthodox
**Languages:** Greek, English, French

## Grenada

**Area:** 133 sq mi (344 sq km)
**Population:** 100,000
**Capital:** St. George's, pop. 39,000
**Currency:** East Caribbean dollar
**Religions:** Roman Catholic, Anglican, other Protestant
**Languages:** English, French patois

## Guatemala

**Area:** 42,042 sq mi (108,889 sq km)
**Population:** 17,200,000
**Capital:** Guatemala City, pop. 2,851,000
**Currency:** quetzal
**Religions:** Roman Catholic, Protestant, indigenous Maya beliefs
**Languages:** Spanish, 23 official Amerindian languages

## Guinea

**Area:** 94,926 sq mi (245,857 sq km)
**Population:** 11,900,000
**Capital:** Conakry, pop. 1,843,000
**Currency:** Guinean franc
**Religions:** Muslim, Christian, indigenous beliefs
**Languages:** French, ethnic languages

## Guinea-Bissau

**Area:** 13,948 sq mi
(36,125 sq km)
**Population:** 1,900,000
**Capital:** Bissau, pop. 558,000
**Currency:** Communauté Financière Africaine franc
**Religions:** indigenous beliefs, Muslim, Christian
**Languages:** Portuguese, Crioulo, African languages

## Guyana

**Area:** 83,000 sq mi
(214,969 sq km)
**Population:** 800,000
**Capital:** Georgetown, pop. 110,000
**Currency:** Guyanese dollar
**Religions:** Christian, Hindu, Muslim
**Languages:** English, Amerindian dialects, Creole, Hindustani, Urdu

## Haiti

**Area:** 10,714 sq mi (27,750 sq km)
**Population:** 10,800,000
**Capital:** Port-au-Prince, pop. 2,637,000
**Currency:** gourde
**Religions:** Roman Catholic, Protestant (Baptist, Pentecostal, other)
**Languages:** French, Creole

## Honduras

**Area:** 43,433 sq mi
(112,492 sq km)
**Population:** 9,000,000
**Capital:** Tegucigalpa, pop. 1,363,000
**Currency:** lempira
**Religions:** Roman Catholic, Protestant
**Languages:** Spanish, Amerindian dialects

## Hungary

**Area:** 35,919 sq mi (93,030 sq km)
**Population:** 9,800,000
**Capital:** Budapest, pop. 1,759,000
**Currency:** forint
**Religions:** Roman Catholic, Calvinist, Lutheran
**Language:** Hungarian

## Iraq

**Area:** 168,754 sq mi
(437,072 sq km)
**Population:** 40,200,000
**Capital:** Baghdad, pop. 6,812,000
**Currency:** Iraqi dinar
**Religions:** Shiite Muslim, Sunni Muslim
**Languages:** Arabic, Kurdish, Assyrian, Armenian

## Iceland

**Area:** 39,769 sq mi
(103,000 sq km)
**Population:** 400,000
**Capital:** Reykjavík, pop. 216,000
**Currency:** Icelandic krona
**Religion:** Lutheran Church of Iceland
**Languages:** Icelandic, English, Nordic
languages, German

## Ireland (Éire)

**Area:** 27,133 sq mi
(70,273 sq km)
**Population:** 4,900,000
**Capital:** Dublin, pop. 1,201,000
**Currency:** euro
**Religions:** Roman Catholic, Church of Ireland
**Languages:** Irish (Gaelic), English

## India

**Area:** 1,269,221 sq mi (3,287,270 sq km)
**Population:** 1,371,300,000
**Capital:** New Delhi, pop. 28,514,000
(part of Delhi metropolitan area)
**Currency:** Indian rupee
**Religions:** Hindu, Muslim
**Languages:** Hindi, 21 other official languages,
Hindustani (popular Hindi/Urdu variant in the north)

## Israel

**Area:** 8,550 sq mi (22,145 sq km)
**Population:** 8,500,000
**Capital:** Jerusalem, pop. 907,000
**Currency:** new Israeli sheqel
**Religions:** Jewish, Muslim
**Languages:** Hebrew, Arabic, English

## Indonesia

**Area:** 742,308 sq mi
(1,922,570 sq km)
**Population:** 265,200,000
**Capital:** Jakarta, pop. 10,517,000
**Currency:** Indonesian rupiah
**Religions:** Muslim, Protestant, Roman Catholic
**Languages:** Bahasa Indonesia (modified form of Malay),
English, Dutch, Javanese, local dialects

## Italy

**Area:** 116,345 sq mi
(301,333 sq km)
**Population:** 60,600,000
**Capital:** Rome, pop. 4,210,000
**Currency:** euro
**Religions:** Roman Catholic, Protestant, Jewish, Muslim
**Languages:** Italian, German, French, Slovene

## Iran

**Area:** 636,296 sq mi
(1,648,000 sq km)
**Population:** 81,600,000
**Capital:** Tehran, pop. 8,896,000
**Currency:** Iranian rial
**Religions:** Shiite Muslim, Sunni Muslim
**Languages:** Persian, Turkic, Kurdish, Luri,
Baluchi, Arabic

## Jamaica

**Area:** 4,244 sq mi
(10,991 sq km)
**Population:** 2,900,000
**Capital:** Kingston, pop. 589,000
**Currency:** Jamaican dollar
**Religions:** Protestant (Church of God, Seventh-day
Adventist, Pentecostal, Baptist, Anglican, other)
**Languages:** English, English patois

## Japan

**Area:** 145,902 sq mi (377,887 sq km)
**Population:** 126,500,000
**Capital:** Tokyo, pop. 37,393,000
**Currency:** yen
**Religions:** Shinto, Buddhist
**Language:** Japanese

## Kazakhstan

**Area:** 1,049,155 sq mi (2,717,300 sq km)
**Population:** 18,400,000
**Capital:** Astana, pop. 1,068,000
**Currency:** tenge
**Religions:** Muslim, Russian Orthodox
**Languages:** Kazakh (Qazaq), Russian

## Jordan

**Area:** 34,495 sq mi (89,342 sq km)
**Population:** 10,200,000
**Capital:** Amman, pop. 2,065,000
**Currency:** Jordanian dinar
**Religions:** Sunni Muslim, Christian
**Languages:** Arabic, English

## Kenya

**Area:** 224,081 sq mi (580,367 sq km)
**Population:** 51,000,000
**Capital:** Nairobi, pop. 4,386,000
**Currency:** Kenyan shilling
**Religions:** Protestant, Roman Catholic, Muslim, indigenous beliefs
**Languages:** English, Kiswahili, many indigenous languages

# SNAPSHOT
# Jamaica

Children dance in Kingston, Jamaica, wearing yellow, green, and black—Jamaica's national colors.

● Asia  ● Europe  ● North America  ● **South America**

## Kiribati

**Area:** 313 sq mi (811 sq km)
**Population:** 100,000
**Capital:** Tarawa, pop. 64,000
**Currency:** Australian dollar
**Religions:** Roman Catholic, Protestant (Congregational)
**Languages:** I-Kiribati, English

## Kuwait

**Area:** 6,880 sq mi (17,818 sq km)
**Population:** 4,200,000
**Capital:** Kuwait City, pop. 2,989,000
**Currency:** Kuwaiti dinar
**Religions:** Sunni Muslim, Shiite Muslim
**Languages:** Arabic, English

## Kosovo

**Area:** 4,203 sq mi (10,887 sq km)
**Population:** 1,800,000
**Capital:** Pristina, pop. 205,000
**Currency:** euro
**Religions:** Muslim, Serbian Orthodox, Roman Catholic
**Languages:** Albanian, Serbian, Bosnian, Turkish, Roma

## Kyrgyzstan

**Area:** 77,182 sq mi (199,900 sq km)
**Population:** 6,100,000
**Capital:** Bishkek, pop. 996,000
**Currency:** som
**Religions:** Muslim, Russian Orthodox
**Languages:** Kyrgyz, Uzbek, Russian

# SNAPSHOT Luxembourg

Pretzel from Grevenmacher, Luxembourg

**COLOR KEY** ● Africa ● Australia, New Zealand, and Oceania

## Laos

**Area:** 91,429 sq mi
(236,800 sq km)
**Population:** 7,000,000
**Capital:** Vientiane, pop. 665,000
**Currency:** kip
**Religions:** Buddhist, animist
**Languages:** Lao, French, English, various ethnic languages

## Libya

**Area:** 679,362 sq mi
(1,759,540 sq km)
**Population:** 6,500,000
**Capital:** Tripoli, pop. 1,158,000
**Currency:** Libyan dinar
**Religion:** Sunni Muslim
**Languages:** Arabic, Italian, English

## Latvia

**Area:** 24,938 sq mi
(64,589 sq km)
**Population:** 1,900,000
**Capital:** Riga, pop. 637,000
**Currency:** Latvian lat
**Religions:** Lutheran, Roman Catholic, Russian Orthodox
**Languages:** Latvian, Russian, Lithuanian

## Liechtenstein

**Area:** 62 sq mi (160 sq km)
**Population:** 40,000
**Capital:** Vaduz, pop. 5,000
**Currency:** Swiss franc
**Religions:** Roman Catholic, Protestant
**Languages:** German, Alemannic dialect

## Lebanon

**Area:** 4,036 sq mi (10,452 sq km)
**Population:** 6,100,000
**Capital:** Beirut, pop. 2,385,000
**Currency:** Lebanese pound
**Religions:** Muslim, Christian
**Languages:** Arabic, French, English, Armenian

## Lithuania

**Area:** 25,212 sq mi
(65,300 sq km)
**Population:** 2,800,000
**Capital:** Vilnius, pop. 536,000
**Currency:** litas
**Religions:** Roman Catholic, Russian Orthodox
**Languages:** Lithuanian, Russian, Polish

## Lesotho

**Area:** 11,720 sq mi (30,355 sq km)
**Population:** 2,300,000
**Capital:** Maseru, pop. 202,000
**Currencies:** loti; South African rand
**Religions:** Christian, indigenous beliefs
**Languages:** Sesotho, English, Zulu, Xhosa

## Luxembourg

**Area:** 998 sq mi (2,586 sq km)
**Population:** 600,000
**Capital:** Luxembourg,
pop. 120,000
**Currency:** euro
**Religions:** Roman Catholic, Protestant, Jewish, Muslim
**Languages:** Luxembourgish, German, French

## Liberia

**Area:** 43,000 sq mi
(111,370 sq km)
**Population:** 4,900,000
**Capital:** Monrovia,
pop. 1,418,000
**Currency:** Liberian dollar
**Religions:** Christian, indigenous beliefs, Muslim
**Languages:** English, some 20 ethnic languages

## Macedonia

**Area:** 9,928 sq mi
(25,713 sq km)
**Population:** 2,100,000
**Capital:** Skopje, pop. 584,000
**Currency:** Macedonian denar
**Religions:** Macedonian Orthodox, Muslim
**Languages:** Macedonian, Albanian, Turkish

## Madagascar

**Area:** 226,658 sq mi
(587,041 sq km)
**Population:** 26,300,000
**Capital:** Antananarivo,
pop. 3,058,000
**Currency:** Madagascar ariary
**Religions:** indigenous beliefs, Christian, Muslim
**Languages:** English, French, Malagasy

## Malta

**Area:** 122 sq mi (316 sq km)
**Population:** 500,000
**Capital:** Valletta, pop. 213,000
**Currency:** euro
**Religion:** Roman Catholic
**Languages:** Maltese, English

## Malawi

**Area:** 45,747 sq mi
(118,484 sq km)
**Population:** 19,100,000
**Capital:** Lilongwe, pop. 1,030,000
**Currency:** Malawian kwacha
**Religions:** Christian, Muslim
**Languages:** Chichewa, Chinyanja, Chiyao, Chitumbuka

## Marshall Islands

**Area:** 70 sq mi (181 sq km)
**Population:** 60,000
**Capital:** Majuro, pop. 31,000
**Currency:** U.S. dollar
**Religions:** Protestant, Assembly of God,
Roman Catholic
**Language:** Marshallese

## Malaysia

**Area:** 127,355 sq mi (329,847 sq km)
**Population:** 32,500,000
**Capital:** Kuala Lumpur,
pop. 7,564,000
**Currency:** ringgit
**Religions:** Muslim, Buddhist, Christian, Hindu
**Languages:** Bahasa Malaysia, English, Chinese, Tamil,
Telugu, Malayalam, Panjabi, Thai, indigenous languages

## Mauritania

**Area:** 397,955 sq mi
(1,030,700 sq km)
**Population:** 4,500,000
**Capital:** Nouakchott, pop. 1,205,000
**Currency:** ouguiya
**Religion:** Muslim
**Languages:** Arabic, Pulaar, Soninke, French,
Hassaniya, Wolof

## Maldives

**Area:** 115 sq mi (298 sq km)
**Population:** 400,000
**Capital:** Male, pop. 177,000
**Currency:** rufiyaa
**Religion:** Sunni Muslim
**Languages:** Maldivian Dhivehi, English

# 3 cool things about MAURITANIA

1. Nouakchott was designated as Mauritania's
capital when the country gained independence
in 1960, making it one of the world's newest
capitals. Once a tiny fishing village, Nouakchott
is now the country's largest city.

2. "The Eye of Africa"—a 30-mile (50-km)-wide
bull's-eye rock formation in the Sahara in
Mauritania can be seen from space. The
natural phenomenon was likely formed by
geological shifts and exposed over time
by wind and water erosion.

3. The rusty remains of some 300 ships once
bobbed along in Mauritania's Bay of
Nouadhibou. It was one of the world's biggest
ship cemeteries, and boats from all over the
world were abandoned there during the 1980s.

## Mali

**Area:** 478,841 sq mi (1,240,192 sq km)
**Population:** 19,400,000
**Capital:** Bamako, pop. 2,447,000
**Currency:** Communauté
Financière Africaine franc
**Religions:** Muslim, indigenous beliefs
**Languages:** Bambara, French, numerous
African languages

## Mauritius

**Area:** 788 sq mi (2,040 sq km)
**Population:** 1,300,000
**Capital:** Port Louis, pop. 149,000
**Currency:** Mauritian rupee
**Religions:** Hindu, Roman Catholic, Muslim, other Christian
**Languages:** Creole, Bhojpuri, French

## Mexico

**Area:** 758,449 sq mi (1,964,375 sq km)
**Population:** 130,800,000
**Capital:** Mexico City, pop. 21,782,000
**Currency:** Mexican peso
**Religions:** Roman Catholic, Protestant
**Languages:** Spanish, Mayan, other indigenous languages

## Micronesia

**Area:** 271 sq mi (702 sq km)
**Population:** 100,000
**Capital:** Palikir, pop. 7,000
**Currency:** U.S. dollar
**Religions:** Roman Catholic, Protestant
**Languages:** English, Trukese, Pohnpeian, Yapese, other indigenous languages

## Moldova

**Area:** 13,050 sq mi (33,800 sq km)
**Population:** 3,500,000
**Capital:** Chișinău, pop. 510,000
**Currency:** Moldovan leu
**Religion:** Eastern Orthodox
**Languages:** Moldovan, Russian, Gagauz

## Monaco

**Area:** 0.8 sq mi (2 sq km)
**Population:** 40,000
**Capital:** Monaco, pop. 39,000
**Currency:** euro
**Religion:** Roman Catholic
**Languages:** French, English, Italian, Monegasque

## Mongolia

**Area:** 603,909 sq mi (1,564,116 sq km)
**Population:** 3,200,000
**Capital:** Ulaanbaatar, pop. 1,520,000
**Currency:** togrog/tugrik
**Religions:** Buddhist Lamaist, Shamanist, Christian
**Languages:** Khalkha Mongol, Turkic, Russian

## Montenegro

**Area:** 5,333 sq mi (13,812 sq km)
**Population:** 600,000
**Capital:** Podgorica, pop. 177,000
**Currency:** euro
**Religions:** Orthodox, Muslim, Roman Catholic
**Languages:** Serbian (Ijekavian dialect), Bosnian, Albanian, Croatian

**MONTENEGRO—WHICH MEANS "BLACK MOUNTAIN"—is home to many DARK MOUNTAIN FORESTS.**

## Morocco

**Area:** 172,414 sq mi (446,550 sq km)
**Population:** 35,200,000
**Capital:** Rabat, pop. 1,847,000
**Currency:** Moroccan dirham
**Religion:** Muslim
**Languages:** Arabic, Berber dialects, French

## Mozambique

**Area:** 308,642 sq mi (799,380 sq km)
**Population:** 30,500,000
**Capital:** Maputo, pop. 1,102,000
**Currency:** metical
**Religions:** Roman Catholic, Muslim, Zionist Christian
**Languages:** Emakhuwa, Xichangana, Portuguese, Elomwe, Cisena, Echuwabo, other local languages

## Myanmar (Burma)

**Area:** 261,218 sq mi
(676,552 sq km)
**Population:** 53,900,000
**Capital:** Nay Pyi Taw,
pop. 500,000
**Currency:** kyat
**Religions:** Buddhist, Christian, Muslim
**Languages:** Burmese, minority ethnic languages

## Nauru

**Area:** 8 sq mi (21 sq km)
**Population:** 11,000
**Capital:** Yaren, pop. 11,000
**Currency:** Australian dollar
**Religions:** Protestant, Roman Catholic
**Languages:** Nauruan, English

## Namibia

**Area:** 318,261 sq mi
(824,292 sq km)
**Population:** 2,500,000
**Capital:** Windhoek, pop. 404,000
**Currencies:** Namibian dollar;
South African rand
**Religions:** Lutheran, other Christian, indigenous beliefs
**Languages:** Afrikaans, German, English

## Nepal

**Area:** 56,827 sq mi
(147,181 sq km)
**Population:** 29,700,000
**Capital:** Kathmandu, pop. 1,330,000
**Currency:** Nepalese rupee
**Religions:** Hindu, Buddhist, Muslim, Kirant
**Languages:** Nepali, Maithali, Bhojpuri, Tharu,
Tamang, Newar, Magar

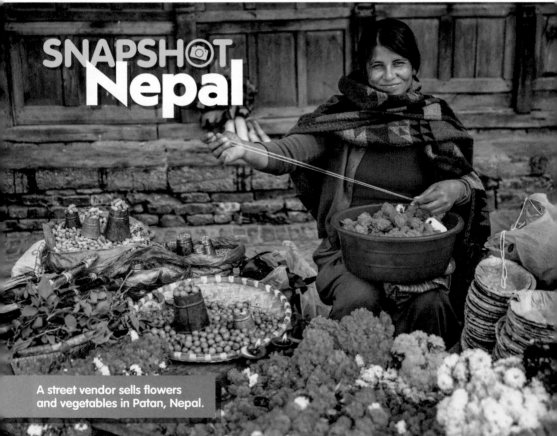

# SNAPSHOT Nepal

A street vendor sells flowers
and vegetables in Patan, Nepal.

**COLOR KEY** ● Africa ● Australia, New Zealand, and Oceania

## Netherlands

**Area:** 16,034 sq mi
(41,528 sq km)
**Population:** 17,200,000
**Capital:** Amsterdam, pop. 1,132,000;
The Hague, pop. 685,000
**Currency:** euro
**Religions:** Roman Catholic, Dutch Reformed,
Calvinist, Muslim
**Languages:** Dutch, Frisian

## North Korea

**Area:** 46,540 sq mi
(120,538 sq km)
**Population:** 25,600,000
**Capital:** Pyongyang,
pop. 3,038,000
**Currency:** North Korean won
**Religions:** Buddhist, Confucianist, some Christian
and syncretic Chondogyo
**Language:** Korean

## New Zealand

**Area:** 104,454 sq mi
(270,534 sq km)
**Population:** 4,900,000
**Capital:** Wellington, pop. 411,000
**Currency:** New Zealand dollar
**Religions:** Anglican, Roman Catholic, Presbyterian,
other Christian
**Languages:** English, Maori

## Norway

**Area:** 125,004 sq mi
(323,758 sq km)
**Population:** 5,300,000
**Capital:** Oslo, pop. 1,012,000
**Currency:** Norwegian krone
**Religion:** Church of Norway (Lutheran)
**Languages:** Bokmal Norwegian, Nynorsk
Norwegian, Sami

## Nicaragua

**Area:** 50,193 sq mi
(130,000 sq km)
**Population:** 6,300,000
**Capital:** Managua, pop. 1,048,000
**Currency:** gold cordoba
**Religions:** Roman Catholic, Evangelical
**Language:** Spanish

## Oman

**Area:** 119,500 sq mi
(309,500 sq km)
**Population:** 4,700,000
**Capital:** Muscat, pop. 1,447,000
**Currency:** Omani rial
**Religions:** Ibadhi Muslim, Sunni Muslim,
Shiite Muslim, Hindu
**Languages:** Arabic, English, Baluchi, Urdu, Indian dialects

## Niger

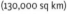

**Area:** 489,191 sq mi (1,267,000 sq km)
**Population:** 22,200,000
**Capital:** Niamey, pop. 1,214,000
**Currency:** Communauté
Financière Africaine franc
**Religions:** Muslim, other (includes indigenous
beliefs and Christian)
**Languages:** French, Hausa, Djerma

## Pakistan

**Area:** 307,374 sq mi
(796,095 sq km)
**Population:** 200,600,000
**Capital:** Islamabad, pop. 1,061,000
**Currency:** Pakistani rupee
**Religions:** Sunni Muslim, Shiite Muslim
**Languages:** Punjabi, Sindhi, Siraiki, Pashto, Urdu,
Baluchi, Hindko, English

## Nigeria

**Area:** 356,669 sq mi
(923,768 sq km)
**Population:** 195,900,000
**Capital:** Abuja, pop. 2,919,000
**Currency:** naira
**Religions:** Muslim, Christian, indigenous beliefs
**Languages:** English, Hausa, Yoruba, Igbo (Ibo), Fulani

## Palau

**Area:** 189 sq mi (489 sq km)
**Population:** 20,000
**Capital:** Melekeok, pop. 11,000
**Currency:** U.S. dollar
**Religions:** Roman Catholic, Protestant, Modekngei,
Seventh-day Adventist
**Languages:** Palauan, Filipino, English, Chinese

## Panama

**Area:** 29,157 sq mi (75,517 sq km)
**Population:** 4,200,000
**Capital:** Panama City, pop. 1,783,000
**Currencies:** balboa; U.S. dollar
**Religions:** Roman Catholic, Protestant
**Languages:** Spanish, English

## Papua New Guinea

**Area:** 178,703 sq mi (462,840 sq km)
**Population:** 8,500,000
**Capital:** Port Moresby, pop. 367,000
**Currency:** kina
**Religions:** indigenous beliefs, Roman Catholic, Lutheran, other Protestant
**Languages:** Melanesian Pidgin, 820 indigenous languages

## Paraguay

**Area:** 157,048 sq mi (406,752 sq km)
**Population:** 6,900,000
**Capital:** Asunción, pop. 3,222,000
**Currency:** guarani
**Religions:** Roman Catholic, Protestant
**Languages:** Spanish, Guarani

## Peru

**Area:** 496,224 sq mi (1,285,216 sq km)
**Population:** 32,200,000
**Capital:** Lima, pop. 10,391,000
**Currency:** nuevo sol
**Religion:** Roman Catholic
**Languages:** Spanish, Quechua, Aymara, minor Amazonian languages

## Philippines

**Area:** 115,831 sq mi (300,000 sq km)
**Population:** 107,000,000
**Capital:** Manila, pop. 13,482,000
**Currency:** Philippine peso
**Religions:** Roman Catholic, Muslim, other Christian
**Languages:** Filipino (based on Tagalog), English

## Poland

**Area:** 120,728 sq mi (312,685 sq km)
**Population:** 38,400,000
**Capital:** Warsaw, pop. 1,768,000
**Currency:** zloty
**Religion:** Roman Catholic
**Language:** Polish

## Portugal

**Area:** 35,655 sq mi (92,345 sq km)
**Population:** 10,300,000
**Capital:** Lisbon, pop. 2,927,000
**Currency:** euro
**Religion:** Roman Catholic
**Languages:** Portuguese, Mirandese

## Qatar

**Area:** 4,448 sq mi (11,521 sq km)
**Population:** 2,700,000
**Capital:** Doha, pop. 633,000
**Currency:** Qatari rial
**Religions:** Muslim, Christian
**Languages:** Arabic; English commonly a second language

## Romania

**Area:** 92,043 sq mi (238,391 sq km)
**Population:** 19,500,000
**Capital:** Bucharest, pop. 1,821,000
**Currency:** new leu
**Religions:** Eastern Orthodox, Protestant, Roman Catholic
**Languages:** Romanian, Hungarian

## Russia

**Area:** 6,592,850 sq mi (17,075,400 sq km)
**Population:** 147,300,000
**Capital:** Moscow, pop. 12,538,000
**Currency:** ruble
**Religions:** Russian Orthodox, Muslim
**Languages:** Russian, many minority languages
*Note: Russia is in both Europe and Asia, but its capital is in Europe, so it is classified here as a European country.*

**COLOR KEY** ● Africa ● Australia, New Zealand, and Oceania

## Rwanda

**Area:** 10,169 sq mi
(26,338 sq km)
**Population:** 12,600,000
**Capital:** Kigali, pop. 1,058,000
**Currency:** Rwandan franc
**Religions:** Roman Catholic, Protestant,
Adventist, Muslim
**Languages:** Kinyarwanda, French, English, Kiswahili

## San Marino

**Area:** 24 sq mi (61 sq km)
**Population:** 30,000
**Capital:** San Marino, pop. 4,000
**Currency:** euro
**Religion:** Roman Catholic
**Language:** Italian

## Samoa

**Area:** 1,093 sq mi (2,831 sq km)
**Population:** 200,000
**Capital:** Apia, pop. 36,000
**Currency:** tala
**Religions:** Congregationalist, Roman Catholic,
Methodist, Church of Jesus Christ of Latter-day
Saints, Assembly of God, Seventh-day Adventist
**Languages:** Samoan (Polynesian), English

## Sao Tome and Principe

**Area:** 386 sq mi (1,001 sq km)
**Population:** 200,000
**Capital:** São Tomé,
pop. 80,000
**Currency:** dobra
**Religions:** Roman Catholic, Evangelical
**Language:** Portuguese

# SNAPSHOT
# Papua New Guinea

Children ride in a homemade canoe in
Kavieng, New Ireland, Papua New Guinea.

## Saudi Arabia

**Area:** 756,985 sq mi
(1,960,582 sq km)
**Population:** 33,400,000
**Capital:** Riyadh, pop. 6,907,000
**Currency:** Saudi riyal
**Religion:** Muslim
**Language:** Arabic

## Senegal

**Area:** 75,955 sq mi
(196,722 sq km)
**Population:** 16,300,000
**Capital:** Dakar, pop. 2,978,000
**Currency:** Communauté
Financière Africaine franc
**Religions:** Muslim, Christian (mostly Roman Catholic)
**Languages:** French, Wolof, Pulaar, Jola, Mandinka

## Serbia

**Area:** 29,913 sq mi (77,474 sq km)
**Population:** 7,000,000
**Capital:** Belgrade, pop. 1,389,000
**Currency:** Serbian dinar
**Religions:** Serbian Orthodox, Roman Catholic, Muslim
**Languages:** Serbian, Hungarian

## Seychelles

**Area:** 176 sq mi (455 sq km)
**Population:** 100,000
**Capital:** Victoria, pop. 28,000
**Currency:** Seychelles rupee
**Religions:** Roman Catholic, Anglican, other Christian
**Languages:** Creole, English

## Sierra Leone

**Area:** 27,699 sq mi (71,740 sq km)
**Population:** 7,700,000
**Capital:** Freetown, pop. 1,136,000
**Currency:** leone
**Religions:** Muslim, indigenous beliefs, Christian
**Languages:** English, Mende, Temne, Krio

## Singapore

**Area:** 255 sq mi (660 sq km)
**Population:** 5,800,000
**Capital:** Singapore, pop. 5,792,000
**Currency:** Singapore dollar
**Religions:** Buddhist, Muslim, Taoist, Roman Catholic, Hindu, other Christian
**Languages:** Mandarin, English, Malay, Hokkien, Cantonese, Teochew, Tamil

## Slovakia

**Area:** 18,932 sq mi
(49,035 sq km)
**Population:** 5,400,000
**Capital:** Bratislava, pop. 430,000
**Currency:** euro
**Religions:** Roman Catholic, Protestant, Greek Catholic
**Languages:** Slovak, Hungarian

## Slovenia

**Area:** 7,827 sq mi
(20,273 sq km)
**Population:** 2,100,000
**Capital:** Ljubljana,
pop. 286,000
**Currency:** euro
**Religions:** Roman Catholic, Muslim, Orthodox
**Languages:** Slovene, Croatian, Serbian

# 3 cool things about SLOVENIA

1. Some 54 percent of Slovenia's land is forest. Kočevje, a town that is made up of about 90 percent forest, is also known as Slovenia's Bear Forest, as it's home to much of the country's 500-strong brown bear population.

2. There are about 10,000 caves in Slovenia, including Postojna Cave, which has 15 miles (24 km) of passages, galleries, and chambers that started forming some three million years ago.

3. A 1,181-foot (360-m)-tall chimney soars above the city of Trbovlje, Slovenia. The tallest chimney in Europe, it's part of the old Trbovlje Power Station and is a destination for climbers, who scale the more than 50-year-old tower.

## Solomon Islands

**Area:** 10,954 sq mi (28,370 sq km)
**Population:** 700,000
**Capital:** Honiara, pop. 82,000
**Currency:** Solomon Islands dollar
**Religions:** Church of Melanesia, Roman Catholic, South Seas Evangelical, other Christian
**Languages:** Melanesian pidgin, 120 indigenous languages

## Somalia

**Area:** 246,201 sq mi (637,657 sq km)
**Population:** 15,200,000
**Capital:** Mogadishu, pop. 2,082,000
**Currency:** Somali shilling
**Religion:** Sunni Muslim
**Languages:** Somali, Arabic, Italian, English

## South Africa

**Area:** 470,693 sq mi (1,219,090 sq km)
**Population:** 57,700,000
**Capitals:** Pretoria (Tshwane), pop. 2,378,000; Bloemfontein, pop. 546,000; Cape Town, pop. 4,430,000
**Currency:** rand
**Religions:** Zion Christian, Pentecostal, Catholic, Methodist, Dutch Reformed, Anglican, other Christian
**Languages:** IsiZulu, IsiXhosa, Afrikaans, Sepedi, English

## South Korea

**Area:** 38,321 sq mi (99,250 sq km)
**Population:** 51,800,000
**Capital:** Seoul, pop. 9,963,000
**Currency:** South Korean won
**Religions:** Christian, Buddhist
**Languages:** Korean, English

## South Sudan

**Area:** 248,777 sq mi (644,329 sq km)
**Population:** 13,000,000
**Capital:** Juba, pop. 369,000
**Currency:** South Sudan pound
**Religions:** animist, Christian
**Languages:** English, Arabic, regional languages (Dinke, Nuer, Bari, Zande, Shilluk)

## Spain

**Area:** 195,363 sq mi (505,988 sq km)
**Population:** 46,700,000
**Capital:** Madrid, pop. 6,497,000
**Currency:** euro
**Religion:** Roman Catholic
**Languages:** Castilian Spanish, Catalan, Galician, Basque

## Sri Lanka

**Area:** 25,299 sq mi (65,525 sq km)
**Population:** 21,700,000
**Capitals:** Colombo, pop. 600,000; Sri Jayewardenepura Kotte, pop. 103,000
**Currency:** Sri Lankan rupee
**Religions:** Buddhist, Muslim, Hindu, Christian
**Languages:** Sinhala, Tamil

## St. Kitts and Nevis

**Area:** 104 sq mi (269 sq km)
**Population:** 50,000
**Capital:** Basseterre, pop. 14,000
**Currency:** East Caribbean dollar
**Religions:** Anglican, other Protestant, Roman Catholic
**Language:** English

## St. Lucia

**Area:** 238 sq mi (616 sq km)
**Population:** 200,000
**Capital:** Castries, pop. 22,000
**Currency:** East Caribbean dollar
**Religions:** Roman Catholic, Seventh-day Adventist, Pentecostal
**Languages:** English, French patois

## St. Vincent and the Grenadines

**Area:** 150 sq mi (389 sq km)
**Population:** 100,000
**Capital:** Kingstown, pop. 27,000
**Currency:** East Caribbean dollar
**Religions:** Anglican, Methodist, Roman Catholic
**Languages:** English, French patois

## Sudan

**Area:** 718,722 sq mi
(1,861,484 sq km)
**Population:** 41,700,000
**Capital:** Khartoum, pop. 5,534,000
**Currency:** Sudanese pound
**Religions:** Sunni Muslim, indigenous beliefs, Christian
**Languages:** Arabic, Nubian, Ta Bedawie, many diverse dialects of Nilotic, Nilo-Hamitic, Sudanic languages

## Suriname

**Area:** 63,037 sq mi (163,265 sq km)
**Population:** 600,000
**Capital:** Paramaribo, pop. 239,000
**Currency:** Suriname dollar
**Religions:** Hindu, Protestant (predominantly Moravian), Roman Catholic, Muslim, indigenous beliefs
**Languages:** Dutch, English, Sranang Tongo, Hindustani, Javanese

## Sweden

**Area:** 173,732 sq mi
(449,964 sq km)
**Population:** 10,200,000
**Capital:** Stockholm, pop. 1,583,000
**Currency:** Swedish krona
**Religion:** Lutheran
**Languages:** Swedish, Sami, Finnish

## Switzerland

**Area:** 15,940 sq mi
(41,284 sq km)
**Population:** 8,500,000
**Capital:** Bern, pop. 422,000
**Currency:** Swiss franc
**Religions:** Roman Catholic, Protestant, Muslim
**Languages:** German, French, Italian, Romansh

## Syria

**Area:** 71,498 sq mi (185,180 sq km)
**Population:** 18,300,000
**Capital:** Damascus, pop. 2,320,000
**Currency:** Syrian pound
**Religions:** Sunni, other Muslim (includes Alawite, Druze), Christian
**Languages:** Arabic, Kurdish, Armenian, Aramaic, Circassian

## Tajikistan

**Area:** 55,251 sq mi
(143,100 sq km)
**Population:** 9,100,000
**Capital:** Dushanbe, pop. 873,000
**Currency:** somoni
**Religions:** Sunni Muslim, Shiite Muslim
**Languages:** Tajik, Russian

### There's a flag pole as high as a 50-story building in DUSHANBE, TAJIKISTAN.

## Tanzania

**Area:** 364,900 sq mi (945,087 sq km)
**Population:** 59,100,000
**Capitals:** Dar es Salaam, pop. 6,048,000; Dodoma, pop. 262,000
**Currency:** Tanzanian shilling
**Religions:** Muslim, indigenous beliefs, Christian
**Languages:** Kiswahili, Kiunguja, English, Arabic, local languages

## Thailand

**Area:** 198,115 sq mi
(513,115 sq km)
**Population:** 66,200,000
**Capital:** Bangkok, pop. 10,156,000
**Currency:** baht
**Religions:** Buddhist, Muslim
**Languages:** Thai, English, ethnic dialects

## Timor-Leste (East Timor)

**Area:** 5,640 sq mi
(14,609 sq km)
**Population:** 1,200,000
**Capital:** Dili, pop. 281,000
**Currency:** U.S. dollar
**Religion:** Roman Catholic
**Languages:** Tetum, Portuguese, Indonesian, English, indigenous languages

## Togo

**Area:** 21,925 sq mi (56,785 sq km)
**Population:** 8,000,000
**Capital:** Lomé, pop. 1,746,000
**Currency:** Communauté Financière Africaine franc
**Religions:** indigenous beliefs, Christian, Muslim
**Languages:** French, Ewe, Mina, Kabye, Dagomb

## Turkey

**Area:** 300,948 sq mi (779,452 sq km)
**Population:** 81,300,000
**Capital:** Ankara, pop. 4,919,000
**Currency:** new Turkish lira
**Religion:** Muslim (mostly Sunni)
**Languages:** Turkish, Kurdish, Dimli (Zaza), Azeri, Kabardian, Gagauz

## Tonga

**Area:** 289 sq mi (748 sq km)
**Population:** 100,000
**Capital:** Nuku'alofa, pop. 23,000
**Currency:** pa'anga
**Religion:** Christian
**Languages:** Tongan, English

## Turkmenistan

**Area:** 188,456 sq mi (488,100 sq km)
**Population:** 5,900,000
**Capital:** Ashgabat, pop. 810,000
**Currency:** Turkmen manat
**Religions:** Muslim, Eastern Orthodox
**Languages:** Turkmen, Russian, Uzbek

## Trinidad and Tobago

**Area:** 1,980 sq mi (5,128 sq km)
**Population:** 1,400,000
**Capital:** Port of Spain, pop. 544,000
**Currency:** Trinidad and Tobago dollar
**Religions:** Roman Catholic, Hindu, Anglican, Baptist
**Languages:** English, Caribbean Hindustani, French, Spanish, Chinese

## Tuvalu

**Area:** 10 sq mi (26 sq km)
**Population:** 10,000
**Capital:** Funafuti, pop. 7,000
**Currencies:** Australian dollar; Tuvaluan dollar
**Religion:** Church of Tuvalu (Congregationalist)
**Languages:** Tuvaluan, English, Samoan, Kiribati

**LEATHERBACK SEA TURTLES nest on the beaches of TRINIDAD and TOBAGO.**

**Tuvalu's land area has grown by about 3 PERCENT since the EARLY 1970s.**

## Tunisia

**Area:** 63,170 sq mi (163,610 sq km)
**Population:** 11,600,000
**Capital:** Tunis, pop. 2,291,000
**Currency:** Tunisian dinar
**Religion:** Muslim
**Languages:** Arabic, French

## Uganda

**Area:** 93,104 sq mi (241,139 sq km)
**Population:** 44,100,000
**Capital:** Kampala, pop. 2,986,000
**Currency:** Ugandan shilling
**Religions:** Protestant, Roman Catholic, Muslim
**Languages:** English, Ganda, other local languages, Kiswahili, Arabic

## Ukraine

**Area:** 233,030 sq mi
(603,550 sq km)
**Population:** 42,300,000
**Capital:** Kiev, pop. 2,957,000
**Currency:** hryvnia
**Religions:** Ukrainian Orthodox, Orthodox, Ukrainian
Greek Catholic
**Languages:** Ukrainian, Russian

## United Kingdom

**Area:** 93,788 sq mi
(242,910 sq km)
**Population:** 66,400,000
**Capital:** London, pop. 9,046,000
**Currency:** British pound
**Religions:** Anglican, Roman Catholic,
Presbyterian, Methodist
**Languages:** English, Welsh, Scottish form of Gaelic

## United Arab Emirates

**Area:** 30,000 sq mi
(77,700 sq km)
**Population:** 9,500,000
**Capital:** Abu Dhabi,
pop. 1,420,000
**Currency:** Emirati dirham
**Religion:** Muslim
**Languages:** Arabic, Persian, English, Hindi, Urdu

## United States

**Area:** 3,794,083 sq mi
(9,826,630 sq km)
**Population:** 328,000,000
**Capital:** Washington, D.C.,
pop. 5,207,000
**Currency:** U.S. dollar
**Religions:** Protestant, Roman Catholic
**Languages:** English, Spanish

# SNAPSHOT
# Zambia

Victoria Falls on the border of
Zambia and Zimbabwe

**COLOR KEY**   ● Africa   ● Australia, New Zealand, and Oceania

## Uruguay

**Area:** 68,037 sq mi
(176,215 sq km)
**Population:** 3,500,000
**Capital:** Montevideo, pop. 1,737,000
**Currency:** Uruguayan peso
**Religion:** Roman Catholic
**Language:** Spanish

There are about **FOUR TIMES MORE COWS in Uruguay than people.**

## Uzbekistan

**Area:** 172,742 sq mi
(447,400 sq km)
**Population:** 32,900,000
**Capital:** Tashkent,
pop. 2,464,000
**Currency:** Uzbekistani sum
**Religions:** Muslim (mostly Sunni), Eastern Orthodox
**Languages:** Uzbek, Russian, Tajik

## Vanuatu

**Area:** 4,707 sq mi (12,190 sq km)
**Population:** 300,000
**Capital:** Port Vila, pop. 53,000
**Currency:** vatu
**Religions:** Presbyterian, Anglican, Roman Catholic, other Christian, indigenous beliefs
**Languages:** more than 100 local languages, pidgin (known as Bislama or Bichelama)

## Vatican City

**Area:** 0.2 sq mi (0.4 sq km)
**Population:** 800
**Capital:** Vatican City, pop. 800
**Currency:** euro
**Religion:** Roman Catholic
**Languages:** Italian, Latin, French

## Venezuela

**Area:** 352,144 sq mi
(912,050 sq km)
**Population:** 31,800,000
**Capital:** Caracas, pop. 2,935,000
**Currency:** bolivar
**Religion:** Roman Catholic
**Languages:** Spanish, numerous indigenous dialects

## Vietnam

**Area:** 127,844 sq mi
(331,114 sq km)
**Population:** 94,700,000
**Capital:** Hanoi, pop. 4,283,000
**Currency:** dong
**Religions:** Buddhist, Roman Catholic
**Languages:** Vietnamese, English, French, Chinese, Khmer

## Yemen

**Area:** 207,286 sq mi
(536,869 sq km)
**Population:** 28,900,000
**Capital:** Sanaa, pop. 2,779,000
**Currency:** Yemeni rial
**Religions:** Muslim, including Shaf'i (Sunni) and Zaydi (Shiite)
**Language:** Arabic

## Zambia

**Area:** 290,586 sq mi
(752,614 sq km)
**Population:** 17,700,000
**Capital:** Lusaka, pop. 2,524,000
**Currency:** Zambian kwacha
**Religions:** Christian, Muslim, Hindu
**Languages:** English, Bemba, Kaonda, Lozi, Lunda, Luvale, Nyanja, Tonga, about 70 other indigenous languages

## Zimbabwe

**Area:** 150,872 sq mi
(390,757 sq km)
**Population:** 14,000,000
**Capital:** Harare, pop. 1,515,000
**Currency:** Zimbabwean dollar
**Religions:** Syncretic (part Christian, part indigenous beliefs), Christian, indigenous beliefs
**Languages:** English, Shona, Sindebele, tribal dialects

# THE POLITICAL UNITED STATES

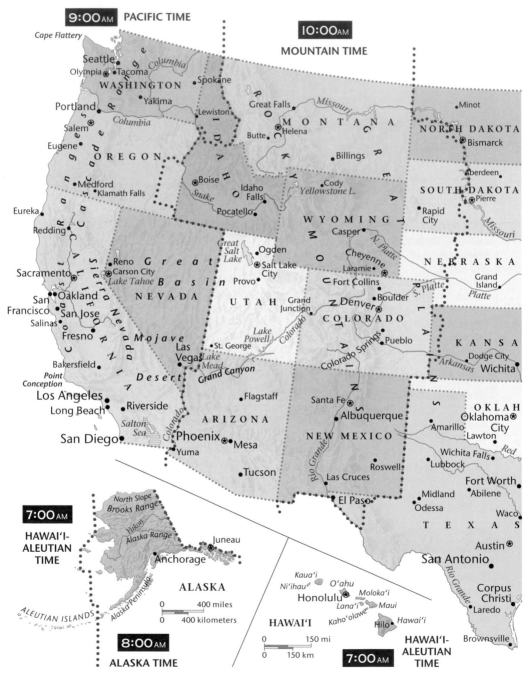

**9:00 AM** PACIFIC TIME

**10:00 AM** MOUNTAIN TIME

Cape Flattery

Seattle
Olympia ⊛ Tacoma
WASHINGTON · Spokane
· Yakima
Portland
Salem ⊛
Columbia
Eugene
OREGON
· Medford
Klamath Falls

Eureka
Redding

Sacramento ⊛
San
Francisco · San Jose
Oakland
Salinas
Fresno
CALIFORNIA
Bakersfield
Point
Conception
Los Angeles
Long Beach
San Diego

· Great Falls
MONTANA
Butte · · Helena
· Billings

· Boise
IDAHO
Idaho
Falls
Snake
Pocatello

Reno ·
Carson City
Lake Tahoe
NEVADA
Sierra Nevada
Mojave
Las
Vegas
Desert
Lake
Mead
Grand Canyon
Colorado

Great
Salt
Lake
· Ogden
⊛ Salt Lake
City
Provo ·
UTAH
Grand
Junction
Lake
Powell
Colorado
St. George ·

WYOMING
· Casper
N. Platte
Cheyenne ⊛
Laramie ·
· Fort Collins
· Boulder
Denver ⊛
COLORADO
Colorado Springs ·
· Pueblo

NORTH DAKOTA
· Minot
⊛ Bismarck

· Aberdeen
SOUTH DAKOTA
· Pierre
Rapid
City ·
Missouri

NEBRASKA
Grand
Island ·
S. Platte
Platte

KANSAS
Dodge City ·
Arkansas
· Wichita

Flagstaff ·
ARIZONA
Phoenix ⊛ · Mesa
· Yuma
· Tucson

Santa Fe ⊛
· Albuquerque
NEW MEXICO
Rio Grande
· Roswell
· Las Cruces
El Paso ·

Oklahoma ⊛
City
· Lawton
OKLAH
Amarillo ·
Wichita Falls · Red
· Lubbock
· Midland · Abilene
· Odessa
TEXAS
Fort Worth
· Waco
Austin ⊛
San Antonio ·
Corpus
Christi
· Laredo
· Brownsville

**7:00 AM**
HAWAI'I-
ALEUTIAN
TIME

North Slope
Brooks Range
Yukon
Alaska Range
Juneau ⊛
· Anchorage
ALASKA
ALEUTIAN ISLANDS
Alaska Peninsula

0   400 miles
0   400 kilometers

**8:00 AM**
ALASKA TIME

Kaua'i
Ni'ihau
O'ahu
Moloka'i
Honolulu
Lana'i · Maui
HAWAI'I
Kaho'olawe
Hilo · Hawai'i

0   150 mi
0   150 km

**7:00 AM**
HAWAI'I-
ALEUTIAN
TIME

The United States is made up of 50 states joined like a giant quilt. Each is unique, but together they make a national fabric held together by a constitution and a federal government. State boundaries, outlined in dotted lines on the map, set apart internal political units within the country. The national capital—Washington, D.C.—is marked by a star in a double circle. The capital of each state is marked by a star in a single circle.

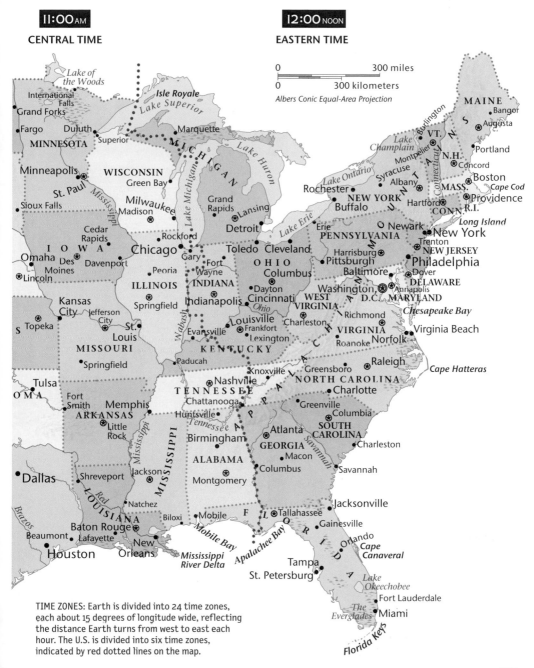

**11:00 AM**
CENTRAL TIME

**12:00 NOON**
EASTERN TIME

0 — 300 miles
0 — 300 kilometers
Albers Conic Equal-Area Projection

TIME ZONES: Earth is divided into 24 time zones, each about 15 degrees of longitude wide, reflecting the distance Earth turns from west to east each hour. The U.S. is divided into six time zones, indicated by red dotted lines on the map.

# THE PHYSICAL UNITED STATES

Mt. St. Helens 8,366 ft, 2,550 m
Mt. Rainier 14,411 ft 4,392 m
Mt. Hood 11,239 ft 3,425 m
CASCADE RANGE
COAST RANGE
Snake
Columbia
Great Sandy Desert
Blue Mountains
Columbia Plateau
Snake
Bitterroot Range
Salmon River Mountains
ROCKY
Flathead Lake
Milk
Missouri
Fort Peck Lake
Yellowstone
Lake Sakakawea
Little Missouri
Heart
Missouri
White Butte 3,506 ft 1,069 m
Lake Oahe
Geographical Center of the 50 United States
White
James
Yellowstone Lake
Grand Teton 13,770 ft 4,197 m
Snake River Plain
Absaroka Range
Bighorn Mts.
Harney Peak 7,242 ft 2,207 m
Black Hills
Niobrara
Sand Hills
N. Platte
Platte
Sierra Nevada
Sacramento Valley
San Joaquin
Lake Tahoe
Great Salt Lake
Great Basin
Wasatch Range
Uinta Mts.
Great Divide Basin
MOUNTAINS
Laramie Mts.
Front Range
S. Platte
Geographical Center of the 48 Contiguous United States.
Smoky Hills
San Joaquin Valley
Mt. Whitney 14,494 ft 4,418 m
Death Valley
Mojave
Lake Powell
Colorado
Mt. Elbert 4,399 m 14,433 ft
Pikes Peak 14,110 ft 4,301 m
San Juan Mts.
Sangre de Cristo Mts.
Arkansas
Red Hills
Lowest Point in North America -282 ft, -86 m
Lake Mead
Grand Canyon
Desert
Colorado
Plateau
Painted Desert
Black Mesa 4,973 ft 1,516 m
GREAT PLAINS
Cimarron
Canadian
Channel Islands
Salton Sea
Imperial Valley
Humphreys Peak 12,637 ft 3,852 m
Colorado
Gila
Sonoran Desert
Salt
Rio Grande
Llano Estacado
Brazos
Guadalupe Peak 8,749 ft 2,667 m
Sacramento Mts.
Pecos
Edwards Plateau
Colorado
Rio Grande

0 400 miles
0 400 kilometers

North Slope
Brooks Range
Yukon
(Mt. McKinley) Denali 6,190 m, 20,310 ft
Highest Point in North America
Alaska Range
Alexander Archipelago
Aleutian Islands
Alaska Peninsula

Kaua'i
Ni'ihau
O'ahu
Moloka'i
Lana'i
Maui
Kaho'olawe
Mauna Kea 13,679 ft 4,169 m
Hawai'i

0 150 miles
0 150 kilometers

ALASKA AND HAWAII:
In addition to the states located on the main landmass, the U.S. has two states—Alaska and Hawaii—that are not directly connected to the other 48 states. If Alaska and Hawaii were shown in their correct relative sizes and locations, the map would not fit on these pages.

Stretching from the Atlantic Ocean in the east to the Pacific Ocean in the west, the United States is the third largest country (by area) in the world. Its physical diversity ranges from mountains to fertile plains and dry deserts. Shading on the map indicates changes in elevation, while colors show different vegetation patterns.

0        400 miles

0        400 kilometers

*Albers Conic Equal-Area Projection*

**NATURAL VEGETATION**

- NEEDLELEAF FOREST
- BROADLEAF FOREST
- MIXED FOREST
- GRASSLAND
- TROPICAL VEGETATION
- DESERT
- TUNDRA

**321**

# THE STATES

**From sea to shining sea,** the United States of America is a nation of diversity. In the 244 years since its creation, the nation has grown to become home to a wide range of peoples, industries, and cultures. The following pages present a general overview of all 50 states in the U.S.

The country is generally divided into five large regions: the Northeast, the Southeast, the Midwest, the Southwest, and the West. Though loosely defined, these zones tend to share important similarities, including climate, history, and geography. The color key below provides a guide to which states are in each region.

The flags of each state and highlights of demography and industry are also included. These details offer a brief overview of each state.

In addition, each state's official flower and bird are identified.

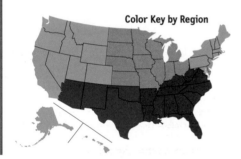

**Color Key by Region**

## Arizona

**Area:** 113,998 sq mi (295,256 sq km)
**Population:** 7,171,646
**Capital:** Phoenix, pop. 1,626,078
**Largest city:** Phoenix, pop. 1,626,078
**Industry:** Real estate, manufactured goods, retail, state and local government, transportation and public utilities, wholesale trade, health services
**State flower/bird:** Saguaro/cactus wren

In Arizona, **CUTTING DOWN A SAGUARO CACTUS** could **RESULT** in **JAIL TIME.**

## Arkansas

**Area:** 53,179 sq mi (137,732 sq km)
**Population:** 3,013,825
**Capital:** Little Rock, pop. 198,606
**Largest city:** Little Rock, pop. 198,606
**Industry:** Services, food processing, paper products, transportation, metal products, machinery, electronics
**State flower/bird:** Apple blossom/mockingbird

## Alabama

**Area:** 52,419 sq mi (135,765 sq km)
**Population:** 4,887,871
**Capital:** Montgomery, pop. 199,518
**Largest city:** Birmingham, pop. 210,710
**Industry:** Retail and wholesale trade, services, government, finance, insurance, real estate, transportation, construction, communication
**State flower/bird:** Camellia/northern flicker

## California

**Area:** 163,696 sq mi (423,972 sq km)
**Population:** 39,557,045
**Capital:** Sacramento, pop. 501,901
**Largest city:** Los Angeles, pop. 3,999,759
**Industry:** Electronic components and equipment, computers and computer software, tourism, food processing, entertainment, clothing
**State flower/bird:** Golden poppy/California quail

## Alaska

**Area:** 663,267 sq mi (1,717,862 sq km)
**Population:** 737,438
**Capital:** Juneau, pop. 32,094
**Largest city:** Anchorage, pop. 294,356
**Industry:** Petroleum products, government, services, trade
**State flower/bird:** Forget-me-not/willow ptarmigan

## Colorado

**Area:** 104,094 sq mi (269,602 sq km)
**Population:** 5,695,564
**Capital:** Denver, pop. 704,621
**Largest city:** Denver, pop. 704,621
**Industry:** Real estate, government, durable goods, communications, health and other services, nondurable goods, transportation
**State flower/bird:** Columbine/lark bunting

**COLOR KEY** ● Northeast ● Southeast

## Connecticut

**Area:** 5,543 sq mi (14,357 sq km)
**Population:** 3,572,665
**Capital:** Hartford, pop. 123,400
**Largest city:** Bridgeport, pop. 146,579
**Industry:** Transportation equipment, metal products, machinery, electrical equipment, printing and publishing, scientific instruments, insurance
**State flower/bird:** Mountain laurel/robin

## Delaware

**Area:** 2,489 sq mi (6,447 sq km)
**Population:** 967,171
**Capital:** Dover, pop. 37,538
**Largest city:** Wilmington, pop. 71,106
**Industry:** Food processing, chemicals, rubber and plastic products, scientific instruments, printing and publishing, financial services
**State flower/bird:** Peach blossom/blue hen chicken

## Florida

**Area:** 65,755 sq mi (170,304 sq km)
**Population:** 21,299,325
**Capital:** Tallahassee, pop. 191,049
**Largest city:** Jacksonville, pop. 892,062
**Industry:** Tourism, health services, business services, communications, banking, electronic equipment, insurance
**State flower/bird:** Orange blossom/mockingbird

## Georgia

**Area:** 59,425 sq mi (153,910 sq km)
**Population:** 10,519,475
**Capital:** Atlanta, pop. 486,290
**Largest city:** Atlanta, pop. 486,290
**Industry:** Textiles and clothing, transportation equipment, food processing, paper products, chemicals, electrical equipment, tourism
**State flower/bird:** Cherokee rose/brown thrasher

## Hawaii

**Area:** 10,931 sq mi (28,311 sq km)
**Population:** 1,420,491
**Capital:** Honolulu, pop. 350,395
**Largest city:** Honolulu, pop. 350,395
**Industry:** Tourism, trade, finance, food processing, petroleum refining, stone, clay, glass products
**State flower/bird:** Hibiscus/Hawaiian goose (nene)

## Idaho

**Area:** 83,570 sq mi (216,447 sq km)
**Population:** 1,754,208
**Capital:** Boise, pop. 226,570
**Largest city:** Boise, pop. 226,570
**Industry:** Electronics and computer equipment, tourism, food processing, forest products, mining
**State flower/bird:** Syringa (Lewis's mock orange)/mountain bluebird

## Illinois

**Area:** 57,914 sq mi (149,998 sq km)
**Population:** 12,741,080
**Capital:** Springfield, pop. 114,868
**Largest city:** Chicago, pop. 2,716,450
**Industry:** Industrial machinery, electronic equipment, food processing, chemicals, metals, printing and publishing, rubber and plastics, motor vehicles
**State flower/bird:** Violet/cardinal

## Indiana

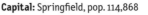

**Area:** 36,418 sq mi (94,322 sq km)
**Population:** 6,691,878
**Capital:** Indianapolis, pop. 863,002
**Largest city:** Indianapolis, pop. 863,002
**Industry:** Transportation equipment, steel, pharmaceutical and chemical products, machinery, petroleum, coal
**State flower/bird:** Peony/cardinal

## Iowa

**Area:** 56,272 sq mi (145,743 sq km)
**Population:** 3,156,145
**Capital:** Des Moines, pop. 217,521
**Largest city:** Des Moines, pop. 217,521
**Industry:** Real estate, health services, industrial machinery, food processing, construction
**State flower/bird:** Wild rose/American goldfinch

An enormous **BALL OF POPCORN**—made from 900 pounds (408 kg) of popcorn—resides in **SAC CITY, IOWA.**

● Midwest ● Southwest ● West

## Kansas

**Area:** 82,277 sq mi (213,097 sq km)
**Population:** 2,911,505
**Capital:** Topeka, pop. 126,587
**Largest city:** Wichita, pop. 390,591
**Industry:** Aircraft manufacturing, transportation equipment, construction, food processing, printing and publishing, health care
**State flower/bird:** Sunflower/western meadowlark

## Kentucky

**Area:** 40,409 sq mi (104,659 sq km)
**Population:** 4,468,402
**Capital:** Frankfort, pop. 27,621
**Largest city:** Louisville, pop. 621,349
**Industry:** Manufacturing, services, government, finance, insurance, real estate, retail trade, transportation, wholesale trade, construction, mining
**State flower/bird:** Goldenrod/cardinal

## Louisiana

**Area:** 51,840 sq mi (134,265 sq km)
**Population:** 4,659,978
**Capital:** Baton Rouge, pop. 225,374
**Largest city:** New Orleans, pop. 393,292
**Industry:** Chemicals, petroleum products, food processing, health services, tourism, oil and natural gas extraction, paper products
**State flower/bird:** Magnolia/brown pelican

## PROFESSIONAL WRESTLING was once BANNED in LOUISIANA.

## Maine

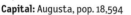

**Area:** 35,385 sq mi (91,646 sq km)
**Population:** 1,338,404
**Capital:** Augusta, pop. 18,594
**Largest city:** Portland, pop. 66,882
**Industry:** Health services, tourism, forest products, leather products, electrical equipment
**State flower/bird:** White pine cone and tassel/chickadee

## Maryland

**Area:** 12,407 sq mi (32,133 sq km)
**Population:** 6,042,718
**Capital:** Annapolis, pop. 39,321
**Largest city:** Baltimore, pop. 611,648
**Industry:** Real estate, federal government, health services, business services, engineering services
**State flower/bird:** Black-eyed Susan/northern (Baltimore) oriole

## Massachusetts

**Area:** 10,555 sq mi (27,336 sq km)
**Population:** 6,902,149
**Capital:** Boston, pop. 685,094
**Largest city:** Boston, pop. 685,094
**Industry:** Electrical equipment, machinery, metal products, scientific instruments, printing and publishing, tourism
**State flower/bird:** Mayflower/chickadee

## Michigan

**Area:** 96,716 sq mi (250,495 sq km)
**Population:** 9,995,915
**Capital:** Lansing, pop. 116,986
**Largest city:** Detroit, pop. 673,104
**Industry:** Motor vehicles and parts, machinery, metal products, office furniture, tourism, chemicals
**State flower/bird:** Apple blossom/robin

## Minnesota

**Area:** 86,939 sq mi (225,172 sq km)
**Population:** 5,611,179
**Capital:** St. Paul, pop. 306,621
**Largest city:** Minneapolis, pop. 422,331
**Industry:** Real estate, banking and insurance, industrial machinery, printing and publishing, food processing, scientific equipment
**State flower/bird:** Showy lady's slipper/common loon

## Mississippi

**Area:** 48,430 sq mi (125,434 sq km)
**Population:** 2,986,530
**Capital:** Jackson, pop. 166,965
**Largest city:** Jackson, pop. 166,965
**Industry:** Petroleum products, health services, electronic equipment, transportation, banking, forest products, communications
**State flower/bird:** Magnolia/mockingbird

**COLOR KEY** ● Northeast ● Southeast

## Missouri

**Area:** 69,704 sq mi (180,534 sq km)
**Population:** 6,126,452
**Capital:** Jefferson City, pop. 42,895
**Largest city:** Kansas City, pop. 488,943
**Industry:** Transportation equipment, food processing, chemicals, electrical equipment, metal products
**State flower/bird:** Hawthorn/eastern bluebird

## Montana

**Area:** 147,042 sq mi (380,840 sq km)
**Population:** 1,062,305
**Capital:** Helena, pop. 31,429
**Largest city:** Billings, pop. 109,642
**Industry:** Forest products, food processing, mining, construction, tourism
**State flower/bird:** Bitterroot/western meadowlark

## Nebraska

**Area:** 77,354 sq mi (200,346 sq km)
**Population:** 1,929,268
**Capital:** Lincoln, pop. 284,736
**Largest city:** Omaha, pop. 466,893
**Industry:** Food processing, machinery, electrical equipment, printing and publishing
**State flower/bird:** Goldenrod/western meadowlark

## Nevada

**Area:** 110,561 sq mi (286,352 sq km)
**Population:** 3,034,392
**Capital:** Carson City, pop. 54,745
**Largest city:** Las Vegas, pop. 641,676
**Industry:** Tourism and gaming, mining, printing and publishing, food processing, electrical equipment
**State flower/bird:** Sagebrush/mountain bluebird

## New Hampshire

**Area:** 9,350 sq mi (24,216 sq km)
**Population:** 1,356,458
**Capital:** Concord, pop. 43,019
**Largest city:** Manchester, pop. 111,196
**Industry:** Machinery, electronics, metal products
**State flower/bird:** Purple lilac/purple finch

## New Jersey
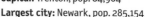
**Area:** 8,721 sq mi (22,588 sq km)
**Population:** 8,908,520
**Capital:** Trenton, pop. 84,964
**Largest city:** Newark, pop. 285,154
**Industry:** Machinery, electronics, metal products, chemicals
**State flower/bird:** Violet/American goldfinch

## New Mexico

**Area:** 121,590 sq mi (314,917 sq km)
**Population:** 2,095,428
**Capital:** Santa Fe, pop. 83,776
**Largest city:** Albuquerque, pop. 558,545
**Industry:** Electronic equipment, state and local government, real estate, business services, federal government, oil and gas extraction, health services
**State flower/bird:** Yucca/roadrunner

## New York

**Area:** 54,556 sq mi (141,300 sq km)
**Population:** 19,542,209
**Capital:** Albany, pop. 98,251
**Largest city:** New York City, pop. 8,622,698
**Industry:** Printing and publishing, machinery, computer products, finance, tourism
**State flower/bird:** Rose/eastern bluebird

**Coyotes, skunks, deer, rabbits, opossum, and snapping turtles have all been spotted in NEW YORK CITY'S PARKS.**

## North Carolina

**Area:** 53,819 sq mi (139,390 sq km)
**Population:** 10,383,620
**Capital:** Raleigh, pop. 464,758
**Largest city:** Charlotte, pop. 859,035
**Industry:** Real estate, health services, chemicals, tobacco products, finance, textiles
**State flower/bird:** Flowering dogwood/cardinal

## North Dakota

**Area:** 70,700 sq mi (183,113 sq km)
**Population:** 760,077
**Capital:** Bismarck, pop. 72,865
**Largest city:** Fargo, pop. 122,359
**Industry:** Services, government, finance, construction, transportation, oil and gas
**State flower/bird:** Wild prairie rose/western meadowlark

## Ohio

**Area:** 44,825 sq mi (116,097 sq km)
**Population:** 11,689,442
**Capital:** Columbus, pop. 879,170
**Largest city:** Columbus, pop. 879,170
**Industry:** Transportation equipment, metal products, machinery, food processing, electrical equipment
**State flower/bird:** Scarlet carnation/cardinal

## Oklahoma

**Area:** 69,898 sq mi (181,036 sq km)
**Population:** 3,943,079
**Capital:** Oklahoma City, pop. 643,648
**Largest city:** Oklahoma City, pop. 643,648
**Industry:** Manufacturing, services, government, finance, insurance, real estate
**State flower/bird:** Mistletoe/scissor-tailed flycatcher

## Oregon

**Area:** 98,381 sq mi (254,806 sq km)
**Population:** 4,190,713
**Capital:** Salem, pop. 169,798
**Largest city:** Portland, pop. 647,805
**Industry:** Real estate, retail and wholesale trade, electronic equipment, health services, construction, forest products, business services
**State flower/bird:** Oregon grape/western meadowlark

## Pennsylvania

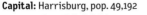

**Area:** 46,055 sq mi (119,283 sq km)
**Population:** 12,807,060
**Capital:** Harrisburg, pop. 49,192
**Largest city:** Philadelphia, pop. 1,580,863
**Industry:** Machinery, printing and publishing, forest products, metal products
**State flower/bird:** Mountain laurel/ruffed grouse

## Rhode Island

**Area:** 1,545 sq mi (4,002 sq km)
**Population:** 1,057,315
**Capital:** Providence, pop. 180,393
**Largest city:** Providence, pop. 180,393
**Industry:** Health services, business services, silver and jewelry products, metal products
**State flower/bird:** Violet/Rhode Island red

## South Carolina

**Area:** 32,020 sq mi (82,932 sq km)
**Population:** 5,084,127
**Capital:** Columbia, pop. 133,114
**Largest city:** Charleston, pop. 134,875
**Industry:** Service industries, tourism, chemicals, textiles, machinery, forest products
**State flower/bird:** Yellow jessamine/Carolina wren

# 3 cool things about SOUTH CAROLINA

1. The world's largest fire hydrant is in Columbia, South Carolina. The public work of art, known as Busted Plug, is as tall as a four-story building and is said to be sturdy enough to withstand a tornado.

2. The hottest pepper on the planet is grown on a farm on Fort Mill, South Carolina. The Carolina Reaper is said to be more than 200 times hotter than the spiciest jalapeño pepper.

3. South Carolina's Morgan Island is home to a population of some 3,500 Rhesus monkeys. Only researchers are allowed on the federally protected "Monkey Island," which is closed off to the general public.

## South Dakota

**Area:** 77,117 sq mi (199,732 sq km)
**Population:** 882,235
**Capital:** Pierre, pop. 14,004
**Largest city:** Sioux Falls, pop. 176,888
**Indus try:** Finance, services, manufacturing, government, retail trade, transportation and utilities, wholesale trade, construction, mining
**State flower/bird:** Pasqueflower/ring-necked pheasant

**COLOR KEY** ● Northeast ● Southeast

## Tennessee

**Area:** 42,143 sq mi (109,151 sq km)
**Population:** 6,770,010
**Capital:** Nashville, pop. 667,560
**Largest city:** Nashville, pop. 667,560
**Industry:** Service industries, chemicals, transportation equipment, processed foods, machinery
**State flower/bird:** Iris/mockingbird

## Texas

**Area:** 268,581 sq mi (695,624 sq km)
**Population:** 28,701,845
**Capital:** Austin, pop. 950,715
**Largest city:** Houston, pop. 2,312,717
**Industry:** Chemicals, machinery, electronics and computers, food products, petroleum and natural gas, transportation equipment
**State flower/bird:** Bluebonnet/mockingbird

## Utah

**Area:** 84,899 sq mi (219,888 sq km)
**Population:** 3,161,105
**Capital:** Salt Lake City, pop. 200,544
**Largest city:** Salt Lake City, pop. 200,544
**Industry:** Government, manufacturing, real estate, construction, health services, business services, banking
**State flower/bird:** Sego lily/California gull

## Vermont

**Area:** 9,614 sq mi (24,901 sq km)
**Population:** 626,299
**Capital:** Montpelier, pop. 7,484
**Largest city:** Burlington, pop. 42,239
**Industry:** Health services, tourism, finance, real estate, computer components, electrical parts, printing and publishing, machine tools
**State flower/bird:** Red clover/hermit thrush

## Virginia

**Area:** 42,774 sq mi (110,785 sq km)
**Population:** 8,517,685
**Capital:** Richmond, pop. 227,032
**Largest city:** Virginia Beach, pop. 450,435
**Industry:** Food processing, communication and electronic equipment, transportation equipment, printing, shipbuilding, textiles
**State flower/bird:** Flowering dogwood/cardinal

## Washington

**Area:** 71,300 sq mi (184,666 sq km)
**Population:** 7,535,591
**Capital:** Olympia, pop. 51,609
**Largest city:** Seattle, pop. 724,745
**Industry:** Aerospace, tourism, food processing, forest products, paper products, industrial machinery, printing and publishing, metals, computer software
**State flower/bird:** Coast rhododendron/Amer. goldfinch

**WASHINGTON STATE FERRIES carry 22 million passengers per year—making them the WORLD'S MOST POPULAR ferry system.**

## West Virginia

**Area:** 24,230 sq mi (62,755 sq km)
**Population:** 1,805,832
**Capital:** Charleston, pop. 47,929
**Largest city:** Charleston, pop. 47,929
**Industry:** Tourism, coal mining, chemicals, metal manufacturing, forest products, stone, clay, oil, glass products
**State flower/bird:** Rhododendron/cardinal

## Wisconsin

**Area:** 65,498 sq mi (169,639 sq km)
**Population:** 5,813,568
**Capital:** Madison, pop. 255,214
**Largest city:** Milwaukee, pop. 595,351
**Industry:** Industrial machinery, paper products, food processing, metal products, electronic equipment, transportation
**State flower/bird:** Wood violet/robin

## Wyoming

**Area:** 97,814 sq mi (253,337 sq km)
**Population:** 577,737
**Capital:** Cheyenne, pop. 63,624
**Largest city:** Cheyenne, pop. 63,624
**Industry:** Oil and natural gas, mining, generation of electricity, chemicals, tourism
**State flower/bird:** Indian paintbrush/western meadowlark

● Midwest ● Southwest ● West

# THE TERRITORIES

**The United States has 14 territories—** political divisions that are not states. Three of these are in the Caribbean Sea, and the other 11 are in the Pacific Ocean.

St. John, U.S. Virgin Islands

Convention Center, San Juan, Puerto Rico

Talofofo Falls, Guam

## U.S. CARIBBEAN TERRITORIES

### Puerto Rico

**Area:** 3,508 sq mi (9,086 sq km)
**Population:** 3,337,177
**Capital:** San Juan, pop. 2,454,000
**Languages:** Spanish, English

### U.S. Virgin Islands

**Area:** 149 sq mi (386 sq km)
**Population:** 106,977
**Capital:** Charlotte Amalie, pop. 52,000
**Languages:** English, Spanish or Spanish Creole, French or French Creole

## U.S. PACIFIC TERRITORIES

### American Samoa

**Area:** 77 sq mi (199 sq km)
**Population:** 50,826
**Capital:** Pago Pago, pop. 49,000
**Language:** Samoan

### Guam

**Area:** 217 sq mi (561 sq km)
**Population:** 167,772
**Capital:** Hagåtña (Agana), pop. 147,000
**Languages:** English, Chamorro, Philippine languages

### Northern Mariana Islands
**Area:** 184 sq mi (477 sq km)
**Population:** 51,994
**Capital:** Saipan, pop. 51,000
**Languages:** Philippine languages, Chinese, Chamorro, English

### Other U.S. Territories
Baker Island, Howland Island, Jarvis Island, Johnston Atoll, Kingman Reef, Midway Islands, Palmyra Atoll, Wake Island, Navassa Island (in the Caribbean)

*Figures for capital cities vary widely between sources because of differences in the way the area is defined and other projection methods.*

## THE U.S. CAPITAL

### District of Columbia
**Area:** 68 sq mi (177 sq km)
**Population:** 702,455

Abraham Lincoln, who was president during the Civil War and a strong opponent of slavery, is remembered in the Lincoln Memorial, located at the opposite end of the National Mall from the U.S. Capitol Building.

**COLOR KEY** ● Territories ● Northeast

# BY THE NUMBERS!

## RECORD SETTERS IN THE NATIONAL PARKS

**Highest, longest, hottest, most visited:** Our national parks are not only natural wonders—they're record setters! Check out the titles that these parks hold.

### 20,320 FEET (6,194 M)

**THE FEAT:** Highest Point in North America
**THE PLACE:** Denali National Park & Preserve (Mt. McKinley)

Rising from the Alaska Range, Denali is a block of granite that is half covered in permanent snowfields. Its name comes from the Athabaskan Indians and means "Great One."

### 134°F (57°C)

**THE FEAT:** Hottest Place on Earth
**THE PLACE:** Death Valley National Park

Death Valley holds the record for world's highest air temperature—recorded at Furnace Creek in 1913. It's also the lowest place in North America—the park's Badwater Basin is 282 feet (86 m) below sea level. The average annual rainfall in Death Valley, which is located in California and Nevada, is less than two inches (5 cm), making it the driest place in North America.

### 400 MILES (644 KM)

**THE FEAT:** Longest Known Cave System in the World
**THE PLACE:** Mammoth Cave system, Mammoth Cave National Park

Some 400 miles (644 km) of Kentucky's Mammoth Cave system have been explored, but no one really knows how far it extends, as new caverns continue to be discovered. Over 4,000 years ago, the first humans entered the cave, which contains more than 1,000 stalactite formations.

### 10,099,276 PEOPLE

**THE FEAT:** Most Visited National Park
**THE PLACE:** Great Smoky Mountains National Park

Attracting more than 10 million visitors per year, Great Smoky Mountains is the nation's busiest national park! Its central location in North Carolina and Tennessee is within a day or two's drive for two-thirds of the U.S. population. Famous for its diversity of plant and animal life, the park is home to some 65 species of mammals, more than 200 varieties of birds, 67 native fish species, and more than 80 types of reptiles and amphibians!

# Wacky World ←

check out these **bizarre roadside** attractions from around the globe.

Hop in your car and get out your camera—you'll definitely want some selfies with these strange sights. Found all over the globe, bizarre roadside attractions draw visitors who want to add a little wackiness to their vacations. Take a glimpse at five of the world's weirdest stop-and-stare spots.

## SHIN-YOKOHAMA RAMEN MUSEUM
**Yokohama, Japan**

Slurp up some fun at a museum dedicated to the beloved noodle dish. Popular in Japan for more than half a century, ramen today comes in different styles specific to the country's regions. Taste them all at the museum's nine restaurants, decide which you like best, and then purchase as many packets as you like to take home. In between bites, watch how the noodles are made, read about their history, and stroll sets made to mimic a 1950s Tokyo neighborhood.

## SUSPENDED WATER TAP
**Ypres, Belgium**

What's the trick to this floating faucet? A clear pipe inside the falling water creates the illusion. The supportive pipe carries water from a pool on the ground to the rear of the faucet. The water loops around and is spewed back out into the pool. That's why it looks like an unending flow of water. Now we're thirsty.

**Check out the book!**

125 WACKY Roadside Attractions

## DRAGON BRIDGE
**Da Nang, Vietnam**

Drivers cruising through one Vietnamese metropolis can see a pretty epic sight: a mythical monster perched on one of the city's bridges. The six-lane crossing, which is the length of 55 school buses, was designed to resemble a dragon. (In Vietnamese culture, dragons symbolize good fortune.) The beastly bridge even "breathes" fire! A blowtorch-like device in the dragon's mouth can be timed to spew flames. This dragon-shaped bridge is really slaying it.

## LUCY THE ELEPHANT
### Margate City, New Jersey, U.S.A.

No, you're not seeing things. That is a giant elephant on the horizon at the Jersey Shore. Her name is Lucy, and she's not your average pachyderm. All elephants are huge, but Lucy, made of wood and tin, stands 65 feet (19.8 m) high—taller than a six-story building. Built in 1881, Lucy has served as a jumbo-size billboard, a beach house, and a tavern. How do visitors get in? Her 22-foot (6.7-m)-tall legs hide spiral staircases that lead the way.

Over the years, Lucy has withstood fires, hurricanes, and raging parties in her belly.

"Floating" faucets can also be found in Canada, England, Spain, Switzerland, and the United States.

The sculpture is as tall as some trees, but this tree won't be doing any growing.

## TRAFFIC LIGHT TREE
### London, England, U.K.

Money doesn't grow on trees—but traffic lights might! This 26-foot (8-m)-high treelike structure is made of 75 sets of traffic lights controlled by computers. The sculpture, created by a French artist to represent the energy of the city around it, has been a big hit with locals. Sounds like this fake tree has really taken root.

# HOW TALL IS IT?

**Burj Khalifa, located in Dubai** in the United Arab Emirates, soars over half a mile (0.8 km) high. But how does that compare to other cool sights around the globe? Check out this lineup to find out!

The Willis Tower has **16,100** windows.

More than **36,000** stones make up the Washington Monument.

**BURJ KHALIFA**
**2,717** FEET (828 m)

**WILLIS TOWER** (WITH TWIN ANTENNAS)
**1,730** FEET (530 m)

**EMPIRE STATE BUILDING** (WITH ANTENNAS)
**1,454** FEET (443 m)

**EIFFEL TOWER** (WITH ANTENNAS)
**1,063** FEET (324 m)

**WASHINGTON MONUMENT**
**555** FEET (169 m)

**GREAT PYRAMID**
**455** FEET (139 m)

3,000
2,500
2,000
1,500
1,000
500

# NUMBER **CASCADE**

**Victoria Falls, fed by the Zambezi River** and located on the border of Zambia and Zimbabwe, is one of Africa's most famous and natural wonders and one of the most impressive waterfalls found on Earth. Explore some of the amazing stats behind this thunderous wall of water, which has shaped the land and ecosystem for millions of years.

**142.7 BILLION GALLONS** (540 billion L)
of water drop over the falls per minute when the river is in full flood

**354 FEET HIGH** (108 M)

**5,538 FEET WIDE** (1,688 M)

**1.25 MILES** (2 KM) width of Zambezi River at the falls

**0.3 MILE HIGH** (0.5 KM) maximum height of the spray plume

**12 MILES** (20 KM) distance mist can be seen for

**2,000,000 YEARS AGO** time when the falls started to form

**3,000,000 YEARS OLD** age of stone artifacts made by early humans found near the falls

# EXTREME WEIRDNESS

## VADER RULES THE SKY

**WHAT** León International Balloon Festival

**WHERE** León, Mexico

**DETAILS** This might be the Rebels' worst nightmare. Participants at this festival soared across the sky in giant hot-air balloons, such as this one shaped like Darth Vader's mask. More than a hundred balloons fly each year—anything from pandas to bees to scarecrows. But don't worry. This Vader's only full of hot air.

THE FORCE IS STRONG WITH THIS ONE.

DON'T MOW THIS GRASS.

## WEAR YOUR LAWN

**WHAT** Grass-covered flip-flops

**WHERE** New South Wales Coast, Australia

**DETAILS** Want to feel the grass between your toes? Just plant your feet in these grass-topped flip-flops, designed to give you the sensation of being outdoors anytime. Don't worry about watering the sandals—the grass is actually a layer of artificial turf. You'll have some happy feet!

YOU'RE IN THE COLD SEAT.

## ICE CUBE ON WHEELS

**WHAT** Truck made of ice

**WHERE** Hensall, Canada

**DETAILS** It's going to be an icy ride. This functional truck has a body made of 11,000 pounds (4,990 kg) of ice. Built over a base frame with wheels, the icy exterior covers a real engine, brakes, and steering wheel. It runs on a battery that's specially designed to start in frigid conditions that would keep most cars from revving up. The car can only go short distances—but what a great place to chill!

# WILD VACATION

**ENTER HERE!**

**SLEEP HERE!**

## Tree Hotel
### NESTLING INTO NATURE

**WHERE** Dalat, Vietnam

**HOW MUCH** About $35 to $80 a night

**WHY IT'S COOL** One look at this hotel and you'll understand its nickname: "Crazy House." The bizarre lodging is designed to resemble a giant tree stump from the outside. The structure's cozy interior is filled with twisting passageways and 10 cavelike rooms, each with a different animal, insect, or plant theme. Visitors can unwind next to a fireplace shaped like a kangaroo or drift to sleep while staring at the stars through skylights in the Gourd Room. Guests can also wander through the garden, where eerie metal spiderwebs hang. More daring individuals can climb the winding walkways to the roof of the building and take in views of the surrounding city. From top to bottom, this hotel is insanely awesome.

## COOL THINGS ABOUT VIETNAM

About 40 percent of the people in Vietnam have the last name Nguyen.

Grilled squid teeth are a popular snack in the country's coastal towns.

Vietnam is only 30 miles (48 km) wide at its narrowest point.

## THINGS TO DO IN VIETNAM

Explore the bustling Cai Rang floating market, where boats are colorfully packed with fruits and vegetables for sale.

Sample traditional noodle soup called pho (pronounced FUH) from shops in Hanoi, the country's capital city.

Discover the palaces of former emperors inside the walls of the Hue Citadel, along the Perfume River.

335

# QUIZ WHIZ

**Is your geography knowledge off the map? Quiz yourself to find out!**

Write your answers on a piece of paper. Then check them below.

**1** Each year, monarch butterflies migrate from Mexico to _____.
a. Europe
b. Canada and the United States
c. Asia
d. Australia

**2** A 5,500-year-old leather _____ was once discovered in an Armenian cave.
a. handbag
b. briefcase
c. shoe
d. wallet

**3** The Traffic Light Tree is a wacky roadside attraction found in which city?
a. London, England
b. Chicago, Illinois
c. Prague, Czech Republic
d. Lima, Peru

**4** **True or false?** An adult gentoo penguin makes as many as 450 dives a day looking for food.

**5** Which speedy animal lives in Africa?
a. cheetah
b. antelope
c. wildebeest
d. all of the above

Not **STUMPED** yet? Check out the *NATIONAL GEOGRAPHIC KIDS QUIZ WHIZ* collection for more crazy **GEOGRAPHY** questions!

**ANSWERS:**
1. b; 2. c; 3. a; 4. True; 5. d

## HOMEWORK HELP

# Finding Your Way Around

**Every map has a story to tell,** but first you have to know how to read one. Maps represent information by using a language of symbols. Knowing how to read these symbols provides access to a wide range of information. Look at the scale and compass rose or arrow to understand distance and direction (see box below).

To find out what each symbol on a map means, you must use the key. It's your secret decoder—identifying information by each symbol on the map.

90°N (North Pole)
75°N
60°N
45°N
30°N
15°N
0° (Equator)
15°S
30°S
45°S

30°E
45°E
60°E
75°E
90°E
105°E
120°E
135°E

Latitude

Longitude

75°N
60°N
45°N
30°N
15°N
0° (Equator)
15°S
30°S
45°S
75°W
60°W
45°W
30°W
15°W
0° (Prime Meridian)
15°E
30°E
45°E
60°E
75°E

## LATITUDE AND LONGITUDE

Latitude and longitude lines (above) help us determine locations on Earth. Every place on Earth has a special address called absolute location. Imaginary lines called lines of latitude run west to east, parallel to the Equator. These lines measure distance in degrees north or south from the Equator (0° latitude) to the North Pole (90° N) or to the South Pole (90° S). One degree of latitude is approximately 70 miles (113 km).

Lines of longitude run north to south, meeting at the poles. These lines measure distance in degrees east or west from 0° longitude (prime meridian) to 180° longitude. The prime meridian runs through Greenwich, England.

## SCALE AND DIRECTION

The scale on a map can be shown as a fraction, as words, or as a line or bar. It relates distance on the map to distance in the real world. Sometimes the scale identifies the type of map projection. Maps may include an arrow or compass rose to indicate north on the map.

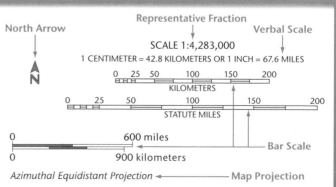

North Arrow

Representative Fraction

Verbal Scale

SCALE 1:4,283,000
1 CENTIMETER = 42.8 KILOMETERS OR 1 INCH = 67.6 MILES

N

0    25    50         100         150         200
KILOMETERS

0      25      50              100              150              200
STATUTE MILES

0                         600 miles
0                         900 kilometers

Bar Scale

*Azimuthal Equidistant Projection* ◄——— Map Projection

# GAME ANSWERS

## What in the World?
page 164

Top row: **mud, snowdrifts, lava**
Middle row: **moss, stones, palm leaf**
Bottom row: **tree trunk, iceberg, sand dunes**

## Find the Hidden Animals
page 165

1. **E**, 2. **D**, 3. **A**, 4. **B**, 5. **F**, 6. **C**

## Signs of the Times
page 166

Signs **5** and **8** are fake.

## Stump Your Parents
page 168

1. **D**, 2. **B**, 3. **B**, 4. **C**, 5. **B**, 6. **C**, 7. **A**,
8. **A-5, B-4, C-2, D-3, E-1**, 9. **A**, 10. **B**

## What in the World?
page 170

Top row: **balloon, swimming pool, dreidel**
Middle row: **clam, butterfly, macaw**
Bottom row: **stadium seats, sponge, toothbrush**

## Are You a Garbage Genius?
page 172

1. **True**, 2. **True**, 3. **B**, 4. **C**, 5. **D**

## Find the Hidden Animals
page 173

1. **B**, 2. **D**, 3. **E**, 4. **F**, 5. **A**, 6. **C**

## Stump Your Parents
page 175

1. **C**, 2. **C**, 3. **D**, 4. **A**, 5. **B**, 6. **A**, 7. **D**,
8. **C**, 9. **C**, 10. **B**

## Movie Madness
page 176

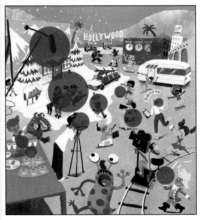

## What in the World?
page 178

Top row: **galaxy, astronaut, moon**
Middle row: **space shuttle, sun, comet**
Bottom row: **Saturn, Mars rover, satellite**

# Want to Learn More?

Find more information about topics in this book in these National Geographic Kids resources.

**Absolute Expert series**

**Weird But True series**

**Just Joking series**

**5,000 Awesome Facts (About Everything!) series**

**The Ultimate Book of Sharks**
*Brian Skerry*
May 2018

**Animal Smackdown**
*Emily Krieger*
August 2018

**Why Not?: Over 1,111 Answers to Everything**
*Crispin Boyer*
August 2018

**Dog Science Unleashed**
*Jodi Wheeler-Toppen*
August 2018

**How Things Work: Then and Now**
*T. J. Resler*
October 2018

**1,000 Facts About Ancient Egypt**
*Nancy Honovich*
February 2019

**Funny Animals**
April 2019

**125 True Stories of Amazing Animal Friendships**
May 2018

**Extreme Records**
*Julie Beer and Michelle Harris*
June 2018

**Animal Zombies!**
*Chana Stiefel*
August 2018

**Food Fight!**
*Tanya Steel*
September 2018

**Ultimate Predatorpedia**
*Christina Wilsdon*
October 2018

**340**

kwest/SS; 86 (UP); FotograFFF/SS; 86 (LO), Craig Tuttle/Corbis/GI; 87 (UP), Lori Epstein/NG Staff; 87 (LO LE), Lori Epstein/NG Staff; 87 (LO RT), Science Picture Co/Collection Mix: Subjects RM/GI; 87 (CTR), Lori Epstein/NG Staff; 88-89, Simon Fraser/Science Source; 90 (UP), Roger Harris/Science Source; 90 (LO), Shaber/SS; 91, Tim Vernon/SPL/Science Source; 92 (UP), Cynthia Turner; 92 (LO), cobalt88/SS; 93 (CTR), Heritage Image Partnership Ltd/AL; 93 (LO), bgblue/IS/GI; 94 (UP LE), Dimarion/SS; 94 (UP), Eraxion/IS; 94 (CTR LE), Microfield Scientific Ltd./Science Source; 94 (CTR), mrfiza/SS; 94 (LO), iLexx/IS; 95 (UP), Jani Bryson/IS; 95 (CTR), MyImages - Micha/SS; 95 (LO), RapidEye/IS; 96-97 (all), Matthew Rakola; 98 (UP), FotograFFF/SS; 98 (CTR RT), Ted Kinsman/Science Source; 98 (LO LE), VINCENT CALLEBAUT ARCHITECTURES, PARIS; 99, Klaus Vedfelt/GI

## Going Green (100–115)

100-101, Stefano Boeri Architetti; 102 (UP), Gemma Atwal; 102 (inset), Peter Anthony; 103 (UP), Streliuk Aleksei/DRMS; 103 (LO), Todd Paris/UAF; 104-105 (background), Wildlife in Crisis; 104 (UP), Wildlife in Crisis; 105 (UP & CTR LE), Marie De Stefanis/The Marine Mammal Center; 105 (CTR RT & LO), Wildlife in Crisis; 106 (UP), Scanrail/DRMS; 106 (CTR), Sean Pavone/DRMS; 106 (LO), Rodrigo Kristensen/SS; 107 (background), Caters News Agency; 107 (CTR RT), Jamie Squire/GI; 107 (CTR), Joao Sabino/Solent News/REX/SS; 107 (LO RT), Courtesy of Austin-Mergold; 107 (LO LE), Dirty Sugar Photography; 108, Cnora/GI; 109 (UP), Rich Carey/SS; 109 (LO), Jimmy Cumming/GI; 111 (UP), James Stone/Chasing Light Photography/GI; 111 (LO), James Balog/NGIC; 112 (CTR), Rebecca Hale/NG Staff; 112 (photo collage—redwood), FogStock LLC/Index Stock; 112 (photo collage—cat), Digital Vision/Punchstock; 112 (photo collage—ball), Royalty-Free/Corbis; 112 (photo collage—ice cream), Photodisc Green/GI; 112 (photo collage—dog), Royalty-Free/Corbis; 112 (photo collage—fire hydrant), Burke/Triolo/Brand X Pictures/Jupiter Images; 112 (photo collage—genie lamp), Burke/Triolo/Brand X Pictures/Jupiter Images; 112 (photo collage—girl), Rubberball Productions/GI; 112 (photo collage—WHOA sign), Thinkstock/Jupiter Images; 113, Rebecca Hale/NG Staff; 114 (UP), Scanrail/DRMS; 114 (CTR), Jim Cumming/GI; 114 (LO), Rich Carey/SS

## Culture Connection (116–139)

116-117, Douglas Peebles/GI; 118 (UP), Nick Kato; 118 (inset), Kauila Barber; 119 (UP), Nick Kato; 119 (LO), Elizabeth Lindsey; 120-121 (UP), fotohunter/SS; 120 (UP LE), CreativeNature.nl/SS; 120 (UP RT), pattarastock/SS; 120 (LO LE), Tubol Evgeniya/SS; 120 (LO RT), imageBROKER/AL; 121 (UP), Jeremy Villasis/Demotix/Corbis; 121 (CTR), Zee/AL; 121 (LO), wacpan/SS; 122 (UP), Ajay Verma/Reuters; 122 (LO), Rubens Chaves/Tips Italia/Photolibrary; 123, Chonnanit/SS; 124 (UP LE), Splash News/NewsCom; 124 (UP RT), Fuse/GI; 124 (LO LE), Timothy A. Clary/

AFP/GI; 124 (LO RT), Timothy A. Clary/AFP/GI; 125-127 (all), Rebecca Hale/NG Staff; 128 (UP LE), Ivan Vdovin/AL; 128 (UP CTR), maogg/GI; 128 (UP RT), Paul Poplis/GI; 128 (CTR LE), Mlenny/IS; 128 (CTR RT), Jack Guez/AFP/GI; 128 (LO LE), Courtesy of The Banknote Book; 128 (LO RT), Ninette Maumus/AL; 129 (UP LE), Numismatic Guaranty Corporation (NGC); 129 (UP RT), Comstock/GI; 129 (UP CTR LE), Igor Stramyk/SS; 129 (LO CTR LE), Splash News/Newscom; 129 (LO CTR RT), D. Hurst/AL; 129 (LO CTR), "MoneyDress" with "Colonial Dress" behind. Paper currency and frame, Lifesize © Susan Stockwell 2010. © photo Colin Hampden-White 2010; 129 (LO RT), Kelley Miller/NG Staff; 130, Mark Thiessen/NG Staff; 131 (both), Mark Thiessen/NG Staff; 133, fcknimages/IS/GI; 134 (LE), John Hazard; 134 (RT), Jose Ignacio Soto/SS; 135 (LE), Corey Ford/DRMS; 135 (RT), Photosani/SS; 136 (UP), Randy Olson; 136 (LO LE), Martin Gray/NGIC; 136 (LO RT), Sam Panthaky/AFP/GI; 137 (UP), Filippo Monteforte/GI; 137 (LO LE), Reza/NGIC; 137 (LO RT), Richard Nowitz/NGIC; 138 (UP), fcknimages/IS/GI; 138 (LO LE), "MoneyDress" with "Colonial Dress" behind. Paper currency and frame, Lifesize © Susan Stockwell 2010. © photo Colin Hampden-White 2010; 138 (LO RT), Mark Thiessen/NG Staff; 139 (UP LE), spatuletail/SS; 139 (UP RT), PictureLake/SS; 139 (CTR), cifotart/SS; 139 (LO), zydesign/SS

## Space and Earth (140–161)

140-141, SpaceX/GI; 142 (UP), Kim Huppert; 142 (inset), Jordan Krcmaric; 143 (UP), Rafal Cichawa/SS; 143 (CTR & LO), Christine Y. Chen; 144-145 (UP), Mark Garlick/Science Photo Library; 144 (LO), NASA/CXC/IOA/A FABIAN ETAL/Science Photo Library; 145 (UP), NASA, ESA and M.J. Jee (Johns Hopkins University); 145 (LO), M. Markevitch/CXC/CFA/NASA/Science Photo Library; 146-147, David Aguilar; 148 (UP), David Aguilar; 149 (all), Mondolithic Studios; 150 (background UP), Alexxandar/GI; 150 (UP RT), Walter Myers/Stocktrek Images/Corbis/GI; 150 (CTR RT), Tony & Daphne Hallas/Photo Researchers, Inc.; 150 (LO RT), Don Smith/GI; 151 (UP), NASA/Science Faction/SuperStock; 151 (LO), NASA; 152 (UP), Ralph Lee Hopkins/NGIC; 152 (UP LE and RT), Visuals Unlimited/GI; 152 (CTR LE), Visuals Unlimited/Corbis; 152 (CTR RT), Dirk Wiersma/Photo Researchers, Inc.; 152 (LO LE), Charles D. Winters/Photo Researchers, Inc.; 152 (LO RT), Theodore Clutter/Photo Researchers, Inc.; 153 (UP), NGIC; 154 (UP LE), Panoramic Stock Images/NGIC; 154 (UP RT), Charles D. Winters/Photo Researchers, Inc.; 154 (CTR), Ted Clutter/Photo Researchers, Inc.; 154 (LO LE), Jim Lopes/SS; 154 (LO RT), Jim Richardson/NGIC; 155 (UP LE), Scenics & Science/AL; 155 (UP RT), Mark A. Shneider/Photo Researchers, Inc.; 155 (UP CTR LE), Ken Lucas/Visuals Unlimited; 155 (UP CTR RT), Carsten Peter/NGIC; 155 (LO CTR), Dirk Wiersma/Photo Researchers, Inc.; 155 (LO LE), Arturo Limon/SS; 155 (LO RT), Goran Bogicevic/SS; 156, Illustration by Frank Ippolito; 157 (UP LE), All Canada Photos/AL; 157 (UP RT), Salvatore Gebbia/National

Geographic My Shot; 157 (CTR LE), NASA; 157 (CTR RT), Diane Cook & Len Jenshel/NGIC; 157 (LO LE), Image Science and Analysis Laboratory, NASA-Johnson Space Center. "The Gateway to Astronaut Photography of Earth."; 157 (LO RT), Douglas Peebles Photography/AL; 158-159 (all), Denis Budkov/Caters News; 160 (UP), Don Smith/GI; 160 (CTR), All Canada Photos/AL; 160 (LO), Visuals Unlimited/Corbis; 161, pixhook/IS

## Fun and Games (162–181)

162-163, Anup Shah/MP; 164 (UP LE), Punchstock; 164 (UP RT), Photodisc Blue/GI; 164 (UP RT), PictureQuest; 164 (CTR LE), Pal Hermansen/GI; 164 (CTR), Punchstock; 164 (CTR RT), Vibe Images/SS; 164 (LO LE), Anthony Ise/GI; 164 (LO CTR), Punchstock; 164 (LO RT), Denis Burdin/SS; 165 (UP LE), EEI_Tony/GI; 165 (UP RT), Joel Sartore/NGIC; 165 (CTR LE), Tui De Roy/MP; 165 (CTR RT), Jack Goldfarb/Design Pics/Corbis/GI; 165 (LO LE), Fabio Liverani/NPL/MP; 165 (LO RT), Exactostock/SuperStock; 166 (#1), Charles Gullung/GI; 166 (#2), Photo Resource Hawaii/AL; 166 (#3), Slim Aarons/Hulton Archive/GI; 166 (#4), Joseph Sohm/Visions of America/Corbis; 166 (#5), Thinkstock Images/Jupiter Images; 166 (#6), Owaki/Kulla/GI; 166 (#7), Jack Sullivan/AL; 166 (#8), Dale O'Dell 2008; 166 (#9), Jeff Greenberg/UIG/GI; 167, Dan Sipple; 168 (UP LE), Sergey Alimov/GI; 168 (UP RT), Sorin Rechitan/EyeEm/GI; 168 (CTR RT), NASA/Paolo Nespoli; 168 (LO RT), Globe Photos/ZUMAPRESS; 168 (LO LE), Michael and Patricia Fogden/MP; 169, Chris Ware; 170 (UP LE), artpartner-images.com/AL; 170 (UP LE), napocska/SS; 170 (UP RT), PNC/Photodisc/GI; 170 (CTR LE), Khoroshunova Olga/SS; 170 (CTR), Dobermaraner/SS; 170 (CTR RT), Ian Duffield/SS; 170 (LO LE), Medioimages/Jupiterimages; 170 (LO CTR), LWA/Photodisc/GI; 170 (LO RT), Esa Hiltula/AL; 171 (UP), Kitchin & Hurst/leesonphoto; 171 (CTR), Elvele Images Ltd/AL; 171 (CTR), Pioneer111/DRMS; 171 (LO LE), Fuse/GI; 171 (LO RT), RubberBall/SuperStock; 172 (UP CTR), Rita Kochmarjova/SS; 172 (UP RT), Autthaphol Khoonpijit/DRMS; 172 (UP CTR RT), Nerthuz/SS; 172 (CTR LE), Mdorottya/DRMS; 172 (CTR), Skypixel/DRMS; 172 (CTR RT), Melinda Fawver/SS; 172 (LO LE), Domiciano Pablo Romero Franco/DRMS; 172 (LO CTR), Martinmark/DRMS; 173 (UP), Robert Fowler/SS; 173 (CTR LE), Valerie Taylor/Ardea; 173 (UP CTR RT), DARIYASINGH/IS/GI; 173 (LO LE), Iren Silence/SS; 173 (LO RT), Don Johnston/GI; 173 (LO RT), Rafael Martos Martins/SS; 174, Dan Sipple; 175 (UP LE), Rinus Baak/DRMS; 175 (UP RT), Richard Susanto/SS; 175 (CTR LE), weerapong worranam/SS; 175 (CTR RT), M. Unal Ozmen/SS; 175 (LO LE), Dobermaraner/SS; 175 (LO RT), somchaij/SS; 176, MIGY; 177 (UP RT), Tim Laman/NGIC; 177 (A), Stephen St. John/NGIC; 177 (B), Joel Sartore/NGIC; 177 (C), Robert Harding/NGIC; 177 (UP RT INSET), Uwe Bergwitz/SS; 177 (UP CTR RT), Ellen Goff/Danita Delimont/SS; 177 (CTR LE), Westend61 Premium/SS; 177 (CTR RT), Westend61 Premium/SS; 177 (LO RT), Michael Durham/MP; 178 (UP LE), David Herraez

Calzada/SS; 178 (UP CTR), Andrey Armyagov/SS; 178 (UP RT), Kei Shooting/SS; 178 (CTR LE), Mikephotos/DRMS; 178 (CTR), NASA/SDO; 178 (CTR RT), NASA/MSFC/MEO/AAron Kingery; 178 (LO LE), MarcelClemens/SS; 178 (LO CTR), NASA; 178 (LO RT), Andrey Armyagov/SS; 179, Dan Sipple; 180-181, Strika Entertainment

## Awesome Exploration (182-199)

182-183, Pat Morrow/NGIC; 184 (LE), Marco Grob/NGIC; 184 (RT), Jenny Nichols; 185 (all), Brian Ford; 186-187 (UP), Brian J. Skerry/NGIC; 186 (LO), Brian J. Skerry/NGIC; 187 (CTR), Mark D. Conlin/NGIC; 187 (LO), Brian J. Skerry/NGIC; 188 (background & UP), Paul Nicklen/NGIC; 188 (LO), James C. Chatters; 189 (UP), HI-SEAS/Sian Proctor; 189 (CTR), AP Photo/Hi-Seas; 189 (LO), AP/Rex/SS; 190 (UP RT), Joel Sartore/NGIC; 190 (LO LE), Elliott Ross/NGIC; 190 (LO RT), created by John Gurche/photographed by Mark Thiessen/NGIC; 191 (UP), izusek/GI; 191 (CTR UP), Jim Cumming/GI; 191 (CTR LE), Imgorthand/GI; 191 (CTR CTR), Getman/SS; 191 (CTR RT), Tony Anderson/GI; 192 (both), Ben Arnst/Squaw Valley Alpine Meadows; 193 (UP), Renee Lynn/GI; 193 (LO), Barbara Kinney; 194 (UP LE), Pictures Colour Library/Newscom; 194 (UP RT), Marius Bøstrand; 194 (LO LE), Channi Anand/AP Photo; 194 (LO RT), Bigfoot Hostel/Barcroft Media/GI; 195 (UP LE), Michael Clark/AL; 195 (UP RT), EPA/Newscom; 195 (CTR LE), Anthony Devlin/PA Images/AL; 195 (LO RT), Lucas Jackson/Reuters; 196-197 (all), Annie Griffiths; 198 (UP), Brian J. Skerry/NGIC; 198 (CTR), AP Photo/Hi-Seas; 198 (LO), Bigfoot Hostel/Barcroft Media/GI; 199, Grady Reese/IS

## Wonders of Nature (200-219)

200-201, RooM RF/GI; 202 (UP), Manu San Félix; 202 (inset), Rebecca Hale/NG Staff; 203 (all), Enric Sala/NGIC; 205 (UP), Stephanie Sawyer/GI; 205 (LO), Grant Dixon/MP; 206 (UP), Stuart Armstrong; 206 (LO), Franco Tempesta; 207 (UP LE), Leonid Tit/SS; 207 (UP RT), Lars Christensen/SS; 207 (CTR LE), Frans Lanting/NGIC; 207 (CTR RT), Daniel Loretto/SS; 207 (LO), Richard Peterson/SS; 208-209, 3dmotus/SS; 210 (UP), Stephen M. Katz/The Virginian-Pilot via AP; 210 (CTR LE), Carlos Giusti/AP; 210 (CTR RT), Melvin Levongo/AFP/GI; 210 (LO) Australia Broadcasting Corporation via AP; 211 (UP LE), Lori Mehmen/Associated Press; 211 (UP RT & RT CTR), Susan Law Cain/SS; 211 (UP CTR), Brian Nolan/IS; 211 (CTR LE), Judy Kennamer/SS; 211 (LO LE), Jim Reed; 211 (LO CTR & LO RT), jam4travel/SS; 212 (LE), AVTG/IS; 212 (RT), Brad Wynnyk/SS; 213 (UP LE), Rich Carey/SS; 213 (UP RT), Richard Walters/IS; 213 (LO LE), Karen Graham/IS; 213 (LO RT), Michio Hoshino/MP/NGIC; 214-215 (UP), Jason Edwards/NGIC; 214 (LO LE), cbpix/SS; 214 (LO RT), Mike Hill/Photographer's Choice/GI; 215 (LO LE), Wil Meinderts/Buitenbeeld/MP; 215 (LO RT), Paul Nicklen/NGIC; 216-217 (background), John A. Anderson/IS; 216 (UP), Vilainecrevette/SS; 216 (LO), Brandon Cole; 217 (UP), Paul Souders/GI; 217 (LO), Rebecca Hale/NG Staff; 218 (UP), Frans Lanting/NGIC; 218 (CTR), John A. Anderson/IS; 218 (LO), SS

## History Happens (220-251)

220-221, Nicola Forenza/IS/GI; 222 (UP), Paul Nicklen/NGIC; 222 (inset), Karla Ortega; 222 (LO), Karla Ortega; 223 (UP), Paul Nicklen/NGIC; 223 (LO), Karla Ortega; 224-225 (background), Pius Lee/SS; 225 (UP LE), Providence Pictures; 225 (UP RT), HOPE PRODUCTIONS/Yann Arthus Bertrand/GI; 225 (LO RT), Hulton Archive/GI; 226 (UP), James L. Stanfield/NGIC; 226 (LO), Photoservice Electa/Universal Images/SuperStock; 227 (all), Joe Rocco; 228, Wang da Gang; 229 (UP LE, UP RT & LO RT), O. Louis Mazzatenta/NGIC; 229 (CTR RT), O. Louis Mazzatenta; 229 (LO LE), Wang da Gang; 230-231 (background), Corey Ford; 230 (LO), Disney Enterprises, Inc./Walden Media, LLC; 231 (UP RT), Ocean/Corbis; 231 (LO), Mark Thiessen/NG Staff; 232 (all), Chris Wass; 233 (UP RT), Index Stock Imagery/Jupiterimages/GI; 233 (CTR), Chip Clark/NMNH/Smithsonian Institution; 233 (LO), Superstock, Inc./SuperStock; 234, U.S. Air Force photo/Staff Sgt. Alexandra M. Boutte; 235, Corbis/GI; 236, Scott Rothstein/SS; 237 (UP), AleksandarNakic/IS/GI; 237 (CTR RT), Zack Frank/SS; 237 (LO LE), Gary Blakely/SS; 238 (UP & CTR), AFP/GI; 238 (LO), Education Images/UIG/GI; 239 (all), White House Historical Association; 240 (LO RT), DRMS; 240 (all others), White House Historical Association; 241 (CTR LE), Krissi Lundgren/SS; 241 (all others), White House Historical Association; 242 (LO RT), Francis Miller/Time Life Pictures/GI; 242 (all others), White House Historical Association; 243 (LO CTR RT), lazyllama/SS; 243 (LO RT), Clint Spaulding/WWD/REX/SS; 243 (all others), White House Historical Association; 244-245 (all), Adrian Lubbers; 246 (UP), Bettmann/Corbis/GI; 246 (inset), Science Source/GI; 247 (UP), Charles Kogod/NGIC; 247 (LO LE), iStock Editorial/GI; 247 (LO RT), Chip Somodevilla/GI; 248, Bettmann Archive/GI; 249 (UP LE), Scott Eisen/GI; 249 (UP RT), Mark Wilson/GI; 249 (LO), Bettmann Archive/GI; 250 (UP), Providence Pictures; 250 (CTR), Chris Wass; 250 (LO), Photoservice Electa/Universal Images/SuperStock; 251, Christopher Furlong/GI

## Geography Rocks (252-337)

252-253, MelindaChan/GI; 254 (UP), Jon Bowen; 254 (inset), Becky Hale/NG Staff; 255 (UP), International Mapping Inc/NGIC; 255 (LO), Chin Kit Sen/SS; 261 (UP RT), Lori Epstein/NG Staff; 261 (CTR LE), NASA; 262 (background), Fabiano Rebeque/GI; 262 (valley), Thomas J. Abercrombie/NGIC; 262 (river), Maria Stenzel/NGIC; 262 (mountain), Gordon Wiltsie/NGIC; 262 (glacier), James P. Blair/NGIC; 262 (canyon), Bill Hatcher/NGIC; 262 (desert), Carsten Peter/NGIC; 263, f11photo/SS; 264, Amelandfoto/SS; 265 (UP RT), Glowimages/GI; 265 (CTR LE), keyvanchan/GI; 265 (CTR RT), Jean-Jacques Hublin; 265 (LO RT), Dimitri Vervitsiotis/GI; 268, Yva Momatiuk and John Eastcott/MP; 269 (UP RT), Achim Baque/SS; 269 (CTR LE), Alex Tehrani; 269 (CTR RT), iCreative3D/SS; 269 (LO RT), Aurora Creative/GI; 272, Nguyen Anh Tuan/SS; 273 (UP RT), Jon Arnold Images/Danita Delimont.com; 273 (CTR LE), Ilin Sergey/age fotostock; 273 (CTR RT), Nancy Brown/Photographer's Choice/GI; 273 (LO RT), Daniel Heuclin/NPL/MP; 276, The Image Bank/GI; 277 (UP LE), Mika Stock/Danita Delimont.com; 277 (UP RT), Andrew Watson/John Warburton-Lee Photography Ltd/GI; 277 (CTR RT), FiledIMAGE/SS; 277 (LO), Robert Harding World Imagery/GI; 280, Christian Mueller/SS; 281 (UP RT), Roy Pedersen/SS; 281 (CTR LE), RomarioIen/SS; 281 (CTR RT), Annette Hopf/IS; 281 (LO RT), Mark Gillow/GI; 284, Stone Sub/GI; 285 (UP RT), Rodrigo Arangua/GI; 285 (CTR LE), Gail Shotlander/GI; 285 (CTR RT), Yiming Chen/GI; 285 (LO RT), Janie Blanchard/GI; 288, GI South America/GI; 289 (UP RT), Soberka Richard/hemis.fr/GI; 289 (CTR LE), David Tipling/AL; 289 (CTR RT), DC_Colombia/GI; 289 (LO RT), Walter Diaz/AFP/GI; 295, Maya Karkalicheva/GI; 296, Ondrej Prosicky/SS; 300, MehmetO/SS; 303, Tim Graham/GI; 304, EyeEm/GI; 308, Bartosz Hadyniak/GI; 311, Peter Cade/GI; 316, Westend61/GI; 328 (UP RT), Panoramic Images/GI; 328 (UP CTR LE), TexPhoto/SS; 328 (UP CTR RT), Harold G Herradura/SS; 328 (LO RT), PhotoDisc; 329 (UP LE), John Warburton Lee/AWL Images; 329 (LO LE), Sumikophoto/DRMS; 329 (RT), Danita Delimont/GI; 330 (UP), Tony McNicol/AL; 330 (CTR), Pioneron/SS; 330-331(LO), Bob Henry/AL; 331 (UP), Walter Bibikow/GI; 331 (CTR LE), Alistair Scott/AL; 331 (LO RT), Stuart Miles/DRMS; 332 (LE), Ilona Ignatova/SS; 332 (CTR LE), Songquan Deng/SS; 332 (CTR), Dokic Dojan/SS; 332 (CTR RT), Roman Sigaev/SS; 332 (LO CTR RT), Iesapi images/SS; 332 (LO RT), Brian Kinney/SS; 333, Galyna Andrushko/SS; 334 (UP), Shane Talbot/Solent News/REX/SS; 334 (CTR), Mario Armas/Reuters/AL; 334 (LO), ZJAN/Canadian Tire Corporation/WENN/Newscom; 335 (UP), John S Lander/LightRocket/GI; 335 (inset UP), John S Lander/LightRocket/GI; 335 (inset LO), WENN Ltd/AL; 336 (UP), Janie Blanchard/GI; 336 (CTR), Stuart Miles/DRMS; 336 (LO), keyvanchan/GI

Since 1888, the National Geographic Society has funded more than 12,000 research,
exploration, and preservation projects around the world.
The Society receives funds from National Geographic Partners, LLC,
funded in part by your purchase. A portion of the proceeds from this book
supports this vital work. To learn more, visit natgeo.com/info.

NATIONAL GEOGRAPHIC and Yellow Border Design are trademarks of the
National Geographic Society, used under license.

For more information, visit nationalgeographic.com,
call 1-800-647-5463, or write to the following address:

National Geographic Partners
1145 17th Street N.W.
Washington, D.C. 20036-4688 U.S.A.

Visit us online at nationalgeographic.com/books

For librarians and teachers: ngchildrensbooks.org

More for kids from National Geographic: natgeokids.com

*National Geographic Kids* magazine inspires children to explore their world with fun
yet educational articles on animals, science, nature, and more. Using fresh storytelling and
amazing photography, Nat Geo Kids shows kids ages 6 to 14 the fascinating truth about
the world—and why they should care. **kids.nationalgeographic.com/subscribe**

For information about special discounts for bulk purchases, please contact
National Geographic Books Special Sales: specialsales@natgeo.com

For rights or permissions inquiries, please contact
National Geographic Books Subsidiary Rights: bookrights@natgeo.com

Designed by Kathryn Robbins and Ruthie Thompson

**National Geographic supports K–12 educators with ELA Common Core Resources.
Visit natgeoed.org/commoncore for more information.**

Trade paperback ISBN: 978-1-4263-3281-4
Hardcover ISBN: 978-1-4263-3282-1

Printed in the United States of America
19/WOR-PCML/1

The publisher would like to thank everyone who worked to make this book come together:
Angela Modany, associate editor; Mary Jones, project editor; Sarah Wassner Flynn,
writer; Michelle Harris, researcher; Lori Epstein, photo director; Hillary Leo, photo editor;
Mike McNey, map production; Stuart Armstrong, illustrator; Sean Philpotts, production
director; Anne LeongSon and Gus Tello, design production assistants;
Sally Abbey, managing editor; Joan Gossett, editorial production manager;
and Alix Inchausti and Molly Reid, production editors.